D1613414

LANGUAGE, ELITES, AND THE STATE

Nationalism in Puerto Rico and Quebec

AMÍLCAR A. BARRETO

Westport, Connecticut
London

#37731659

Library of Congress Cataloging-in-Publication Data

Barreto, Amílcar Antonio.
    Language, elites, and the state : nationalism in Puerto Rico and
Quebec / Amílcar A. Barreto.
        p.   cm.
    Includes bibliographical references and index.
    ISBN 0–275–96183–4 (alk. paper)
    1. Nationalism—Puerto Rico—History—20th century.
2. Nationalism—Québec (Province)—History—20th century.   3. Puerto
Rico—Politics and government—1952– .   4. Québec (Province)—Politics
and government—1960– .   5. Spanish language—Political aspects—
Puerto Rico.   6. French language—Political aspects—Québec
(Province)   7. Puerto Rico—Relations—United States.   8. United
States—Relations—Puerto Rico.   9. Federal government—Canada.
I. Title.
F1976.B87   1998
    303.48′27295073—dc21   97–38541

British Library Cataloguing in Publication Data is available.

Library of Congress Catalog Card Number: 97–38541
ISBN: 0–275–96183–4

First published in 1998

Praeger Publishers, 88 Post Road West, Westport, CT 06881
An imprint of Greenwood Publishing Group, Inc.

Printed in the United States of America

The paper used in this book complies with the
Permanent Paper Standard issued by the National
Information Standards Organization (Z39.48–1984).

10 9 8 7 6 5 4 3 2

Dedicado a mis padres, Amílcar y Eloina

Contents

Acknowledgments

Our prosperity or detriment is often attributable to our social milieu as much as to our physical environment. I have been extremely fortunate to be blessed with a strong network of family, friends, and colleagues who have helped to make this work possible. The first order of thanks goes to my mentor Aline Frambes-Buxeda at the Universidad Interamericana de Puerto Rico. Throughout the years she has consistently supported my work and constantly encouraged me to pursue excellence. She taught me that to question is not to transgress, but is a service to humanity.

Many of the key ideas in this work took their form after multiple conversations with close friends. Hours of discussions and debates with Vesna Danilović and Joanna Drzewieniecki helped me immeasurably to question my own assumptions and consider what seemed impossible. They played a pivotal role in both my personal and intellectual development. More than friends they were and remain family. Together we discussed politics, society, and life, and I am by far the richer for it.

The research in this project would not have been possible without the assistance of the libraries and staffs of the State University of New York at Buffalo, York University, the New York Public Library, Northeastern University, Boston University, Boston College and the Universidad Interamericana de Puerto Rico. I also want to thank my friends Emerson Barr, David, Joan and Robert Brand, Sriram Kulkarni, James and Tanya Peck who on many occasions opened up their homes and thus allowed me to complete my research in a timely manner. I was also extremely fortunate to have the help of three incredible research assistants: my aunt Olga Iris Barreto, my grandmother Ana Delia Castro, and Luis Tulier. On little notice and with little fanfare, they went out of their way to send me valuable documents, saving me several research trips. Additionally, I am thankful for the help and support from two great secretaries Margaret Kasprzyk and Frances Ricker.

This manuscript went through two major phases. I can never fully express my deepest appreciation for the time and energy spent by an outstanding group of scholars at the State University of New York at Buffalo. They gave me extremely valuable feedback on the first draft of this project. They were D. Munroe Eagles, Gary Hoskin, Claude E. Welch, Jr., and Wolfgang Wölck. A special order of thanks goes to Claude Welch. Despite his grueling schedule he meticulously scrutinized even major idea and minute detail of the first draft. His philosophy was that good was not good enough—*Gracias*. In addition the first draft would have never come to light without the help of Frederic Fleron and Frank Zinni. Regarding the second version I am indebted to two colleagues at Northeastern University who took the time to read and comment on individual chapters—Felix Matos-Rodríguez and David Schmitt. In the midst of a very trying academic term, they found the time to make extremely helpful suggestions. I appreciate the assistance of three more colleagues who helped me to improve various parts of this work—Christopher Bosso, William Crotty, and William Kay. I also thank Marsha Havens and Marc Sadowsky for helping me polish the final draft.

Finally, I am grateful for all the moral support I have received over the years. Their encouragement is what sustained my work at those times when I considered throwing in the towel. My colleagues Leslie Armijo, Robert Cord, Robert Gilbert, and Lynn Stephen have been a godsend. I also count myself among the most fortunate to have received moral support from Myrna Berrios, Eric Cherry, Karla Cunningham, Ramón Carlos Díaz, Rosalind Diaz, Maude Duquella, Joanne Fahey, Melitta Fort, Joan Gross, Gary Haigh, Dorothea Johnson, Kimi King, Steve Levine, Valeska McDonald, Miriam Mitchell, John McGuire, Karina Rinsky, John Sacco, and Anwar Syed Safvi. A special round of thanks goes to a truly wonderful family, the Berliners—Heidi, Otto, and Karen. My family has also been extremely supportive of my work throughout the years. In particular I would like to express my deepest gratitude to Rubén and Gisela Márquez, and Ferdinand, Aida and Eduardo Quiñones. Finally, but surely not least, I thank my parents Amílcar and Eloina Barreto. Their love and support made this work possible.

1

Introduction

Throughout the twentieth century numerous scholars and policy-makers have celebrated a requiem for the phenomenon known as *nationalism*. Like the renowned phoenix, nationalism seems to disprove its detractors and rise from the ashes to challenge the supremacy of the sacrosanct modern state.[1] Where they did not previously exist, nationalists requested or insisted on the creation of ethnically based political units. Moderate territorial demands amounted to the establishment of autonomous regions within the confines of the existing state apparatus. More militant demands insisted on the secession of the ethnic enclave, thus creating a new independent country. How leaders reacted to nationalist demands varied tremendously by country, time period, and administration. In most cases, and throughout most of the past two centuries, governments have vehemently resisted negotiating with any incipient nationalist demands, relying on their armed forces to maintain the state's supremacy.

But not all regimes fought their respective nationalists. Negotiations for autonomy proceeded in many countries as did agreements on eventual secession. While they are fewer in number than their more sanguineous counterparts, they do point out that not all requests for greater self-rule are met by the barrel of a gun. A relatively recent example of peacefully accorded autonomy was the creation of the canton of Jura. Since its break from Bern, this entity has showed no notable signs of trying to leave the Helvetian Federation. On the other hand all-out independence was the goal of others. Norway quietly severed its union with Sweden early in the twentieth century. Nor did the partition of the Czechoslovakia in the latter part of the twentieth century involve bloodshed.

To its opponents nationalism is an irrational and outdated doctrine that counters the ordained trajectory of historic evolution. Their underlying premise asserts that history follows a linear and evolutionary path from primitive tribal organizations to more advanced and culturally heterogeneous states. Nationalism's critics see modern states as necessary vehicles for technological and economic advancement; they also insist that these political units are intrinsic guarantors of political, civic, and cultural rights for their numerous citizens. Advocating a redistribution of political power, based on ethnic or cultural criteria, is seen as the mark of devolution and regression, not progress.

On the other hand, to its proponents nationalism and political evolution are not necessarily contradictory phenomena. They counter that states have often served the interests of particular groups at the expense of others. Far from ensuring political rights and promoting an equitable distribution of economic opportunities, nationalists assert that governments have all too often used their resources to actively benefit the few while mobilizing a host of institutions to protect the *status quo*. In defense of the existing order, nationalists usually claim that the state gives some an unfair advantage due to its impressive arsenal of government bureaucracies and agencies, and ultimately the command of the armed forces. Both as an ideology and an object of study, nationalism has continued to generate controversy and debate.

Among those who routinely resist the resurrection of nationalist movements are policy-makers in ethnically plural states. Their privileges and livelihoods are intimately tied to the existence of a territorially expansive, demographically extensive, and largely centralized polity. For years the more enlightened among them have diligently persisted in their quest for the full integration of society's varied groups. In some cases they even promoted members of traditionally subjugated and oppressed groups into their ranks in the hopes of fulfilling their vision of a serene heterogeneous society. These bureaucrats and their respective government leaders struggled to reinforce the notion that all those within their frontiers pertain to one indivisible family.

To this end many rulers targeted key institutions. One such target was society's formal news outlets. Manipulating the media is an easier task in authoritarian regimes, but a democratic system does not automatically immunize the media from government influence or interference. Regardless of regime type television, radio, and newspapers have been used in the hopes of creating a "new individual" who would cast aside primordial feelings toward the home region or ethnic group in favor of the larger society. If the media aimed its message primarily at the adult population, it was the responsibility of the educational system to instill the values of the central government among its progeny. To this end school systems promoted saluting flags, singing anthems, and establishing clubs or civic organizations that rewarded those who demonstrated loyalty to the country. Despite impressive efforts these measures did not save the heterogeneous colonial empires that collapsed in the twentieth century. Nor did they keep the Pakistani, Soviet, Yugoslav, Ethiopian, and Czechoslovak states from disintegrating in the past few decades.

Increased trade, more extensive systems of transportation and communication, compulsory public education, and in some cases multiparty elections were believed sufficient to crush the convictions of those who would strive for smaller political units, or for more regional autonomy within existing frontiers. The failure of these peaceful methods has encouraged more hawkish policy-makers to augment repression in order to quell nationalistic passions. Fear that nationalism would inevitably lead to the disintegration of the state was the justification for these actions. In order to maintain the integrity of the state political parties, clubs and other organizations were banned, the press was restricted or controlled directly by the state, and various leaders were imprisoned. These measures "settled" the problem, but only for a short time. Such measures rarely resolved the nationalist question in the long term.

The existence of nationalist groups in developing states was not a surprise to many observers. Many of these new countries were unqualified artificial constructs, born of cartographers and policy-makers in Europe's colonial empires. Thus, they were often seen as immature societies, vulnerable to an array of internal cleavages. Nationalism in developing countries was often times assumed to be symptomatic of a state's "growing pains." This being the case, nationalism was viewed as a temporary phenomenon. Economic prosperity, technological advancements, urbanization and secularization were accepted "cures" for modernization's ills. Nonetheless, the existence of vibrant nationalist movements in advanced industrial states challenged this diagnosis. Autonomist and separatist groups endure in the Basque country, Catalonia, Corsica, northern Italy, Ulster, Scotland, Wales, Flanders, Wallonia, Quebec, Puerto Rico, and other cultural peripheries of developed countries. The presumed institutionalization of the state after decades, if not centuries, meant little to nationalists proposing to alter their relationships with their sovereigns. Living under someone's political roof does not create, in and of itself, a mutually hospitable environment. Nationalists often view their relationship to the state as a lopsided union in which one partner has a greater say in their affairs than it should. Recall that at times the dominant group in a state has sought to smother the identity of the minority or peripheral group. For many nationalists, the end result of this perceived imbalance is a demand either to renegotiate the terms of their political association or to dissolve them entirely. This desire to reset their political, economic, and social relationship with the state results from nationalists' insistence that they are not full and equal partners in their respective countries. They see themselves as second-, if not third-, class citizens. Even with increased material benefits descending from the central governing apparatus, many ethnic minorities still feel threatened and conclude that only by distancing themselves from their respective government center can they find tranquillity, if not prosperity.

Yet, not all ethnic minorities behave in the same manner. Some ethnic groups are relatively content with their current status and have little or no desire to change it. They have come to an agreement or an accommodation with their society's dominant group. It might help to view ethnic groups and their sense of nationalism in terms of a continuum. At one end we find nationalists who demand a separate state. Their goal is outright independence and the formation of their own sovereign country. On the other extreme of this spectrum, we find "complacent" ethnic groups. The word "complacent" here implies an ethnic group that collectively feels relatively safe and secure within its present borders and with its current group status. The group makes few demands, if any, for changes in its relations with the central government. Between those two extremes—of complacency and a desire for complete independence—there are a myriad of contemporary nationalist movements in both developed and developing countries.

In an attempt to locate groups along this continuum we should not leave with the impression that levels and intensities of nationalism are stagnant. To the contrary, over time nationalist sentiments intensify or moderate in reaction to the changing circumstances found in society. A central government willing to negotiate its relationship with its various ethnic groups may be able to salvage the state's borders. On the other hand states and their dominant groups can also create an environment that enflames nationalistic passions. The debate over nationalism among scholars and policy-makers has in many ways generated a vast array of questions with only moderate success at answering them. Why are some groups complacent while others are agitating for full independence? Why do still others seek only limited sovereignty? Why has nationalism emerged years after it was presumed to have perished? Are all pluralistic states vulnerable to the powerful currents that nationalism generates?

Toward a greater understanding of nationalism, this work will explore two contemporary movements—one in the Canadian province of Quebec and another in the American territory of Puerto Rico. On the surface these two cases appear to be quite different. Quebec has been geographically and historically linked to Canada and British North America for over two centuries. Its status as a Canadian province, an equal partner in Confederation, gives it a significant degree of input in the federal system. This province sends the second largest bloc of delegates to the federal House of Commons and has been home to many cabinet officers, prime ministers, and justices of the Canadian Supreme Court. Additionally, its internal autonomy is protected, like that of the other nine provinces, by the Canadian Constitution and federal laws. This case appears rather different from the territory of Puerto Rico, a Caribbean island that the United States has controlled for only one century. Since it is an unincorporated territory, insular residents, while citizens of the United States, have no effective legislative representation in Congress[2] nor can they vote for the president. Unlike Quebec's relationship to the federal capital in Ottawa, few of Puerto Rico's sons or daughters can be found on the roster of the powerful in Washington, D.C. What do Quebec and Puerto Rico have in common?

For starters, Quebec and Puerto Rico contain the largest non-English-speaking enclaves for Canada and the United States, respectively. While there are millions of French speakers in various provinces, only in Quebec do they constitute a majority. The Acadians, concentrated primarily in northern and eastern New Brunswick, view theirs as a culture distinct from their Francophone brethren of Quebec. But the Acadians account for only one-third of New Brunswick's population. There are also significant French-speaking minorities in

Ontario and Manitoba. But Quebec represents the sole remaining Francophone majority enclave in North America.³ Their minority status in the rest of the continent was assured when King Louis XV surrendered New France, thus leaving Quebec's fate in the hands of King George III and his heirs. Likewise, there are millions of Spanish speakers throughout the United States who nonetheless view their particular cultures (be they Cuban, Mexican/Chicano, or Puerto Rican) as distinct from one another. Only in the U.S. territory of Puerto Rico do Spanish speakers comprise the majority population. In purely geographic terms Puerto Rico is not a part of North America but rather is a part of the Caribbean. However, since the Spanish-American War of 1898 the island's fate has been in Washington's hands. Unlike its Canadian counterpart Puerto Rico is not an integral part of the American Union. Its official status as a "commonwealth" is a form of nonincorporated territory of the federal government. Unlike those of the "states" of the Union, Puerto Rico's autonomy is not constitutionally protected.

Despite these and other differences, Quebec and Puerto Rico have been captivated by the politics of nationalism. Nationalism represents a key component in the political and social arena of both this province and this territory. For decades their societies have debated the nature and depth of their relationships with their respective federal governments. At times the push was for cultural autonomy, at other periods the drive was for full-fledged independence. In either case politics in these two entities has focused for years on the relationship of the culturally distinct "periphery" to the "center." Additionally, the nature of Québécois and Puerto Rican nationalism has changed over the decades. In the past these movements provided lists of cultural markers that separated "us" from "them"; today they focus primarily (but not exclusively) on one issue—language. This change is not accidental. In order to politicize ethnicity, nationalists had to focus on a small number of cultural traits that would serve as their rallying point. Assuming that these elements distinguish one group from another, nationalists will quite often highlight language as a defining group marker due to its intrinsic qualities. In and of itself a linguistic divide between two groups does not create nationalistic tensions; to the contrary, for it to develop into the forefront of a nationalist's cause, certain key segments of society must intentionally incorporate linguistic differences into their "group myth." This work will argue that three major factors forged the contemporary connection between nationalism and language in Quebec and Puerto Rico.

The first major point is that despite their partition into two distinct political entities, embracing differing political philosophies, the dominant societies of both the United States and Canada shared an important social characteristic—they established a clear hierarchy, elevating the status of the English language and its speakers. The selection of language did not happen per chance. Yes, it was the predominant medium of communication. However, groups have flexibility with regard to what cultural traits they wish to highlight in terms of their group identity. Language, as a social symbol, served to unite individuals who previously saw themselves as pertaining to different groups. As the communication medium of society's elites, social, political, and economic ascendancy would require dominance of this language. Language served as a clear marker, separating the "in" group from the "out" group.

The same cultural trait that brought people together would also, paradoxically, provide elites with a means of restricting membership into their circles. The selection of language as a defining quality of group membership is based on its susceptibility to elite control. Dominant groups in society will promote those cultural traits that they can control or easily manipulate, if not monopolize. Elite input in the standardization process makes language a choice target. Dominant groups in societies hold up their dialect as the *correct* version of the vernacular. This they accomplish by *standardizing* their speech patterns as the accepted linguistic norm. Standard languages are then disseminated by intellectuals, pedagogues, and society's mainstream media. This is not the only cultural trait they can exploit; however, it is one of the few that elites can readily employ and easily direct. Ultimately elites seek to lower the costs of governing by establishing a cultural hegemony whereby the cultural markers they use to define their society are accepted by the population at large as obvious and common sense. Toward this end these elites used the state and its legislative powers to advance their status by promoting their language.

Second, it is argued that the defense of the French language by Québécois nationalists, and of Spanish by Puerto Rican nationalists, was a reaction by elites in the periphery to discriminatory policies and attitudes emanating from the dominant group's government and society at large. These policies and attitudes from the center served to impede the social and economic mobility of elites in the culturally distinct periphery. Language, along with religion, was one of several defining characteristics of Quebec society vis-à-vis English-speaking Canada. Throughout the twentieth century Roman Catholicism declined as a defining trait of Québécois identity, leaving the French language as the key group identifier. Language became the focus of provincial nationalists in the 1960s with the rise of a new secular technocratic elite. This new elite, created in large measure with the flourishing of technical education in Quebec (particularly in the natural and applied sciences, and in business-related fields) found a linguistic ceiling that limited their career advancements. Puerto Rican nationalism emerged in the nineteenth century while the island was still a colony of Spain. Clearly language did not separate peninsular Spaniards from islanders, though Puerto Ricans did speak a distinct dialect of Castilian. Language was not the focus of Puerto Rican nationalism in the first few years of American rule in Puerto Rico. This changed as the U.S. federal government began implementing its policy of cultural and linguistic assimilation. The Spanish language became one of the main concerns of local nationalists as highly educated Puerto Ricans were limited in participating in the local administration—one of the few avenues for upward mobility available at that time. Spearheading the connection between Puerto Ricanness and the Spanish language were teachers.

In both the Quebec and Puerto Rico cases, barriers to upward mobility served as the catalyst for linking language with politico-cultural demands on the state. However, the successful socialization of most members of an ethnic group to the link between language and their group identity will require the newly formed elite to convince the masses that such a move is in their interests. One available avenue is to convince the masses that their own prospective upward mobility is at stake. Non-Anglophone elites in Puerto Rico and Quebec argued that impediments to their socioeconomic assent (as high-class members of a low-status group) guaranteed the subordination of the non-English-speaking masses (as low-class members of a low-status group). In effect, their prosperity is predicated on the overthrow of the existing socio-politico-economic order that relegates the entire periphery to a subservient status. By embracing the new social link of nation and language, the Puerto Rican and Québécois masses sought to transform their low social status within the larger state to that of a high-status group within the periphery. Elites outside the center are offering the peripheral masses a heightened social standing today that potentially holds the promise of an enhanced economic position tomorrow.

New elites in Puerto Rico and Quebec could not have forged the links between language and nationalism without the help of the dominant group— English speakers. Nationalism in Puerto Rico and Quebec are reactions to a North American hegemonic cultural order that elevated the social standing, political power, and economic opportunities of English speakers. This is not to say that governments or elites from the state's center intentionally participated in the creation of the local nationalist movements. Rather, nationalism in Quebec and Puerto Rico was an unanticipated byproduct of policies and attitudes in English Canada and the United States, respectively. There can be no "us" unless there is simultaneously a "them." In the Canadian case, the reservation of choice positions in commerce and industry for English speakers relegated Quebec's French-speaking majority to performing manual labor. This discriminatory attitude in the private sector preceded attempts by the British Crown to assimilate French-speaking Canadians in the late eighteenth and early nineteenth centuries. Previous attempts at cultural assimilation would be subsequently used by nationalists in their myth-making project of fomenting a new *Québécois* identity as opposed to a *French Canadian* identity. Defenders of the French language in Canada would also highlight, in their nationalist litany, federal policies that limited the spread of their language outside Quebec.

The American federal government was also a key (though unwitting) actor in the crystallization of a distinct Puerto Rican identity. Federal policy early in the twentieth century placed a great emphasis on "Americanization" and cultural assimilation for both immigrants and territorial residents. Toward that end a high priority was given to the perfusion of public education in the English language. The implementation of this policy would require a multitude of Anglophone, or at least English-proficient, teachers. As a result, this policy remained a constant threat to the livelihood of most Puerto Rican educators and would also prevent their ascent within the magisterial bureaucracy. Additionally, choice positions in the local administration, aside from teachers, were reserved for those fluent in English.

Barriers to upward mobility for local elites fueled resentment. This indignation, in time, would be channeled into the development of a nationalist movement. Just as elites in the dominant society forged links with their masses, so would elites in the culturally distinct periphery. Through nationalism elites in Quebec and Puerto Rico offered their masses a change in status. The transition they offered is one of a low-status group in the larger society to that of a high-status group in a geographically smaller enclave. In North America various elites endeavored to establish a cultural hegemony. Similarly elite members of subordinate groups struggled to enact a "counter-hegemony." This counter-hegemony would aspire to overthrow the existing hegemonic order. For nationalists, however, their intended field of action is not the entire breadth of the state, but only the periphery.

Third, it is contended that a key instrument of peripheral elites to promote their status is the use of the substate entity—the political sphere where they have the greatest leverage. Of all legislation enacted at the substate level, only a small percentage concerns issues related to culture. Such legislation in a culturally distinct periphery is evidence of attempts to institutionalize a counter-hegemony. Many social scientists have focused a great deal of attention on the central government and its many institutions. Yet, substate polities, whether they be territorial, provincial, or departmental legislatures are often at the forefront of cultural defense. This is often the case where the group under study represents either a majority or a significant plurality in a substate jurisdiction. As one of the few administrative units that peripheral elites dominate, it is the logical locus for the institutionalization of the peripheral group's counter-hegemony.

French-speaking legislators in Ottawa and Spanish-speaking legislators in Washington, D.C. are in the minority. However, this numerically inferior status does not carry over into local legislatures. Francophones clearly dominate the National Assembly in Quebec City and Hispanophones unquestionably control the territorial legislature in San Juan. Their status as "local majorities" has been used to enact policies at the local level that would bolster the linguistic-national nexus. How far local majorities go in terms of pushing their cultural agenda will depend upon the limits of their lawmaking abilities as defined by statute or central constitution (a "brake"), combined with their perceived cultural threat (an "accelerator"). The greater the number and kinds of perceived cultural threats, the more numerous and extensive will be the demands made by the group in question on the center.

This book will endeavor to demonstrate how these factors contributed to the development and sustenance of contemporary nationalism in the Quebec and Puerto Rico cases. The following chapter provides an overview of ongoing debates among scholars. Nations, like ethnicity, are *invented* identities, based on malleable myths of common ancestry or kinship. Whereas ethnic groups may or may not be conscious of their existence, nations must be. In addition, nations make political demands for a devolution of power from the central state. This definition leaves open the question of why nationalist groups make such demands. Culturalists, or primordialists, argue that the answer lies in the cultural traits themselves. Rational choice approaches to the study of ethnic conflict counter this view. One influential variant of this school of thought suggests that nationalism is a direct consequence of a "cultural division of labor" that results as ethnic status coincides with class and social status. Rational choice approaches usually assume a continuous recalculation of the benefits for supporting the nationalist agenda. Thus, this approach implies a short-term view of the commitment to a nationalist cause while most research points to nationalist identity and commitment to the endeavor as a rather long-term project. Other scholars challenge this point, suggesting that the nationalist enterprise is predicated on long-term strategies based on the establishment of a cultural hegemony.

Chapter 3 explores the links between language and elites. Key actors in the development of the national identity are elites who endeavor to forge cultural links with their populations. Such links, by creating a sense of common identity, benefit elites by entrenching their status in society and allowing them, with popular support, to restrict the participation of rivals. In exchange for popular support, elites offer the masses a higher social status; however, elites also want to maintain their privileges and power. One way of accomplishing both of these seemingly diametrical goals is through the selection of language as a cultural marker. A medium of communication can distinguish one group from another. At the same time it also differentiates between elites who speak its standard variant or dialect and the masses who speak a lower-class or unstandardized version of a language. Thus, language is a cultural trait that has the interesting duality of both separating the "in" and "out" groups while preserving the social hierarchy within the "in" group.

Chapter 4 explores the connection between the English language and American identity. Early on language was viewed as one of the elements uniting the inhabitants of the thirteen colonies and was used to distinguish the American colonists from others—particularly the German colonists. At the same time the American variant of English distinguished the colonists from the British. In time, American society would embrace Germans and other European immigrants on the condition that they first acquire its language. Learning this language was a requirement for becoming an American citizen. Elites from other societies would first have to learn English before they could be accepted as members of the dominant society here. At the collective level members of the dominant society imposed a linguistic litmus test on would-be members of the Union. Thus, evidence of a linguistic hegemonic order can be found in the popular acceptance of this linguistic requirement for both individuals aspiring to become Americans and territories seeking admittance into the Union. In time this language would also be imposed on the non-English-speaking peoples living in overseas territories.

The fifth chapter will look at how the British regime in North America also established a clear linguistic hierarchy, placing the King's language on top. It is true that from the beginning Canada was a country with two "founding" languages—English and French. But one outranked the other. English was the dominant medium of communication in Canada. It was also the language in which most large-scale commerce was conducted, and that included French-speaking Quebec. Montreal, the largest city in the Province of Quebec, was also the business center for English-speaking Canada. Additionally, policies were established that impeded the spread of the French language outside of Quebec and at times policies were implemented with the goal of linguistically assimilating the French-speaking *Canadiens*.

Chapter 6 will investigate how nationalism in Puerto Rico changed over time and how now, under American rule, it embraces the Spanish language as a key defining trait. Language is not the only cultural trait that distinguishes Puerto Ricans from Americans, but it is recognized by many as the most important. The connection between the Spanish language and *Puertorriqueñidad*, or Puerto Ricanness, emerged in the first decades of the twentieth century in response to the federal government's Americanization policy. This policy hindered the upward mobility of an emerging elite, the new pool of college-educated Puerto Ricans who were seeking employment in the territorial government's bureaucracy. One segment of this new elite that stands out in particular was the new batch of public school teachers. Implementing Americanization required a large pool of teachers fluent in English. The careers of these new elites were continuously threatened by education commissioners who preferred Americans over islanders. Pedagogues were among the first to defend the Spanish language in legislation as they pushed to establish a counter-hegemony focusing on the Spanish language as a defining group trait. Their prime target of political action was the legislature in San Juan. The new local elite-mass connection was facilitated by high-ranking bureaucrats who threatened to revoke the diplomas of students who failed to show sufficient mastery of English. Again, to a significant degree twentieth-century Puerto Rican nationalism was an unanticipated byproduct of the U.S. policy of cultural assimilation.

The seventh chapter will explore the evolution of nationalism in Quebec with its current emphasis on the French language. In both the eighteenth and nineteenth centuries, two traits stood out as markers of the *Canadien*: the Catholic faith and secondarily the French language. That religion was a key element in this cultural equation should not be surprising since the conquest of New France by Britain left the Roman Catholic church as one of the fundamental pillars of Quebec society. As such, clerics, who constituted a significant portion of the peripheral elites, sought to peddle a cultural trait that they monopolized. This emphasis on faith changed in the twentieth century as Quebec became more urban and secular and thus created a new elite. Québécois nationalism emerged in its modern guise in the 1960s during the "Quiet Revolution," a period that witnessed the upward mobility of highly educated Francophones. An emphasis on training in the applied and natural sciences, in addition to business-related fields, created a pool of highly trained college graduates. Their ascent was hampered by their lack of proficiency in English—the language of interprovincial and continental commerce. Nationalism was additionally fueled by a large influx of immigrants from abroad in the 1960s. Immigrants to Quebec ordinarily chose to learn English over French, and in so doing could jump ahead of French speakers and present a serious long-term threat to the ascendancy of the new Francophone elites.

Returning to Puerto Rico, chapter 8 will inquire into the various measures taken by the legislature in San Juan to protect Spanish. Puerto Ricans have no effective representation in Washington, leaving the territorial government in San Juan as the logical target for legislative action. Contrary to what some scholars have suggested, it will be argued that protecting or even mandating the use of a particular language *does* augment its social standing and expands the economic parameters of that language's users. At a minimum legislation can reserve choice positions in the local bureaucracy for peripheral language speakers. That restriction is particularly important in Puerto Rico where over one-third of all those employed on the island work for either the Commonwealth or its municipal governments. The legislative output will depend on two primary factors, the perceived cultural threat and the substate's formal legislative parameters. As a U.S. territory Puerto Rico's lawmaking powers are limited by federal statutes. The U.S. Constitution gives Congress broad powers over the territories. On the other hand, the island's distance from the North American mainland limited Anglophone migration and therefore the number of mainland English speakers with whom Puerto Ricans would have to compete for jobs. Local elites have succeeded in defining Puerto Rican identity on the basis of the Spanish language; however, at present there is no direct challenge (by way of direct competition) to the careers or upward mobility of most Puerto Ricans on the basis of language. The end result of these two factors has been the approval of essentially symbolic language laws.

In contrast, the ninth chapter will examine how Québécois elites have used their provincial majority to enact language laws. Linking group identity to language will encourage groups to turn to the only government they can rely on. Dominant groups are effective at utilizing the central state. At times Francophones, while a minority in Canada, have been able to effectively use their seats in the federal parliament to defend Quebec's interests. However, when it comes to pursuing the nationalist agenda, it is the provincial legislature that counts the most. As an equal partner in the Confederation, Quebec has far broader lawmaking powers than does Puerto Rico. To this one must add its constitutional powers to bypass the decisions of the Canadian Supreme Court. A strong perception of threat from the province's Anglophone elite and immigrant communities, coupled with broad lawmaking powers, laid the groundwork for a series of language laws in Quebec that have gone far beyond symbolic declarations to promote the role and usage of French in government, business, and public education, while simultaneously restricting the uses of English in Quebec's public domain.

The last chapter will look to the future of Puerto Rican-American and Québécois-Canadian relations. In the coming years the governments in both Washington and Ottawa will be facing challenges to the *status quo*. The biggest push for a status change in the next few years will come from those advocating statehood in Puerto Rico and those promoting sovereignty in Quebec. In the Puerto Rican case, Congress will have to contend with the issue of admitting a non-English-speaking entity with an active separatist movement into the American Union. But policy-makers in both Washington and Ottawa will need to understand the processes that have led to the development of nationalism in the first place. It may be difficult for them to accept that policies laid forth by their predecessors were primarily responsible for nationalism's genesis and subsequent development. Assuming they were to understand the root causes of it, these political actors may not have the resources, or be willing, to pay the price for fully incorporating their culturally distinctive regions. It is hoped that in addition to exploring the origins and the roles language has played in the articulation of nationalist demands this book will shed light on the future trajectory of relations between the dominant English-speaking societies of North America and their linguistic peripheries. Additionally, the two cases studies here may provide important clues for understanding the rise of nationalism in other parts of the globe.

NOTES

1. In order to maintain consistency with current usage in international relations and the literature on nationalism, the word *state* will refer to sovereign political units/independent countries. When referring to the internal divisions of the United States, the word will appear in quotes.

2. Although insular Puerto Ricans are U.S. citizens, they are also residents of a federal territory as opposed to a member "state" of the Union. As a result, they have no representation in the federal Senate and only a nonvoting *resident commissioner* in the federal House of Representatives. However, their ethnic brethren on the U.S. mainland, sharing both U.S. citizenship and "state" residency, do elect Senators and full members to the House of Representatives.

3. The term "North America," as used in this book, will be used in a cultural and geographic sense; therefore, it will not include Mexico.

2

Conflicting Approaches to the Study of Nationalism

Custom dictates that discussions of a social phenomenon start with a definition. In the social sciences different disciplines and competing approaches far too often employ the same term in contradictory ways, creating terminological confusion. Yet, when it comes to disparate uses of the word "nationalism," scholars are not the only contributors. Writers in the popular presses also utilize the term "nationalism" in a myriad of ways, adding to the terminological clutter. In order to avoid contributing to this lexical, tumult this section will begin with a definition of the terms "nation" and "nationalism," and their relationship to the concept of ethnicity, and discuss when national sentiment first emerged.

NATIONS, ETHNIC GROUPS, AND MODERNITY

Simply put, the term "nationalism" refers to a sense of loyalty to the "nation." Though there have been many definitions of "nations," one of the most popular, disseminated early in the twentieth century, was provided by Joseph Stalin (Conner 1994: 73). He defined it as "a historically evolved, stable community of language, territory, economic life, and psychological make-up manifested in a community of culture" (Stalin 1935: 8). While Hobsbawm (1990: 2) questioned the "intellectual merits" of Stalin's work, he nonetheless acknowledged its profound political influence. Stalin's definition attempted to capture what he considered to be all of the significant cultural traits that went into the formulation of national identity. This trend continued throughout the twentieth century as other definitions of nations, in general and as they applied to particular groups, attempted to characterize national identity on the basis of tangible cultural elements.

More recent scholarship has focused not on the visible components of nations (language, common territory, etc.) but rather on the psychological aspect of this identity. This new generation of scholarship argues that objective cultural traits do not make nations. Rather, they are paraded, once a sense of national identity is created, to prove to the group in question and the world that the nation exists. The focus on the objective traits of a culture—elements that one can clearly point to and observe—is an attempt to provide the requisite evidence that group *A* is different from group *B*. This process of cultural dismemberment of national identity on the basis of its constituent attributes is referred to as objectification (Handler 1988: 13-15).

Western thought holds the natural sciences in high regard for their ability to objectively study and analyze phenomena by rationalization and atomization (Handler 1988: 14). Objectification is an attempt by social scientists and nationalist leaders to attain this status by "proving" that the ethnic group in question is truly distinct. This is accomplished by breaking a culture down into its constituent objective traits. "Mimicking natural science, social scientists attempt to suspend their subjectivity and occupy a neutral and removed position from which to analyze the social world—which must, then, be understood automatically, in terms of its bounded elements or parts and the causal interconnections among them" (Handler 1988: 15). However, objectifying a particular group trait changes it from a "custom" to a "tradition" (Handler 1988: 77). The spontaneous act is now calculated and fixed in time and place.

In the past few decades, many scholarly works have acknowledged that nations are invented social entities (Hobsbawm 1983a). As a result scholars who study nationalism today tend to focus less on describing the particular attributes of a particular group than their academic predecessors did. This is not to say that the cultural attributes of a nation are unimportant. After all, the nationalist justifies political demands and actions on the basis of safeguarding the characteristics in question. However, to say that these traits are important is not the same as arguing that they *caused* the nationalist sentiment in the first instance. Instead, more recent scholarship tends to focus on discovering how that "created" national identity developed in the first place—an identity that afterward may lead to the development of nationalist movements.

One eminent scholar characterized a nation as "an imagined political community" (Anderson, B. 1983: 15). This definition emphasizes that nations are constructed and that they harbor political aspirations. With respect to the first element of this definition, its *imagined* nature, Anderson was not alone in arguing that nations are artificial constructs. Other scholars, including Hechter (1975: 4) and Gellner (1983: 7), also incorporated a notion of psychological construction in the development of national identities. They are imagined because "the members of even the smallest nation will never know most of their fellow members, meet them, or even hear them, yet in the minds of each lives the image of their communication" (Anderson, B. 1983: 15). This solidarity is ultimately based on a myth of common ancestral relationship (Conner 1994: xi; Smith 1989: 344). Though they lack genealogical evidence to confirm their beliefs, members of a particular nation quite often assume that they share blood ties and are therefore members of an extended family (Glazer & Moynihan 1970: 18). This extended family of sorts is always juxtaposed to others. Affirming the existence of "us" is an exercise in comparative analysis that requires the simultaneous presence of "them."

The second part of Anderson's definition refers to a political community. The nationalist asks, at times demands, that political power within the state be partitioned and redistributed on the basis of this national sentiment and presumed blood ties. Gellner (1983: 1) asserted that nationalism "is primarily a political principle, which holds that the political and the national unit should be congruent." The foundation of this political community must be some sort of territorial base (Smith 1981: 69-71); however, land claims by nationalist groups do not preclude rival claims by other groups in society, nor do they rule out disagreements within a given nation as to the parameters of its national boundaries.[1] Nationalist demands can range from moderate requests for additional autonomy to the complete separation of the nationalist's region from the current state structure, thus creating a new sovereign country. Whereas a state *is* inherently a political community, a nation *hopes to become* one. In and of itself the existence of a nationalist identity or even a full-fledged nationalist movement does not assure the attainment of this goal. The realization of that final step will require negotiation, subtle and direct pressure on state and key social actors, and possibly armed conflict as a last resort.

The concept of nationalism is intimately tied to that of ethnicity. Ethnic groups, like nations, also have myths of common origin (Eriksen 1993: 12); thus, members of an ethnic group also share the belief that their relationship is based on common blood ties. "One constructs an ethnic identification using knowledge about ancestries in one's background" (Waters 1990: 19). However, this knowledge is not always based on objective information and is often susceptible to manipulation. In some cases individuals, or even entire groups, can alter their ethnic designation (Waters 1990: 26). These *imagined* communities, as opposed to nations, are not inherently political nor are they necessarily conscious of their distinctiveness. Membership in an ethnic group may be identified by an outside observer; on the other hand membership in a nation requires the individual to be self-aware and thus be self-defined (Conner 1994: 103).

Like ethnic ideologies, nationalism stresses the cultural similarity of its adherents and, by implication, it draws boundaries vis-à-vis others, who thereby become outsiders. The distinguishing mark of nationalism is by definition its relationship to the state. A nationalist holds that political boundaries should be coterminous with cultural boundaries, whereas many ethnic groups do not demand command over a state. When the political leaders of an ethnic movement make demands to this effect, the ethnic movement therefore by definition becomes a nationalist movement. (Eriksen 1993: 6)

Thus, the terms "nation" and "ethnic group," while distinct, are also related. This explains Moynihan's (1993: 4-5) statement designating nations as the "highest" form of ethnic group. Once an ethnic group begins making political demands on the state, based on its cultural distinctiveness, it has crossed the threshold and become a nation.

While ethnic groups have existed for eons and in all parts of the globe, nations are relatively recent creations that first emerged in the West. There is a strong consensus among social scientists that the phenomenon we call "nationalism" first emerged in Europe (Hobsbawm 1983, 1990; Kedourie 1993; Kohn 1962; Smith 1981), and that subsequently the nationalist ideal spread to its colonies. Agreement as to the origin of nationalism has not translated into a consensus on its timing—when nations and national identity first emerged. Some date nationalism to the start of the nineteenth century (Kedourie 1993: 1).[2] Others push its genesis back to the latter part of the eighteenth century and claim that it emerged with the French Revolution (Kohn 1962; Smith 1981: 23).[3]

National identities that appear to be ancient are in fact of recent origin. As a part of the myth of common ancestry, groups will selectively include and exclude bits and pieces of their own histories, even their ancient histories, giving an antiquated feel to a relatively recent phenomenon. While a distinctive Welsh culture and language may have existed for many centuries, Welsh nationalism goes back only as far as the late eighteenth century and the formation of Welsh literary societies (Smith 1981: 23). Similarly, despite claims of ancient animosities, Hobsbawm (1983a: 13-14) argued that Israeli and Palestinian nationalism are also recent constructions. Anderson defined nations as "imagined political communities," and there are other researchers who concur and add that groups, at times, even *invent* histories (or parts of their histories), weaving the innovation into the collective's myth of common ancestry and adding to the group's arsenal of *invented traditions* (Hobsbawm 1983a; Roosens 1989).

CULTURALIST VIEWS OF NATIONALISM

Contrasting theories of nationalism can be divided into two main branches. There are those who focus on nationalism's constructed nature and the choices involved in selecting national identities. This perspective is challenged by cultural theorists, also referred to as the primordialist school, who focus on the cultural traits that are highlighted by the nationalists themselves. One of their preeminent advocates within political science is Inglehart, who said that

[t]he political culture approach today constitutes the leading alternative to rational choice theory as a general explanatory framework for political behavior. The political culture approach is distinctive in arguing that (1) people's responses to their situation are shaped by subjective orientations, which vary cross-culturally and within subcultures; *and* (2) these variations in subjective orientations reflect differences in one's socialization experience, with early learning conditioning later learning, making the former more difficult to undo. Consequently, action can *not* be interpreted as simply the result of external situations: Enduring differences in cultural learning also play an essential part in shaping what people think and do. (Inglehart 1990: 19) [emphasis in the original]

First, and foremost, cultural theories argue that cultures "cannot be changed overnight" (Inglehart 1990: 19). That is because "cultural changes reflect the socialization of enduring habits and attitudes" (Inglehart 1990: 17). Culturalists generally focus on the continuity of the objective characteristics that constitute a cultural group such as its language, religion, folk traditions, or other such attributes. This is not to say that cultures do not mutate, merely that they change rather slowly (Inglehart 1988: 1203). Followers of this approach often assume that the persistence of cultural differences is due to "the relative isolation of the peripheral group from the mainstream culture of the core" (Hechter 1975: 23). When changes do take place they usually occur among the younger segments of society; thus cultural shifts take generations to take effect (Inglehart 1990: 19).

Almond (1980: 2) claimed that the importance of culture, when it comes to analyzing social and political phenomena goes back to Plato's *Republic*. However, among contemporary scholars the trend toward focusing on culture more likely emerged with Max Weber (1958) and one of his most influential works that argued that the theological differences between Catholicism and Protestantism played a significant role in the development of early agricultural capitalism in northwestern Europe. Almond and Verba's (1963) study is perhaps one of the most cited in the culturalist perspective. They contended that the commitment to democracy in the United States and United Kingdom, as opposed to West Germany, Italy, and Mexico, was due primarily to a "civic culture" that permeated these Anglophone states—a culture that encouraged consensus while tolerating diversity (Almond & Verba 1963: 8). Their study was predated by Banfield's (1958) research into enduring attitudes in southern Italy. He argued that this particular region was characterized by an extensive emphasis on family ties over nonfamilial relations (such as civil associations), low levels of interpersonal trust, and a parochial attitude toward the larger society. This culture was caught up in a syndrome that he labeled "amoral familism."

Subsequently many scholars attacked the culturalist perspective for its allegedly ethnocentric praise of the cultural attributes of advanced industrial societies, particularly those pertaining to the Anglo-American cultural family, and for its static concept of culture (Inglehart 1988: 1204). Conceptually, however, the culturalist perspective has been criticized on more substantial grounds. Culturalist theories often emerged as a result of observing many failed integration processes in the developing world. Some began to question their applicability to the more industrialized North Atlantic region. As Hechter (1975: 26) noted, it would be difficult to argue that peripheral groups in Western societies are economically, politically, or even culturally isolated from the core. Regions in West European countries experiencing ethnic revivals and witnessing increased demands for greater political autonomy are areas that lost their isolation ages ago. Nationalist movements in Scotland, Wales, and Catalonia cannot be attributed to core penetration of peripheral regions when many of these regions had been economically, socially, and politically incorporated into the core state for centuries. In addition, many from the cultural periphery were key players in the colonial exploits of their host states. Many were settlers, some were soldiers and clerics, and a few were even high-ranking administrators and bureaucrats in the colonial apparatus, both at home and abroad.

Additionally, others have attacked the culturalist perspective for focusing on cultural traits themselves. Culturalists focus on the long-term maintenance of an objective group marker. Their perspective, emphasizing the primacy of the cultural traits themselves, would logically lead us to believe that alteration in these traits would lead to breakdowns and reconfigurations in group solidarity. Yet, it is remarkable that group unity survives changes in these attributes. Both Connor (1994: 44) and Edwards (1985: 160) contended that national or ethnic cohesion can persist despite the loss of any objective group marker. "In the final analysis, the coincidence of the customary tangible attributes of nationality, such as common language or religion, is not determinative. The prime requisite is subjective and consists of the self-determination of people with a group—its past, its present, and what is most important, its destiny" (Conner 1994: 4). As Conner (1994: 104) pointed out, Irish and Scottish identity remained intact despite the loss of Gaelic as their vernacular. Common ancestry myths for these two communities adjusted to the loss of a clearly distinguishable cultural marker just as other group myths have altered legends of their origin and historical travails.[4]

A case in point is Roosen's (1989) study of the Hurons (or Wedat) of Quebec that documented a deliberate change in the group's myth by its grand chief—a shift that failed to disrupt the community's sense of social cohesion. His research illustrated a clear example of historical revision by Chief Max Gros-Louis whose account of the Huron past omitted references to his nation's persecution at the hands of the Iroquois centuries earlier in order to conform to a new pan-Native American identity. This new emphasis on aboriginal unity required the downplaying of historic rivalries and even the quelling of past wrongs committed by other aboriginal peoples. Narratives explaining why the group migrated to its present location had to be deleted in order to present a united front against the dominant society. Simultaneously, local whites, particularly the French, were blamed by the Hurons for territorial deprivation when the historical record shows that Huron settlements in Canada were a gift from the French in the aftermath of the Huron exodus from what is today New York State (Roosens 1989: 57-63).[5] Roosens noted: "In the ethnic arsenal you can partially forget what you know if others do not notice or do not mind" (1989: 161).

The failure to account for nationalist revivals in advanced industrial states where the core penetrated the periphery well in the past and the persistence of group solidarity despite significant modifications in group myths and changes in group traits cast serious doubts on the power of cultural approaches to explain nationalism. A rival explanation tried to combat the weakness in the culturalist perspective by arguing instead that national identities are a deliberate choice and not innate. Key to this creation process is the economic (and subsequent social) division of groups in society on the basis of objective cultural traits.

NATIONALISM AND THE "CULTURAL DIVISION OF LABOR"

Contrasting the culturalist perspective is its main rival—according to Inglehart (1990: 19)—the rational choice school. Though it has been subsequently applied to various branches of the social sciences, it originated within economics. As Morrow (1994: 304) pointed out, there is no one rational choice theory. Instead, this is an approach that assumes that "people have goals and that they attempt to realize those goals through their actions" (Morrow 1994: 7). Additionally, this approach presupposes that individuals have some freedom of choice despite the fact that the available choices may be unpleasant (Morrow 1994: 7-8). As applied to the study of nationalism, the rational choice approach would state that individuals have a choice in selecting their ethnic identity. The availability to choose does not guarantee that one will avoid unpleasant alternatives. This approach counters the culturalist perspective that takes culture as a given rather than as something that is created.

The rational choice approach has worked its way into many disciplines in the social sciences. Some who used this approach in the past have argued that nationalism develops as a response to the economic exploitation and deprivation of one group at the hands of another. One of this approach's main proponents in the study of nationalism is Hechter, who employed a notion of "internal colonialism." As he conceptualized it, the core region's penetration of the state's periphery is not unlike Europe's penetration of its overseas colonies. In much the same way as colonial regimes exploited both the people and the natural resources of their territorial possessions in the Americas, Asia, Africa, and Oceania, these same colonial systems also abused their own hinterlands. Structurally, Hechter argued, England's exploitation of India and Nigeria was paralleled by its exploitation of Wales and Ireland. The intensity of exploitation was greater overseas, but it was still prevalent in Britain's Celtic perimeter.

Industrialization begins in the core region and diffuses to the outlying areas of the state. This pattern of technological diffusion establishes a clear hierarchy of an industrialized center exploiting its domestic periphery for its natural resources. The industries that eventually develop in the periphery do not cater to local needs and markets but complement and serve the needs of the country's core. This model of economic development creates, in the provinces, an "internal colony." Internal colonialism thus posits that exploitation of the periphery by the core region is analogous to bourgeois exploitation of the working class.

A geographical hierarchy ensues where the core emerges in a superior position to its periphery. The foundation of this hierarchy is economic, though it quickly develops important social and political dimensions. The peripheral population, elite and mass alike, becomes associated with the economic station of the region. Implicit in Hechter's thesis is that economic submission translates into social subservience. Downturns in the peripheral economy, particularly those of a long-term nature, will be felt more strongly here than in the state's core, fueling resentment toward the central state. This situation fuels nationalism.

The incorporation of the periphery into the state's economic sphere promotes a "cultural division of labor" that accounts for the development of nationalist movements in advanced industrial democracies.

Agreeing, at least in part, Gellner (1983: 24) echoed the notion that "[n]ationalism is rooted in a *certain kind* of division of labour" [emphasis in the original] as did Rogowski (1985: 87), who connected nationalism with a "social division of labor." As Steinberg put it:

If there is an iron law of ethnicity, it is that when ethnic groups are found in a hierarchy of power, wealth, and status, then conflict is inescapable. However, where there is social, economic, and political parity among the constituent groups, ethnic conflict, when it occurs, tends to be at a low level and rarely spills over into violence. (Steinberg 1981: 170)

Hechter's proposition, influenced by dependency theory, which was at its apex in the 1970s when his work *Internal Colonialism* was published, stated:

The spatially uneven wave of modernization over state territory creates relatively advanced and less advanced groups. As a consequence of this initial fortuitous advantage, there is crystallization of the unequal distribution of resources and power between the two groups. The superordinate group, or core, seeks to stabilize and monopolize its advantages through policies aiming at the institutionalization of the existing stratification system. It attempts to regulate the allocation of social roles such that those roles commonly defined as having high prestige are reserved for its members. Conversely, individuals from the less advanced group are denied access to these roles. This stratification system, which may be termed a cultural division of labor, contributes to the development of distinctive ethnic identification in the two groups. (Hechter 1975: 9)

The gulf that develops between individuals in the periphery and the core resembles the social and economic discrepancies between classes and status groups (Hechter 1975: 37). Regardless of their qualifications individuals from the periphery are limited in their upward mobility. It should be stated at this point that this kind of core discrimination is not absolute but varies in degrees at different periods in history (Hechter 1975: 346). As is often the case in culturally heterogeneous societies, different groups occupy varying positions in the socioeconomic hierarchy, resulting in divergent degrees of ethnic mobilization from one group to the next.

As individuals are denied social mobility, they develop a sense of resentment toward the central region, its culture, and its government. "To the extent that social stratification in the periphery is based on observable cultural differences, there exists the probability that the disadvantaged group will, in time, reactivity assert its own culture as equal or superior to that of the relatively advantaged core" (Hechter 1975: 10). Naturally, this indignation is not felt equally by all in the peripheral society. It most strongly affects those in the periphery who are looking for advancement due to their exceptional skills. Their high local status is nontransferable to the larger society.

One group in particular that will show early signs of growing nationalism are the peripheral notables or elites who are, as a result of their social and economic positions, the most likely to expect an opportunity to ascend the socio-economic-political ladder of the larger state. Rogowski (1985: 92-93) added that "[i]n a CDL [Cultural Division of Labor] any failure to fully assimilate to elite culture and position any substantial number of those of the nonelite who acquire elite skills will be highly likely to inspire nationalism among the nonelite; and the unassimilated or unaccepted upwardly mobile will be the most fervent national-ists."

Not surprisingly, the cultural division of labor argument is not universally accepted by all social scientists. Conner (1994: 47) criticized the entire eco-nomic approach to the study of nationalism, arguing that economic disparities may exacerbate ethnic consciousness but do not cause it. He claimed that to fo-cus on economic differentials between the core and its periphery is to make the same mistake as those who emphasize the objective (and changeable) cultural traits of a nation (Conner 1994: 145). Levels of economic deprivation and de-velopment change over time. Smith (1981: 5) added that economics may rein-force certain trends, or may even act as a catalyst, but it is not the primary cul-prit. He pointed to examples of nationalism in the Spanish Basque region (Euskadi) and in Catalonia (also in Spain) where the periphery, as opposed to the core, represents the more advanced part (in terms of industrialization) of the state (Smith 1982: 21). To this list, and for the same reason, Conner (1994: 148) added the Chinese of Malaysia and the Croats and Slovenes within the pre-1991 Yugoslav Federation. On the same basis Brand (1985: 277) criticized Hechter for his theory's inapplicability to the Scottish case. He countered that Scotland, rather than being a mere colonial outpost of the larger British state, was an inte-gral part of it and for years has been as economically and industrially advanced as the English core. This critique is rather significant when one takes into ac-count that Hechter first tested his internal colonialist model on Britain's Celtic periphery.

In a subsequent work Hechter (1985: 25) acknowledged some of these criti-cisms and suggested that his earlier work was not wrong as much as it was in-complete. On this point McRoberts (1979: 296) agreed. However, in Hechter's defense, the critics failed to take into account Rogowski's (1985) admonition that when exploring a nationalist movement one should pay close attention to peripheral elites. Hechter's critics focused on analyzing the economic status of the periphery as a whole rather than focusing on any social segment within that periphery. Aggregate analyses of a region do not always indicate the state of its elites and, as will later be discussed in greater detail, elites constitute the most susceptible segment in peripheral or even the dominant society to nationalist arguments.

But McRoberts offered constructive criticism that pointed to some of the flaws of Hechter's detractors. The previously mentioned critics pointed to examples of peripheral regions experiencing nationalistic revivals, varying in type and intensity, while at the same time highlighting their relatively privileged economic condition vis-à-vis the state's core. McRoberts noted that this is not the case in Quebec where in terms of industrial development and per capita income this Canadian province's status is analogous to that of wealthier provinces, such as Ontario. The problem is not the cultural division between Quebec and English-speaking Canada, but the cultural division *within* that province (McRoberts 1979: 296). Inside Quebec English speakers enjoy a privileged position over French speakers.[6] As such, Hechter's more general "cultural division of labor" thesis, which can apply both inter- and intraregionally, has more explanatory power than his more specific "internal colonialism" argument, which focuses almost exclusively on peripheral economic subjugation by the core (McRoberts 1979: 314). Additionally, the broader cultural division of labor argument could explain the rise of nationalism in relatively prosperous regions such as Catalonia where the periphery holds an economic advantage over the state's core. In Catalonia there is a clear cultural division of labor. However, here it is the peripheral ethnic group—the Catalans—who enjoy economic preeminence within the region, not Castilian speakers.[7]

Perhaps the most pressing issues regarding Hechter's work came from Laitin. First, when appraising the applicability of rational choice theories to nationalism, one must account for the persistence of ethnic identity without the continuous assessment that normally goes with this approach. Rational choice assumes that individuals, being *rational* actors, will act according to a set of ordered preferences. Assuming that economic benefits are at the top of one's agenda, then the nationalist venture would gain support as individuals saw it in their best interest to identify with the nation over the central state. The obverse of this argument is that a subsequent calculation showing diminishing returns coming from the project would spell an immediate downturn in nationalist support. However, many studies of nationalist movements have documented long-term fidelity to the cause that appears unrelated to short-term economic fluctuations. As Laitin noted: "Because ethnic identity is believed to be a biological 'given,' most people at most times do not calculate how much satisfaction they derive from their ethnic identities. Without calculation and the weighing of satisfactions, economic paradigms lose their explanatory power" (Laitin 1986: 101).

A second problem concerns the so-called free-rider problem (Hechter 1985: 25; Laitin 1986: 102; Olson 1971: 2). Addressing the "free-rider problem," they propose that "truly rational actors will *not* join a group to pursue common ends when, without participating, they can reap the benefit of other people's activity in obtaining them" (Hechter 1987: 27) [emphasis in the original]. Assuming that nationalists will ultimately be successful peripheral elites suggest that they will derive many advantages, both material and social, from their regional government or, in the case of complete separation, from the government of the new country. Thus, elites can distribute among themselves valued "selective" bene-fits, but they usually only offer "collective" benefits to the rank and file of their group (Olson 1971). However, these are benefits that individuals will enjoy re-gardless of their participation in the movement or emotional commitment to the cause. Why should peripheral masses risk potential government reprisals by fol-lowing their regional elites if they can reap the rewards of the efforts of other nationalists? As a partial solution to this problem, Hechter (1987: 52-53) pro-posed that group solidarity "increases to the degree that members are dependent on the group and their behavior is capable of being controlled by the group's agents." Barnes (1992: 263) suggested that this might be accomplished by add-ing "symbolic sanctions" to economic ones. An approach that acknowledges economic disparities as the root of nationalist movements, accounts for the key role of peripheral elites, and addresses these two problems is provided by Laitin, who incorporated Gramsci's notion of cultural hegemony into the study of na-tionalism.

CULTURE, HEGEMONY, AND NATIONALISM

Hechter's study focused on the economic relationship between Britain's Celtic fringe and the English core. On the other hand Laitin's (1986) analysis of the religiously heterogeneous Yorubas of Nigeria was concerned with this coun-try's Christian-Muslim divide, a division that has played a large role in Nigerian politics since the country's independence from the United Kingdom. He was presented with the rather fascinating paradox of a country torn by religious strife minus one of its largest ethnic groups. Among the Yoruba political loyalties to the city of ancestral origin took precedence over political loyalties to religious institutions and their clerics. He argued that local chiefs, with the assistance of the British colonial government,[8] established a cultural hegemony that instituted a clear precedence of loyalty to ancestral city-of-origin over theology (Laitin 1986: 150).[9] Their power was a derivative of the patronage they dispensed—a patronage that rewarded loyalty to the city (and of course its leaders, the chief) as opposed to theologians. Clerics, on the other hand, without an autonomous economic base, could not dispense economic rewards on a large scale and thus could not create an alternative system of political loyalties. The system that local chiefs created became hegemonic to the point where Yoruba society accepted and would not question the "common sense" of subdivisions on the basis of city-origin[10] rather than the alternative apportionment model based on religion.[11] Once established a cultural hegemony functions in much the same way as does a scientific paradigm (Kuhn 1970).

The Yoruba chiefs did not monopolize the means of production in colonial Yorubaland. That role was fulfilled by the British. Yet the chiefs were clearly elites. The status of Yoruba chiefs derived from the dissemination of economic goods. Since chiefs were territorially based, this process fomented loyalties to their particular geographic units. In any society the bourgeoisie are elites because they hold a monopoly (or near monopoly) on the means of production. Power, in this case based on economic assets, is exercised through the control of an indispensable societal commodity. But power can also be exercised by groups other than the bourgeoisie—by those who monopolize other vital resources in society. The modern state performs a vast array of functions, few of which (outside the management of the economy) are carried out directly by the bourgeoisie. Thus, those who monopolize or direct other vital resources—such as education and information (intelligentsia and the media), state-legitimated violence (police and army), and the operation of the state apparatus itself (state administrators and bureaucrats)—are all members of the elite. Additionally, the modern economy also makes elites of those who, through their knowledge, design our work and living spaces and all the implements of modern society (engineers, architects, etc.).

The powerful in any society have various means at their disposal to maintain order. Through use of the state, elites have at their disposal the police and armed forces. But Migdal's (1988) research showed that even with a monopoly on the legitimate use of force, states cannot always direct society as they wish. The ruling classes, outside the state apparatus, can attempt to establish a cultural hegemony in what Gramsci referred to as "civil society" (1971: 52). By cultural hegemony Laitin (1986: 19) meant "the political forging—whether through coercion or elite bargaining—and institutionalization of a pattern of group activity in a state and that concurrent idealization of that schema into a dominant symbolic framework that reigns as common sense." As Gramsci (1971: 57) put it, dominant groups in society reveal their preponderance through "domination" and "intellectual and moral leadership." Dominant groups in society form the backbone of a hegemonic bloc. Elites within the dominant group are the ones who will select the cultural elements that define their group's boundaries (Laitin 1986: 92), and that selection will be based on those cultural traits, that "best coincide with their interests" (Maldonado-Denis 1972: 25). Embracing Gramsci's concept of cultural hegemony Maldonado-Denis went on to say that "[i]n any society, the dominant ideas and beliefs of the society will be those held by the people with economic and political power. These ideas and beliefs, once given credence, will serve as spiritual support for the economic and political policies promulgated by the powerful classes or groups in the society" (Maldonado-Denis 1972: 219). Without necessarily (or at least explicitly) espousing Gramsci's concept of cultural hegemony Weinstein appeared to essentially agree with the main argument in Laitin's and Maldonado-Denis' works on the process of selecting group boundary traits when he posited that

[i]t is the cultural elites and political leaders working together who choose which linguistic, cultural, racial, or class characteristic to emphasize or to discount, depending on their own interests. Their choices contribute significantly to boundary creation, boundary maintenance and disappearance between people, and the economic and political conditions encourage mass acceptance or rejection of the choices. (Weinstein 1983: 12)

The selection of some cultural traits over others embraces some in society and inherently excludes others. Such a decision will naturally create resentment toward the dominant society that is thwarting the upward mobility of peripherals. B. Anderson (1983: 58) noted that high-ranking colonial administrators in Latin America promoted European-born over American-born whites to government posts. Such a policy was advanced in the Iberian peninsula as well as the Americas (Lafaye 1976: 8). Their exclusion from the highest posts in the empire meant that creoles could only aspire to positions at the colonial level of government. This discriminatory policy relegated American-born whites to an inferior social status vis-à-vis their European-born brethren and consequently caused colonists to aspire only to lower-level (colonial) administrative units, thus cementing creole identity with the imperial administrative unit rather than the larger empire.

Among the first peripherals to express resentment are intellectuals who, due to their skills, demand a social status and financial rewards commensurate with their qualifications (Smith 1982: 31).

[T]he crisis of the ruling class's hegemony, which occurs either because the ruling class has failed in some major political undertaking for which it has requested, or forcibly extracted, the consent of the broad masses (war, for example), or because huge masses (especially of peasants and petit-bourgeois intellectuals) have passed suddenly from a state of political passivity to a certain activity, and put forward demands which taken together, albeit not organically formulated, add up to a revolution. (Gramsci 1971: 210)

The rejection of these peripheral elites is the necessary first step in the future establishment of a "counter-hegemony."

The counter-hegemony is a rival hegemonic order that seeks the overthrow of its predecessor. As applied to nationalism, a hegemonic order states that the dominant group is *naturally* on top. Honors, privileges and economic benefits all flow from membership in society's dominant group. The counter-hegemonic project seeks to overthrow this order and replace it with an alternative one. The articulation of this rival order is critical.

Gramsci suggests that counterhegemonic ideas, offering a more comforting and 'parsimonious' mystification of both 'stubborn reality' and elements of irreducible self interest, will be a necessary component in the overthrow of an existing hegemonic conception or an important factor in the failure of some other contender for that status. The point is that no politician, confronted with beliefs honored or advanced as hegemonic, is likely to treat them as problematic unless another available schema can articulate those beliefs as *an interpretation* of reality and the imperatives of national life, rather than as the direct and unavoidable expression of immutable facts and ultimate values. (Lustick 1993: 123) [emphasis in the original]

As the established hegemony is culturally based so shall the counter-hegemony be. Yet, by defining their societies on the basis of their particular cultural attributes, peripheral elites forsake the possibility of forging a common cultural bond within the larger society.[12] In other words, the nationalist counter-hegemony seeks to establish a new hegemonic order. However, since the foundation of this rival order lies on the cultural characteristics prevalent in the periphery, the scope of the nationalist hegemonic project is limited to the periphery. The old hegemonic order will remain and stay in effect, minus the periphery.

As elites in the dominant society were the driving force behind the established hegemonic order so shall peripheral elites usher in the counter-hegemony. New peripheral elites engage in a *nation-building* project in reaction to the discriminatory policies and attitudes of their counterparts in the dominant society (Barth 1969: 33). Their goal is the improvement of their own lot, though this design is not publicly acknowledged.

The new elite which seeks to supersede the old one, or merely to share its power and honors, does not admit to such an intention frankly and openly. Instead it assumes the leadership of all the oppressed, declares that it will pursue not its own good but the good of the many; and it goes to battle, not for the rights of a restricted class, but for the rights of almost the entire citizenry. Of course, once victory is won, it subjugates the erstwhile allies, or, at best, offers them some formal concessions. (Pareto 1991: 36)

The goal of peripheral elites is not to establish a popular order, but a rival elite one. But this process is not particular to nationalism. As Michels (1959: 238) put it: "Every great class-movement in history has arisen upon the instigation, with the co-operation, and under the leadership of men sprung from the very class against which the movement was directed."

While a nationalist movement may start with elites, it cannot hope to succeed unless it has the support of the masses. Elites, whether in the core or in peripheral society, intentionally seek out the support of their masses since their compliance lowers the cost of control (Laitin 1986: 107). Resources that elites would have otherwise been obliged to channel into securing their lot can now be diverted to other endeavors. For elites in the dominant society, this is patronage that can be used to maintain the *status quo*. On the other hand, for their peripheral counterparts, the extra savings can be diverted to shore up the counter-hegemonic order among other key social and political actors in the periphery.

Within their role as promoters of the hegemonic order, the masses are not blind followers. Laitin (1986: 106) argued that "the lower strata should be seen not as merely sharing a dominant ideology with the ruling strata but, instead, as being in simultaneous possession of ideas that support *and* challenge political authority in their society" [emphasis in the original]. Though the masses are "deliberately manipulated" (Toland 1993: 3), they still participate because of the benefits they derive. The lower-class members of the dominant group in society accept their role as active participants since participation promises gains (Laitin 1986: 107).[13] Group solidarity, after all, rests in "individuals' desires to consume goods that are beyond their power either to produce or to secure" (Furtado & Hechter 1992: 172). Embracing the nationalist paradigm or hegemonic order leads to privileges for the masses. The working class of the dominant society, while still subservient to its higher-classed ethnic brethren, now enjoy a high social standing. Such a high social standing allows lower-class individuals to outrank their fellow workers without actually changing their class status. While still workers, lower-class members of a high-status group will demand that they be given greater privileges than their low-social-status low-class counterparts. Thus, the hegemonic order safeguards the jobs of low-skill-low-class individuals. Once the group's boundaries are set and accepted by the vast majority in society, thus becoming the hegemonic order, the admittance of nonelites to positions of power produces a backlash. "In any CDL [Cultural Division of Labor] in which some nonelite positions are held by members of the elite culture, upward movement by members of the nonelite is likely to inspire a 'reactive' nationalism among the less privileged members of the elite culture, who will demand restoration of the status quo ante" (Rogowski 1985: 94). Thus, once the hegemonic order is established, elites are usually bound by it for fear of jeopardizing their command of society. This is particularly the case for elites in the dominant society who constantly hear demands for an expansion of their Ranks (and with that an increased dissemination of their privileges). In essence they become prisoners of their own handywork and victims of their own success. However, for elites, such a hegemonic order provides far more benefits than disadvantages. And for the working class, "[t]hough it grumbles occasionally, the majority is really delighted to find persons who will take the trouble to look after its affairs" (Michels 1959: 53).

The rejected elites from the periphery attempt to break this hegemony by creating their own rival group myth. Such a myth is presented as a counter-hegemony that the subordinate elites hope, in time, will become the foundation of a new hegemonic order under their direction. In their struggle they will employ many of the same tactics as elites in the dominant society. They will try to link themselves to the peripheral masses. One prominent historian, Lafaye (1976), documented early attempts by Mexico's creole elite to forge national ties to the country's mestizo and indigenous majority by expropriating images and symbols from the country's pre-Columbian past.[14] The Mexican-born children of Europeans were looked down upon by Spanish émigrés. This resentment continued to grow in Mexico, as it did in other parts of Latin America, and finally took the form of a separatist movement. He contended, among other things, that the paramount national symbol of Mexico, the apparition of the Virgin Mary as Our Lady of Guadalupe, was the result of the creole Catholicization of Tonantzin, mother goddess of the Aztecs and thus a prime example of myth-making (Lafaye 1976: 29). This act was, he argued, the spiritual component of creole disapproval of the colonial regime (Lafaye 1976: 299).

The most remarkable aspect of the matter is the manner in which the creole descendants of Spaniards exalted and took over as their own patrimony the Indian past recorded in Nahuatl sources. The sentiment of the American *patria*, we have seen, arose in part as a reaction to the scorn heaped by Europeans upon both Indians and creoles. Since the creoles were, after all, America's favorite children, they appropriated for themselves America's pre-Columbian history, telluric predestination prevailing over ties of blood. (Lafaye 1976: 191) [emphasis in the original]

Spain's discriminatory policies dissolved the previously existing unity that was based on European extraction and white skin, thus facilitating creole-mestizo/indigenous ties. These bonds were an essential precursor to the ultimately successful Mexican independence movement. Lafaye (1976: 302) concluded that "it was Spain—however unwillingly—that made Mexico a nation."

For reasons that will be explained shortly, elites often choose to define their culture on the basis of their particular language. They will define their culture on the basis of traits that they control. While elites are not required to use language as a group marker, it does bring them certain advantages. They are also critical actors in the process of deciding which language and dialect will become the accepted communicative norm in society. Though elites are responsible for establishing language as an integral component of society's cultural hegemony, the masses willingly follow because of the direct financial benefits and group-status privileges they receive. This cultural hegemony will be challenged by upwardly mobile peripheral elites who attempt to establish a "counter-hegemony" in their particular region and, like their core counterparts, a nexus with their masses. The following chapter will explore the connection between elites and one cultural trait in particular—language. Certain intrinsic aspects of languages make them alluring targets for elites in the process of myth-making and the establishment of either a cultural hegemonic or cultural counter-hegemonic order.

NOTES

1. This work will focus on Puerto Rico and Quebec where the ethnic groups in question are geographically concentrated and thus share a common territory. However, one should be aware that nationalist sentiments exist even where the group in question is not territorially compact. A noted case in point is that of African Americans and Jews prior to World War II. These groups, while they may have been concentrated in urban enclaves, ghettoes, or small regions were nonetheless spread out over vast distances and lacked a contiguous territorial base from which they could later claim autonomy. This status changed for many Jews following the establishment of the State of Israel. This status did not change for African Americans despite several proposals to bring them under one political roof—such as Marcus Garvey's "Back to Africa" movement early in the twentieth century; Trotsky's (1978) plan for a "Black Republic" within the United States; or the ephemeral "Republic of New Africa" movement in the late 1960s and early 1970s.

2. Anderson (B. 1983: 96), discussing the modernity of nationalism, pointed out that within the Austro-Hungarian Empire, the Hungarian nobility did not commit itself to Magyarization until the 1840s. This, he argued, was not done out of any sense of benevolence or even cultural pride, but to prevent their marginalization in the face of the growing importance of the German language and culture within the realm.

3. The emergence of French national identity with the 1789 revolution did not guarantee its immediate or complete dissemination throughout the country. A noted study pointed out that French national identity did not permeate many parts of the hexagon's hinterland until the early part of the twentieth century (Weber, E. 1976).

4. Language used to separate the English from the Irish back when the latter were Gaelic speakers. In another change of historic fate, religion, which united the Irish in their struggle against the United Kingdom in the nineteenth and twentieth centuries, did not always perform this function. A couple of centuries ago Ireland's Catholic aristocracy, referred to as the "Old English" associated themselves with other nobles in Britain and not with the masses in Ireland (Boyce 1982: 79-81). Elite unity broke down as the British Crown withdrew the privileges of the Irish nobles, surmising that their Catholic faith posed a security threat to London's dominion over Ireland (Lustick 1985: 6-21).

5. Following this original land grant by the Jesuits, parcels of this territory were taken away and then later restored (Roosens 1989: 56). Thus, since their flight from New York State, the Hurons have lost and gained land on several occasions. Unlike most aboriginal communities in Canada, the Huron settlements postdate the European settlement of North America.

6. For readers who are not familiar with discussions in Canada over Québécois nationalism, it is important to point out that one will, at times, see "*the rest of Canada*" (referring to English Canada) abbreviated as "TROC."

7. Woolard's (1989) research pointed out that within the region of Catalonia there is a clear socioeconomic hierarchy whereby those who speak Catalan, the regional language, outrank those who speak Castilian (Spanish). This case reverses the more usual scenario where the state's dominant language is associated with greater prestige and power, even in the peripheral regions. However, she also indicated that most of the Spanish speakers in this region come from the poorer parts of Spain, including a large share from Andalusia.

8. Laitin (1986: 150) suggested that the British were motivated to support local political actors (in this case chiefs) in order to "exert political control at low cost." Indirect rule via local leaders who enjoyed far more legitimacy than Europeans helped to lower colonial administrative costs. However, this was not the case in Northern Nigeria where emirs were recruited as local political leaders over tribal chiefs (Laitin 1986: 163) because Northern society was supposedly more advanced. The British authorities believed that organization by religion was of a higher order than organization by tribal groupings.

9. Marx's (1996: 194) comparative study of Brazil, the United States, and South Africa pointed to another example of British support in the construction of a hegemonic order. He suggested that the British were involved in fomenting a pan-white identity in South Africa that would bring together English settlers and the Boers, thus defusing Afrikaner resistance to British rule. Marx's study, along with Ignatiev's (1995), argued that a similar pan-white unity was forged in the United States in order to bring together formerly disunited Europeans.

10. Laitin's work focused on the alternative preeminence of territoriality over religion and the peripheral people's subsequent political loyalties. Another significant contribution to the understanding of Gramsci's notion of cultural hegemony was provided by Lustick (1993: 41), who argued that the geographical expanse of a polity was also susceptible to inclusion into society's hegemonic order. Once accepted by society as "common sense," mainstream political actors will avoid questioning the country's frontiers. Discussions of state contraction (once a territory is accepted as an inalienable part

of the country) can lead, as was the case with France and the Algerian crisis, to the collapse of the regime and the constitutional order.

11. Once embraced by the scientific community, a paradigm guides fundamental premises and research designs as well as methodological procedures. Regardless of persistent problems or "crises" the original paradigm persists and continues to guide scientific research until successfully challenged by a rival paradigm—a counter-hegemony. As Kuhn (1970: 92) noted, "In both political and scientific development the sense of malfunction that can lead to crisis is prerequisite to revolution." Regarding nationalism, peripheral elites seek to initiate a counter-hegemony (which they hope will become a hegemonic order) over the nationalists' enclave or territory rather than the breadth of the existing state.

12. This strategy does not prevent peripheral elites from forming (or attempting to formulate) political alliances with rivals in the country's core. In both the United Kingdom and Spain, peripheral elites (the Scottish and Welsh, the Basque and Catalans) have hammered power-sharing deals with political parties at the center. These coalitions have varied in duration and stability.

13. By accepting the American racial hegemony that positioned whites above blacks, Irish immigrants in the nineteenth century felt justified in demanding that blacks stay out of certain professions (Ignatiev 1995). Such an attitude fortified the existing elite-created order while benefiting a large class of workers.

14. Elites will not embrace symbols unless they control them. To do otherwise would inevitably empower other sectors of society. Lafaye (1976) noted that Mexican creoles could not embrace symbols from the country's indigenous past until the threat from aboriginal revolts subsided. Once such a menace was eliminated, creoles could appropriate the Aztec's imperial past since the exaltation of Spain's past by the country's Iberian-born elites prevented the colony's rulers from exploiting non-European symbols.

3

Language and Elites

In the United States, for example, there are cultural revival movements that exhibit great pride in the traditions of their forefathers—including their ancestral language. One may find signs, fliers, bumper stickers, or perhaps even books in that idiom. Part of being a hyphenated American is understanding the cultural context associated with the adjective preceding the hyphen. Yet, for the most part, the majority of these Americans who participate in such cultural festivals are monolingual Anglophones. English has such a prominent role in the United States that rarely do other languages survive as vernaculars for more than a generation or two. Outside of a few words or place names, most Americans are ignorant of the language of their ascendants. Somewhere in the past an immigrant parent, grandparent, or great-grandparent chose to forsake his or her ancestral tongue in order to improve his or her standard of living and augment the chances of successfully climbing up the socioeconomic ladder (Edwards 1985: 50).

The choice to exchange one's previous mother tongue for English was not always a desired outcome but maintaining a language other than English on the North American continent, outside of a few significant non-Anglophone enclaves, was exceedingly difficult and lack of fluency in English relegated one's lot in life to low-skill/low-wage jobs. Any hopes of improving one's position depended on learning English. Additionally, the public school system was arguably the most effective of all assimilating agents. With English as the medium of instruction, functional Anglophones were produced within only a generation or two.

The descendants of immigrants described in the previous paragraphs take pride in a language as a symbol of their ancestral culture in much the same way as one is proud of songs, typical dress, and other folk traditions. However, this is not a language that they can speak fluently; thus, it is not a part of their daily lives. Waters (1990: 150) referred to this variety as a "symbolic ethnicity," an ethnicity that one takes on and off like an article of clothing, but which is not a permanent fixture in an individual's life. Such an ethnicity makes dramatic appearances at special events but is otherwise not a pressing issue in the individual's daily life. Symbolic ethnicity differs from one where the cultural traits in question are integral parts of the person's everyday existence—where religion or folk traditions are practiced, or the language is spoken. This distinction is important since the cases discussed here are concerned with nationalism in societies where the periphery does not share the core's vernacular. Between the groups in question there is a barrier to effective communication. For these groups language is not merely a symbol but an integral aspect of daily interaction.

LANGUAGE AND DIALECTS

When discussing the social role of language, one should distinguish between languages and dialects, for this distinction is often taken advantage of by those segments of society that hope to lead a nationalist movement. Though both have important social implications, they are not synonymous.[1] Languages are separate, mutually unintelligible systems of communication (Edwards 1985: 18). As such, a person who speaks one "language" cannot readily be understood by someone who speaks another without some rudimentary knowledge of the other form of speech. Once an oral language has been formally codified and standardized, significant differences with regards to orthography, conjugation, declinations, and other rules of grammar will appear even among closely related forms of speech. In time dialects can evolve into separate languages as happened to the dialects of Latin spoken in Roman Spain and Gaul in Europe, Sanskrit in South Asia, or the various Turkic languages of Central Asia, Caucasia, and Anatolia. Also within the realm of the possible, different languages can (especially if in prolonged contact with one another) fuse to form a single unified language.[2] This is the origin of patois and pidgins. Both languages and dialects can be used in society to distinguish one person and one group from another. Since languages are not mutually intelligible and represent an omnipresent barrier to effective communication, they are often used to demarcate ethnic and group boundaries.[3]

Now, ethnic groups are not required to define themselves on the basis of language. Many successful nationalist movements either omitted or never included language as a significant group marker (Stalin 1935: 6). Nationalism increased in intensity throughout the nineteenth century despite the simultaneous decline of Gaelic as the *lingua franca* of Ireland. It declined as a spoken language despite the efforts of many middle-class Irish in the nineteenth century who worked to maintain and revive it (Edwards 1985: 54-55). One of the few cases of successful linguistic revival—at least in terms of reanimating a dormant or moribund idiom—is the case of Hebrew in the twentieth century. Though it ceased being the *lingua franca* of Jews even before the Diaspora it was brought back as the official language of the State of Israel.[4] Yet, among some nineteenth-century Zionists—including the movement's leader, Theodor Herzl—the role of a common language in a future Jewish state was downplayed as a relatively unimportant issue that would be resolved after the establishment of the Jewish homeland (Herzl 1988: 145).[5]

At the same time a common language, in and of itself, does not create a sense of social unity. Individuals can share a common language yet still see themselves as pertaining to different ethnic groups. Among others, Stalin (1935: 6) observed that Americans, the English, and the Irish shared a common language, yet they did not see themselves as one people. The same applied to Danes and Norwegians. However, in the West language became the single most acknowledged cultural characteristic when defining national groups (Inglehart & Woodward 1967: 27) and the most frequently used criterion when distinguishing between different ethnic and national groups.

The connection between language and nationality was expounded almost two centuries ago by the German philosopher Johann Fichte.[6] In his *Address to the German Nation*, Fichte, arguing from what would today be classified as a culturalist perspective, lauded the "innate superiority" of the German language since, he insisted, it was closer to the original Teutonic language (Fichte 1922: 55). German's genealogy made it a "living language," as opposed to the neo-latin tongues, which he considered to be dead languages (Fichte 1922: 70-71). A language's background impacts the thinking processes of its speakers. "Moreover, in a people with a dead language no truly creative genius can express itself, because they lack the primitive power of designation" (Fichte 1922: 85). His addresses were not concerned exclusively with pedagogical issues but with the articulation of the preeminent basis on which to distinguish German speakers from non-German speakers. In the nineteenth century Germans were alienated from one another due to religion: Catholicism versus Protestantism. In terms of socially significant cultural traits, religious affiliation was a more divisive factor than language. Fichte (1922: 215-216) countered that language was the basis for nationhood and this nationhood implied the right to self-government and self-determination.

Interpersonal contact encouraged the development of a common language. Business and other transactions, whether conducted by farmers, craftsmen, clerics, or even ministers of state, require a common medium of communication. In this sense a language is born out of necessity. At this particular point the upper strata of society are ordinary participants and observers. What elites do create is a *standardized* language that Hobsbawm (1983a: 14) emphasized is another example of an "invented tradition." The standardization of any language will require its formal codification, the establishment of a written script and formal rules of grammar. Prior to standardization communication from one part of a country to another can be exceedingly difficult.[7] As Hobsbawm (1990: 52) noted: "Non-literate vernacular languages are always a complex of local variants or dialects intercommunicating with varying degrees of ease or difficulty, depending on geographical closeness or accessibility." Particularly in the modern era, states deliberately select a common standard in order to facilitate communication from one part of the country to another. The outcome of this decision has far-reaching implications in society for it opens doors to those who speak the elite-anointed standard. "The politics of language is also the process of selecting dialects or separate languages for well-defined functions and the economic and political effects of that choice" (Weinstein 1983: 11).

A question inevitably arises—which one of the many forms of speech will become the basis of the standardized language? This query is based on the observation that few countries are linguistically homogeneous, thereby obligating policy-makers to select a formal language policy. One alternative is to select an idiom for the "practical" reason of reducing communication barriers across the country. Leaders may want to encourage communication in general, or they may favor promoting linguistic intercourse among elites. The selection of Mandarin as the court language in imperial China created a common speech among the country's elites that performed this task (Hobsbawm 1990: 56). Use of Latin by many medieval European governments was, in this sense, also a practical language. As the language of scholarship and the Roman Catholic church, it was one of the few languages which most elites in Europe's linguistically heterogeneous societies could read and communicate in.[8]

When most elites in society speak the same popular language, rulers may want to standardize a local language, selecting one variant or dialect as the "correct" or "proper" communicative norm. Noah Webster, soon after the independence of the United States, favored the standardization of American English in order to facilitate "accuracy in business" (in Crawford 1992: 33). Regardless of which language is chosen, the presumed justification for language selection and its subsequent standardization is based primarily on bureaucratic needs. However, the selection of a language based on "pragmatic" reasons does not alter the fate of its speakers. Those who speak the official language, even if coming from the lower classes, find a straighter path toward upward mobility. "When government language planners and nongovernment elites such as language strategists choose a variety or form of language to resolve what they perceive as communication problems, they affect patterns of participation in power, wealth, and prestige. Who has access to these values, and who is denied access" (Weinstein 1983: 81). Communication in the official idiom facilitates employment in key sectors of both the state bureaucracy and private enterprises that are based in the country's core region. Economic advantages translate over time into social advantages, higher prestige, and political power.

The selection of a linguistic standard could also be based on political reasons. As previously noted, the language of Danes and Norwegians used to be the same. Formal Norwegian (*Nynorsk*) was created by nationalists in the 1850s by combining different dialects in an attempt to further distinguish their language from that spoken by the Danes (Aarebrot 1982: 83). As opposed to the factors mentioned above, the intent here was not to foment unification but separation— of a linguistic kind. Despite its official status Nynorsk is spoken by only 20 percent of the country's population (Hobsbawm 1990: 55). The political purpose behind choosing this linguistic variant was political separation, though there are cases where the dialect chosen was meant to create unity.

Unification was the goal behind the nineteenth-century consecration of the *Štokavian* dialect as the integrative variant of the Serbo-Croatian language in what would become Yugoslavia (Hobsbawm 1990: 54-55). Nineteenth-century Illyrianism (Vojnić 1995: 93), a movement originating in Croatia[9] and Slovenia, sought to linguistically bind southern Slavs with a common language. In light of events in the early 1990s this action may seem ironic, given that its motivation was the unification of southern Slavs. Whether they are officially chosen for political or practical bureaucratic administrative reasons, standardized languages are created or invented despite the claim of many nationalists that they occur naturally. The vast array of dialects and accents within a given language strongly suggests that standardization, by imposing one variant above all the rest, inevitably imposes a linguistic norm on society rather than responding to natural processes. "National languages are therefore almost always semi-artificial constructs and occasionally, like modern Hebrew, virtually invented. They are the opposite of what nationalist mythology supposes them to be, namely the primordial foundations of national culture and the matrices of the national mind" (Hobsbawm 1990: 54).

This criterion is not limited to the revival of dormant languages like Hebrew. Even continuously spoken languages become artificial constructs when standardized. The process of standardization allows elites the flexibility to choose which dialect becomes the official one. Naturally, the center of gravity falls on the dialect of the center. In the case of Spain, it applied to the variant of Spanish spoken in Castile. Commenting on the Spanish case, philosopher José Ortega y Gasset wrote:

The relative homogeneousness of race and tongue which they to-day enjoy—if it is a matter of enjoyment—is the result of the previous political unification. Consequently, neither blood nor language gives birth to the national State, rather it is the national State which levels down the differences arising from the red globule and the articulated sound. And so it has always happened. Rarely, if ever, has the State coincided with a previous identity of blood and language. Spain is not a national State to-day *because* Spanish is spoken throughout the country, nor were Aragon and Catalonia national States *because* at a certain period, arbitrarily chosen, the territorial bounds of their sovereignty coincided with those of Aragonese or Catalan speech. (Ortega y Gasset 1960: 166) [emphasis in the original]

As Ortega y Gasset pointed out, not only are standardized languages imposed (and thus artificial constructs), so too are states.

ELITES AND LANGUAGE

Among elites special attention should be paid to intellectuals—society's guardians of knowledge, its teachers, who also serve as its principal disseminator of group myths. In case after case the intelligentsia have consistently taken the leadership role in nationalist movements (Conner 1994: 158). "In the ethnic community . . . the intelligentsia are welcome because only by means of their skills and specialist knowledge can a 'true' education arise, which will bring self-understanding and self-fulfillment for the whole community" (Smith 1981: 127-128). Myth-makers in both modern and traditional societies play an extremely crucial role. Economic elites, whose position in society are determined by wealth and the dissemination of material resources, need storytellers to inculcate the cultural order they wish to promote on society. Intellectuals are eligible for elite status because of this vital tutorial role they perform. Their version of history and critique of society, bolstered by their array of degrees and other impressive credentials, provides the "spiritual support" that economic elites need to maintain their hegemonic order (Maldonado-Denis 1972: 219).

Intellectuals are usually classified as members of the petite bourgeoisie, thus occupying an intermediate position between the masses and the *haute* bourgeoisie. They also serve as the communicative middlemen between the masses and bourgeoisie. Through their lessons in school, the books and newspaper articles they write, they spread the "common sense" of the cultural order as prescribed by the wealthier segments of society. Diplomas, degrees, and other scholastic honors give their words considerable credence. Their indispensability in maintaining the cultural order qualifies them as elites.[10] Within the dominant society intellectuals are the primary propagators of the hegemonic order to the mass level. Their counterparts in the subordinate society play a similar role. Intellectuals, in the broadest sense, constitute the "habitual infantry" of an ethnic revival movement (Smith 1981: 108). And the bureaucracy was the main vehicle for the intelligentsia's ascent (Smith 1981: 112).

In previous eras the state was staffed with a rather small bureaucracy, the membership of which was primarily restricted on the basis of noble birth and not expertise in governance or administration (Smith 1981: 113). Modern governments, however, perform more functions than their earlier counterparts, requiring a larger bureaucratic system. Modernity necessitated expanding the proportions of the administrative apparatus. Such an augmentation, moreover, required a larger educational system to teach future bureaucrats. Schools and universities became the primary institutions by which the standardized vernacular would be disseminated (Hechter 1975: 37). Standard French, the dialect of Paris, spread deep into the hexagon's hinterland by way of the public school system (Weber, E. 1976: 361-363).[11] Thus, Mayall and Simpson (1992: 7) singled out mass education as the "central ingredient in most contemporary nation-building strategies." In addition to using schools to produce future bureaucrats, states also exploit the school system to diffuse the hegemonic culture and disseminate national myths (Hobsbawm 1990: 91-92).

A frequent consequence of the expansion of public education systems in the modern era is that more technically qualified workers are produced than can be employed in high-status positions, or positions for which they are qualified

(Smith 1981: 117). The scarcity of high-status jobs requires a selection among all qualified candidates. One popular screening process is to select administrators and bureaucrats based on their compatibility with the previously entrenched elites. Compatibility is frequently measured on the basis of shared mannerisms and cultural traits. In this process those who share the same cultural attributes as the dominant culture have an increased likelihood of attaining employment, and once hired they have greater opportunities for upward mobility within the bureaucratic system. Assuming that a hegemonic order has already been established, this preference for members of the dominant society will be accepted and even applauded by the lower-class segments of that group.[12] Again, there is a latent benefit in this system for the masses. If their children attain an extensive education, then the high-status positions they seek will be preferentially given to them over equally qualified individuals from the subordinate society.

Discrimination against an elite segment of society can be a rather dangerous strategy. The risk involves the pivotal roles performed by the intellectual elite in society. This group, unlike peasants and most industrial workers, understands the inner workings of the dominant organs of the state and society. Among their ranks are also found teachers whose task it is to not only educate the population with basic skills but also to disseminate group myths. These are the myths that sustain society's cultural hegemony and the *status quo*. Even among the educated non-pedagogues, their schooling gives their opinions an air of respect that is not accorded that of their less erudite brethren. Referring to the nationalist movements, Stalin (1935: 14) observed that in Europe they were led by the "urban petty bourgeoisie of the oppressed nation against the big bourgeoisie of the dominant nation." It is the frustration of peripheral elites that marks the beginning of a nationalist movement. Again, their wealth or technical competence is not at issue. It is the social stigma of their culture as determined by the dominant groups in society that relegate them to an inferior standing within the larger society, especially the state's core.[13]

One solution to the predicament of these marginalized but highly educated individuals is the establishment of a political unit based on their particular culture. Many positions in the peripheral region are preserved for members of the peripheral society who are familiar with local customs and are fluent in the local language or dialect. The geographic concentration of many of these cultural attributes, especially language, provide peripheral elites with a "ready-made" area for their claims of autonomy and an area where they may claim exclusive rights to government positions (Smith 1981: 126).

LANGUAGE SELECTION

A prominent exponent of the culturalist perspective held that linguistic contact itself was responsible for social tensions (Laponce 1987). People are inherently unilingual, though capable of learning more than language. In order to survive languages must occupy a geographic niche lest a stronger language (one with a more tenacious social, economic, and political standing) displace it (Laponce 1987: 3-4). His argument, like that of other culturalists or primordialists, falls into the trap of assuming that social tensions are derived from the cultural attributes themselves. It is true that linguistic contact has given way to conflict. Yet, there are numerous cases of linguistic contact leading to assimilation or linguistic fusion. Language does not, in and of itself, produce nationalistic tensions. Instead its political significance is as a group marker that separates those who will be given access to power and those who will be restricted from it (Weinstein 1983: 11-12; Williams 1984: 201). Echoing the same sentiment Inglehart and Woodward also agreed that linguistic pluralism in a society did not, by itself, augment nationalistic passions. They stated that linguistic differences were socially divisive to the degree to which social mobility was hindered as a result of pertaining to a linguistic community (Inglehart & Woodward 1967: 28).

Where social mobility is blocked by the existence of one preferred language among several, language differences seem to be politically divisive: the individual must unite with others of his language for political action to raise the group as a whole, as in Belgium and Canada. On the other hand, where all major languages are on an equal footing, as in Switzerland, the presence of several language groups may not necessarily be divisive as an official language in India because all groups there are more or less equally handicapped by it. (Inglehart & Woodward 1967: 33)

As previously mentioned, language is frequently used for political ends. Elites will appropriate language as a marker of group identity in order to prevent the use of alternative symbols to identify their group—substitute symbols that could subsequently undermine their position (Weinstein 1983: 67). Laitin elaborated:

As any elite group (or historical bloc) attempts to achieve domination over society, it will seek to lower the costs of compliance by developing an ideology of its own legitimacy. One method of lowering the costs of control is to view the society from the lens of a single sociocultural divide. All political conflict can then be interpreted in terms of that divide. Cultural hegemony has been established when members of all social strata interpret politics and choose strategies of participation in terms of the divide favored by the elite group. (Laitin 1986: 107)

The question remains which sociocultural divide will be anointed by elites? Elites will define their group on the basis of language if it is a symbol that they can easily control. This was the reason why the leadership of Morocco and Algeria resisted granting any official recognition to any language other than classical Arabic (Weinstein 1983: 86).

For elites choosing a language has clear advantages.[14] First of all, this cultural trait will automatically bar those who do not share it from the halls of power in government, industry, and society. The distribution of selective benefits becomes linguistically based. Language is often chosen as a group identifier where there exists a rival elite who speaks another language. Elites attempting to establish a cultural hegemony will use the state to promote their cause. Choice jobs within the state bureaucracy (ranging from school teachers to posts in government ministries) will be reserved for those who have the training *and* speak the preferred language. Elites also establish cultural hegemonies by means other than the state government apparatus. The same pattern will also be replicated in the private sector and civil society where the most valued positions will be given to those who speak the preferred language. Society at all levels rewards those who accept the hegemonic order, those who resist are cast aside and are marginalized.

Additionally, when the dominant group defines itself on the basis of language, the process of standardization produces, invariably, a superior dialect and accent. Thus, a language not only protects elites from non-vernacular speakers, it also protects them from their own lower-class ethnic brethren who speak a low-status dialect of the preferred language. Those speaking an "inferior" variant of the dominant language will find resistance as they attempt to climb the socioeconomic ladder. The inferior status of that dialect is not a derivative of any attribute of the speech itself. Rather its low standing is conferred by society's elites. Low-standing languages, dialects, and accents, just as their higher-ranking counterparts, inherit this designation. They do not seek it, nor have they earned it. But the barrier to upward mobility for those speaking a low-standing dialect of a high-status language applies only to the ladder's highest rungs. For the most part the dominant group's lower-class members are rewarded with positions and privileges in society—far more so than working class members of subordinate groups.

Marginalized elites from society's periphery react negatively to the established order, which relegates them to positions that fail to adequately reward their social standing, wealth, and education. The incipient elite, by way of nationalism, represents an attempt to counter the entrenched order. Those combating a prevailing elite are struggling to institute a "counter-hegemony" or rival hegemony. Nationalist groups attempt to establish a counter-hegemony in the larger state that they hope will become, in turn, hegemonic in the territorial niche they claim as their homeland.

As mentioned, the dominant group in society derives advantages from demarcating its cultural boundaries on the basis of language. Elites in the subordinate society will also derive one major advantage from their position. They become the bilingual intermediaries between their masses and the dominant group's elites.[15] In a linguistically plural society, the dominant group's language becomes the established norm for communicating with the core's government and leading businesses. As a result of the social, political, and economic strength of their language, members of the dominant society have little incentive to learn another language. This is not the case for individuals belonging to subordinate groups in society. Lower-status groups pay most of the cost of communicating with their dominant counterparts (Laponce 1987: 21).

However, not all lower-status individuals have the same means with which to learn the dominant society's language. Even in cases when low-status, lower-class individuals learn the dominant society's language, as happens frequently in cases of migration, their economic plight obliges them to live in the less well off areas of the center (often in the center's metropolitan regions). The resulting bilinguals, while familiar or even fluent in the dominant society's language, will learn, due to their immediate environment, a lower-class variant (dialect/accent) of the dominant society's language.[16] On the other hand, the resources available to peripheral elites allow them to learn their own standard language in addition to the dominant society's language in a formal setting. For peripheral elites the result is fluency in the elite's variant of the dominant language. In essence, peripheral elites become the bilingual intermediaries between their periphery's masses and the center's elites.

THE ELITE-MASS COMPACT

Notwithstanding their paramount role in the formation of a hegemonic cultural order elites are not the only participants in its maintenance. In fact, a true measure of the strength of any nationalist movement is the extent to which its principles are accepted by all segments of society. Those studying this phenomenon (Stalin 1935: 15) have noticed that "[t]he strength of the national movement is determined by the degree to which the wide strata of the nation, the proletariat and peasantry, participate in it." The benefits for elites in establishing either a cultural hegemony or counter-hegemony are rather abundant. However, elites represent the beginning of nationalist movements, not the end.

Without mass participation a nationalist movement cannot flourish. Indeed, some go as far as to suggest that a nationalist movement does not exist without the participation of the masses. As Huntington (1968: 303) wrote: "The intelligentsia can ally themselves with a revolutionary peasantry but they cannot create a revolutionary peasantry." Nationalist sentiments among elites are, in and of themselves, insufficient to claim that a national consciousness has become entrenched in the popular psyche (Conner 1994: 212). "Vital for any nation is the growth and spread of a 'national sentiment' outwards from the centre and usually downward through the strata of the population" (Smith 1989: 343). What benefit do they derive from a culturally based hegemonic order? Michels's (1959: 24) suggestion that the masses are susceptible to "the eloquence of great popular orators" implies that they do not derive any benefits so much as they are duped.

One question that immediately arises is how elites attain mass support. Members of society's subordinate groups are quite often geographically concentrated (Furtado & Hechter 1992: 173). The same will apply to members of the dominant society. One finds in Spain, for example, Castilian speakers concentrated in the central and southern parts of the country and its linguistic minorities (Galicians, Basques, Catalans) in the northern and eastern regions. In Latin America most indigenous language enclaves are found in the interior, Brazil's west or Peru's eastern jungles and highlands. Even with migration from the periphery to the country's core, expatriates often congregate in the same neighborhoods. As Laponce (1987) noted, linguistically based groups in particular are geographically based since territorial dispersal usually leads to linguistic assimilation. Geographic proximity, along with a shared means of communication, advances the development of a collective identity uniting elites with their masses (Furtado & Hechter 1992: 173).

At the local level ethnically distinct groups usually share common workplaces, houses of worship, schools, and social organizations of various kinds (Hechter 1975: 42). In crass cases of ethnic discrimination, peripheral elites are relegated to positions they are overqualified for. Due to their common language, or other stigmatized cultural traits, these individuals frequently find work in the same places as their lower-class linguistic brethren. The combination of resentment for their inferior standing and their working association with their ethnic kin presents the prime conditions for germinating ethnic consciousness and inciting nationalistic passions. Resentment explains why elites are motivated, and geographic proximity explains how they spread their message.

Yet, this still does not explain why the masses go along with their elites. Successful nationalist leaders are those who convince the masses that their ultimate goal is the uplifting of those shunned by the dominant society (Eriksen 1993: 102). Elites offer their populations two types of rewards, one is psychological—prestige—and the other is economic—a type of ethnic patronage. Prestige is a collective benefit, patronage is a selective benefit. Membership in a high-status group translates into a relatively high social standing. The juxtaposition of two similarly placed individuals, on the basis of class, will reveal a clear hierarchy in favor of the individual belonging to the higher-status group, all things being equal. In an extreme case, the social prestige of the higher-status group may be such that a low-class, high-status individual enjoys more privileges than a high-class member of a subordinate group. The prominence of the dominant group's language automatically descends to all its members—including those in the lower classes. Though they may speak what is considered to be a less prestigious variant of the dominant language, they can still, nonetheless, communicate directly with the elites of the dominant society. As a result, the lower class members of the dominant society have certain expectations.[17]

The second reward is a kind of ethnic patronage. Many analyses of patronage focus entirely on the state sector. Clearly those belonging to the higher-status group have greater access to government jobs, more so than their lower-class companions. However, under a hegemonic regime ethnic patronage permeates all strata of society. In terms of a nonlinguistic example, Ignatiev's (1995) study of nineteenth-century Irish immigration in the United States documented the ire of these newcomers to the news or the threat of low-skilled jobs (which they depended on) being given to black Americans. Their motivation was based on the fear that greater competition for the same number of jobs might bring down their wages. Their justification was that their jobs were the exclusive domain of whites. Ensuing chapters will investigate the consequences of denying positions to highly qualified individuals in Puerto Rico and Quebec on the basis of their lack of English proficiency.

The underlying assumption is that the masses will share a dividend on the hegemonic order. They are expecting collective benefits. In this sense elite promises (including those of peripheral elites to their masses) are interpreted as a form of *latent* selective benefits. Naturally these benefits will increase with one's level of education. An unskilled worker, belonging to the dominant group, expects that his or her job will be protected from a member of a subordinate group. Additionally, one will expect that any raises in pay or job status will fall on oneself and one's equally stationed cohorts. As one climbs the pedagogical ladder, the expectations are that members of the high-status group will enjoy the benefits of the group's place in society. At the very top of social power structure, one finds the very elites who are responsible for mobilizing the nationalist movement.

A paradox that many in the rational choice approach try to skirt is why the working class are often the most vociferous in their support of what are seemingly bourgeois movements. After all, most of the benefits they immediately receive are collective as opposed to the prized selective benefits offered to members of the elite stratum. Part of solution to this question is that the lower strata of society do receive small-scale or limited selective benefits. One must also understand that, generally speaking, they are vulnerable in society. As Michels noted, the well educated are indispensable due to their knowledge. They possess a specialization that is not easily replaced. This is not the case with non-elites, in particular with low-skilled workers (whether urban or rural). Their training is not extensive; therefore, it consumes comparatively little time and does not consti tute a large investment on the part of the employer (whether the state or a private firm). Replacements are readily available. As a result of their vulnerability, non-elites depend, as do elites, on the hegemonic order. The elite-mass compact is a two-way street where, on the one hand, the masses defer to their elites, but on the other hand, where the hegemonic order imposes an obligation on the elites to protect the masses in their group from outsiders.

The biggest difference in Laitin's cultural hegemonic approach, as compared to Hechter's rational choice approach, is precisely the point regarding mass participation in the nationalist endeavor. The rational choice approach presumes a constant recalculation of the costs and benefits of participation. Laitin's alternative, to the contrary, assumes that a hegemony is established by raising the cultural order to the level of "common sense" (Laitin 1986: 92). Immediate economic conditions do change in the short term; however, a hegemony sets up a long-term pattern.

The masses hear that the *status quo* is "natural" and "as things should be" from those at the apex of society. At the same time an identical message is reinforced by society's myth-makers—be they clerics, secular teachers, or others who function as intellectuals. Those who obey these societal norms are celebrated as good members of the ethnic group and model citizens. They and their families are rewarded with accolades and material benefits, be they lands or positions of prestige, honor, and power. On the other hand, those who rebel against the social order risk the scorn of their society for maintaining "wrong thoughts" and they risk the ire of the state. A hegemonic order relies on this "carrot-and-stick" approach to survive in the long run. Once entrenched it acts as the social equivalent of Kuhn's scientific paradigm. It establishes the parameters of political debate and brands as illegitimate or *extremist* any proposals that fall outside its boundaries.

Elites in the dominant society could open the halls of power and prestige to rival elites so long as this second group did not threaten their authority. Under certain circumstances some groups conclude that it is safer to incorporate rivals and be able to keep a closer watch over them. However, this will be difficult if the lower strata of the dominant society are opposed. The masses in the dominant society have a vested interest in maintaining the *status quo*. The endurance of their positions and privileges depends upon it. This is particularly the case for the less skilled among the dominant group for they are the most expendable. Again, it is extremely important to reiterate that in most societies the divide separating the dominant group from its subordinate varies in degrees and intensity.

The following two chapters will argue that elites in both the United States and Canada created a cultural hegemonic order and that at the apogee of this hierarchy were English speakers. A cultural definition grounded partially on the basis of language would have a profound impact on the rise of nationalist movements in the linguistic peripheries of Puerto Rico and Quebec as newly emergent elites in those areas were denied (or restricted in terms of) upward mobility as a direct result of the language. When new elites in North America's linguistic periphery were denied the right to ascend, they turned inward and toward nationalism.

NOTES

1. This book will describe the social, economic, and political interaction of three languages—in particular Spanish (in Puerto Rico), French (in Quebec), and English (in the United States of America and Canada). Clearly these are three separate modes of communication that are not mutually intelligible (despite the common origin of the Romance languages, Spanish and French) and cannot be classified as dialects of some other standardized language.

2. Another possible consequence of the encounter of two or more languages in a common area is the rise of diglossia. Diglossia is a situation whereby languages are segregated on the basis of differing social roles. As Laponce (1993: 25) noted, a common diglossic situation is found where a local language is spoken at home or in the immediate vicinity, and a dominant language is used in the workplace or in official contacts with the government. One can also find a diglossic situation where one language is used in religious ceremonies, such as Arabic in mosques, Hebrew in synagogues, or Latin in Roman Catholic churches (prior to the Vatican II Council).

3. Languages are frequently used to distinguish ethnic groups or ethnic "sets." Since dialects are mutually intelligible they are often used to qualify regional and class perimeters or ethnic "subsets."

4. Katzner (1995: 162-163) noted that Hebrew was displaced as the spoken language of Jews by Aramaic, three centuries before the destruction of the Temple in Jerusalem. Yet, Hebrew maintained a bastion in religious texts and rituals.

5. Prior to the establishment of the State of Israel, Yiddish, a language more closely related to German than Hebrew, was a more likely candidate for the Jewish *lingua franca* as it was spoken or understood by about two-thirds of all Jews (Katzner 1995: 108-109).

6. Birch (1989: 18) wrote that Fichte was influenced by the writings of Herder, who also proposed that linguistic differences implied the existence of a distinctive people, or *Volk*, and for Herder this linguistically based state represented the "only rational form of government"; however, according to Birch, Herder did not articulate a "full theory of nationalism." That task was carried out by Fichte, who superimposed on Herder's linguistic typologies a hierarchy based on the supremacy of certain languages—primarily German (Birch 1989: 19-21).

7. Linguistic standardization, or the social processes associated with codification, does not eliminate the future development of dialects and localisms. As Pei (1984: 53) pointed out, languages have a strong centrifugal tendency that standardization only moderates.

8. One must also keep in mind that the Church's influence on society was greater during this period in history, a condition that advanced the selection of Latin as a court language in many European kingdoms. Since there was only one authorized church in Western Europe, its language held a unique monopoly in religious matters, which translated into the secular realm. Thus, many courts in Western Europe conducted their affairs and even drafted legislation in Latin.

9. That the drive for a unified Serbo-Croatian language came from Ljudevit Gaj, a Croat (Vojnić 1995: 93), is understandable given the linguistic heterogeneity of Croats in the nineteenth century. Croats spoke in the Kajkavian, Čakavian, and Štokavian dialects as opposed to the Serbs, who primarily spoke in the Štokavian dialect of Serbo-Croatian (Banac 1984: 48, 77). Thus, Serbs were essentially united in terms of a common vernacular—a condition Croats of that period had yet to achieve.

10. The role they perform as "myth-makers" may explain the frequency of clashes between secularly based intellectuals and clerics. In traditional societies popular literacy was seen as a luxury. As a result, clerics usually represented one of the few "street-level" literates living in the villages and towns out in the hinterland. Weber's (E. 1976) exploration of the development of French national identity and its spread to the French provinces documented the clashes between parish priests and the new army of secular teachers as both groups defended rival social orders. France's secularly based teachers were the spiritual spearheads of the counter-hegemony inaugurated with the French Revolution—an order that eventually became hegemonic in France.

11. Schools are but one state institution capable of spreading language. Weber (E. 1976: 313-314) argued that the army, via conscription, was principally responsible for popularizing the dialect of Paris and the displacement of the country's regional languages. As literacy spreads throughout a state the print media takes on the added role as an agent actively reinforcing the linguistic standard.

12. Assuming the existence of a cultural hegemonic order that acclaims language as a substantial group marker, one of the most frequently employed stereotypes of those who do not fluently speak the dominant language is that their lack of erudition corroborates

their lower intelligence. Such a stereotype allows the masses within the dominant group to feel superior to many well educated peripheral elites for they can *at least* be understood clearly.

13. There are cases where some peripheral elites, normally rejected by the dominant society on the basis of their cultural attributes, are allowed into the halls of power. Hechter (1975) noted that historically Scottish and Welsh elites were received by their English counterparts so long as they took on English manners of speech and dress. Historically this has also been the case for non-blacks in the United States. However, Woolard (1989: chapter 4) observed that even Castilian speakers who tried to speak Catalan in Barcelona were answered in Castilian. Under the Franco dictatorship languages other than Spanish were proscribed, thus the reaction of Catalans started as a form of self-protection. However, Woolard suggested that in the present context Catalan speaking is viewed as an "in-group" marker that excludes outsiders, even those who take the time and make an effort to learn this regional language.

14. The discussion throughout this book will focus on language. As previously noted, groups do not always define themselves in terms of a distinct language. Additionally, even when groups do characterize themselves on that basis, the vernacular may not be the sole objective cultural trait fixing group boundaries.

15. Their role as bilingual intermediaries will occur whether or not they are rejected from the dominant society on the basis of their cultural attributes.

16. For example, most immigrants who move to large American cities, but who come without technical skills, tend to live in the poorer sectors of the metropolis and are disposed to learn nonstandard variants of English such as "American Black English." This is a marked departure from many highly skilled immigrants who can afford to move to more affluent suburbs. They and their children linguistically gravitate toward speaking more standard variants of American English—variants associated with high social standing and economic prowess.

17. Two societies that offered nonlinguistic examples of this development were South Africa during apartheid and the southern United States (pre-1970s) where the racial hierarchies were so unyielding that even wealthy blacks were denied the franchise, geographic mobility, equal access to educational institutions, and many liberties that were otherwise available to even lower-class whites (Marx 1996).

4

Language and American Identity

In the process of comparing American and Canadian societies, Lipset (1990: 1) reminded readers that the American Revolution did not create one country, but in fact two. The events of 1776 forced King George III's subjects in North America to choose sides in a bitter family feud. Revolutionaries and antimonarchists succeeded in their separation from Great Britain and the creation of the United States of America. This political experiment south of the Great Lakes separated England's established church from the state, decentralized powers between federal and state levels of governments, and separated powers among the executive, legislative, and judicial branches. However, the Founding Fathers of the American Republic failed to convince their more conservative brethren to join them. Despite that historic rift geography and social and economic interactions have maintained strong links between the two countries.

Traditionally the most frequently highlighted difference regards divergent views on the proper role of the state in the everyday lives of individuals. Americans rebelled against Britain's rule in North America, Canadians preserved it. Americans stood for revolution, Canadians for evolutionary change. Canadians' traditional deference toward the state is exemplified with the country's unofficial motto, "Peace, Order, and Good Government" (Berton 1987: 19). This saying is juxtaposed to the American creed of "Life, Liberty and the Pursuit of Happiness" found in the second paragraph of the Declaration of Independence. Distinguishing Americans from their northern cousins, Lipset (1990: 26) commented that "the American creed can be subsumed in four words: antistatism, individualism, populism, and egalitarianism."

Many of these same attributes were observed early in the nineteenth century by Tocqueville. His commentaries and interpretations of life in the early history of the Republic had a profound impact on subsequent scholarship, which tended to see the label "American" more as a loosely organized mass of individuals who were united in terms of their psychological makeup (a shared love of liberty and a common citizenship) as opposed to a culturally cohesive and collective unit. Lipset's description of the American ethos emphasized that "[b]eing an American, however, is an ideological commitment. It is not a matter of birth" (Lipset 1990: 19). Echoing Tocqueville's litany, Kohn (1962: 14) wrote that "[t]he Americans constituted themselves as a nation not on the basis of some peculiar and exclusive biological or traditional characteristics but on the basis of a universal idea." Comparing the United States to Europe, Eriksen (1993: 139) commented that the United States "has no semi-mythical history as a nation." And finally, even Laitin tended to discount the potential for a cultural hegemony in the United States based on a elite-driven myth of collective identity: "In the United States, it would be absurd to suggest that there has been the establishment of hegemony. One sees, for example, both ethnic and class politics existing side by side, each defusing the potential explosion of the other" (Laitin 1986: 168).

The Tocquevillian emphasis on American identity and individualism, as opposed to cultural traits usually associated with a common ancestry, has reached mythological proportions. Nonetheless, individuality as a key component in the "American myth" obscures real collective traits that have been used to define Americanism—though they are rarely articulated openly. As noted earlier, elites select cultural traits that benefit them as part of the power consolidation process. This chapter will argue that American elites, even before the Revolution of 1776, defined themselves on the basis of language, in addition to other traits, and that this cultural element is still used today to separate Americans from "others." While the English language has been used since the eighteenth century to differentiate Americans from others this policy has rarely been stated openly. Laponce (1987: 46) put it well when he said: "If one's language is dominant, one does not think about it any more than one thinks about one's health, provided that this is good."

At least one of the Founding Fathers believed that the peoples of British North America were united by a common culture, which included a shared language. John Jay wrote in the second Federalist, encouraging the subjects of George III to rebel against his rule:

With equal pleasure I have as often taken notice that Providence has been pleased to give this one connected country to one united people—a people descended from the same ancestors, speaking the same language, professing the same religion, attached to the same principles of government, very similar in their manners and customs. (Hamilton, Madison, & Jay 1961: 38)

The country's language was seen as a cohesive element in a decentralized federal system. Tocqueville echoed the notion that language united Americans. In fact, he went so far as to give language center stage in the country's cohesion:

Language is perhaps the strongest and most enduring link which unites men. All the immigrants spoke the same language and were children of the same people. Born in a country shaken for centuries by the struggles of parties, a country in which each faction in turn had been forced to put itself under the protection of the laws, they had learned their political lessons in that rough school, and they had more acquaintance with notions of rights and principles of true liberty than most of the European nations at that time. (Tocqueville 1988: 33)

Non-English speakers were tolerated in the early years of the American Republic, but it was the country's homogeneity that was celebrated, not its cultural diversity (Steinberg 1981: 9). Language was chosen as an important group trait since it served the dual purpose of distinguishing American colonists from the British and separating Americans from non-English speakers.

AMERICAN IDENTITY VIS-À-VIS THE BRITISH

The colonial system provided several West European states with the opportunity to expand their power and influence. It also made large tracts of land available for settlement. As is quite often the case with migration patterns around the world, those who cannot find work, or adequate work, in the home country are the most eager to move on. The economically well-off rarely have any incentive to relocate to another country.[1] From the sixteenth through the seventeenth centuries, the vast majority of these European newcomers were farmers who would benefit from the spoils of conquest. Particularly in the Americas aboriginal peoples would be corralled, pushed aside, or massacred in order to procure more land for large-scale Spanish, Portuguese, Dutch, British, and French settlements.

A direct and perhaps inevitable result of expanding settlements is a change in language. In North America new places, fauna, and species of animals previously unknown to the English, Scottish, Welsh, and Irish settlers had to be named. Similar problems were encountered by colonists from other European states. One common solution was to borrow terms and place names from various indigenous languages. Thus the vocabulary spoken by colonists expanded to include many non-European words (Baron 1990: 28). The English language spoken in Britain was not "purer" in any sense. Linguistic purity is a commonly touted myth. Languages are, by their very nature, dynamic media of communication that are in a constant state of flux. Some words may be dropped from common speech. New words and phrases may be coined and others are borrowed from other languages. The point is that a rift was separating the speech of those coming from the Anglo-Irish Isles and their brethren on the other side of the Atlantic.

In addition to the incorporation of new words into the language of American colonists, the geographic isolation of settlers from the mother country meant that they lost touch with the linguistic novelties that had crept into British English since their departure. Again, as language changes in the periphery, so it also changes in the metropolis. Terms that were commonly used in one century would later fall into disuse. Infrequent contact with the home country prevented most colonists from learning that parts of their lexicon were now "archaic" by the core country's standards. The result was a new variant of English that was distinguishable by its seemingly paradoxical blend of old and new terms—new words from indigenous languages along with what were now outdated expressions from their own language (Baron 1990: 28).

Linguistic differences are often translated into social ones. American society consisted of a social hierarchy of British-born nobles who outranked American-born landowners and merchants.[2] American-born large landowners and merchants, representing the summit of the local bourgeoisie, by extension would outrank smaller landowners and laborers, who in turn would outrank Native Americans, indentured servants, and slaves. The social division between American-born and European-born in North America paralleled a similar situation in Latin America. In this process the lower social rank of the American-born workers and small landowners was extended, by the European nobility, on the wealthier segments of American colonial society. In addition to linguistic snobbery and social differentiation, colonists resented the unequal taxation imposed by London. These duties and customs were passed by the House of Commons[3] (in addition to the House of Lords), which afforded representation for Britain's bourgeoisie but not for their American counterparts. The tax issue reinforced the notion that those on the western side of the Atlantic were "different" from their transoceanic counterparts.

Reiterating a point from the previous chapter, standardized languages are created by elites. In this period before the extension of publicly funded education, literacy was limited, for the most part, to those who were economically well-off. Most of the books were purchased by elites.[4] Printers, tailoring their products to their customers, had no economic incentive to publish in non-elite variants of the language. The publication of books added to the social standing of the "correct" dialect of the language. In the case of the American colonies, this status was awarded to the British variant.

The British rebuked Americans for corrupting *their* language (Baron 1990: 41). This broad generalization was extended to all social classes. Even after the American Revolution, Tocqueville observed the persistence of a transatlantic linguistic hierarchy: "Educated Englishmen, better able to appreciate these fine nuances than I, have often told me that the language of well-educated Americans is decidedly different from that spoken by the same class in Great Britain" (Tocqueville 1988: 477). The relationship between the American and British variants of English persisted in the post-Revolutionary period. As a result of anti-British feelings, some advocated the abandonment of English in favor of another language—possibly Hebrew (Baron 1990: 42). Due to its impracticality this plan, along with others to replace English, was dropped.

While replacing the American vernacular was unrealistic, modifying the language was another matter. One such pioneer was Noah Webster, who promoted the standardization of a "federal language" (Baron 1990: 43). His form of linguistic planning focused on creating a new orthography that would differentiate his popular dictionary from British versions and, in time, the spelling of words on both sides of the Atlantic (Baron 1990: 46).[5] Linguistic change would not come about by way of a linguistic academy,[6] as was advocated by John Adams, but through his dictionary (in Crawford 1992: 31-33).[7] As Webster said in 1789:

As an independent nation, our honor requires us to have a system of our own, in language as well as government. Great Britain, whose children we are, and whose language we speak, should no longer be *our* standard; for the taste of her writers is already corrupted, and her language on the decline. (in Crawford 1992: 34) [emphasis in the original]

The preceding quote uncovers more than just the writings of a rebel against the Crown. It captures an explicit attempt at changing what was an accepted norm of the British society. His words called for the establishment of an American cultural *counter-hegemony* that would offset Britain's cultural hegemonic order on the North American continent. Webster's goal was that this counter-hegemony (from the perspective of His Majesty's government) would eventually become hegemonic in the United States.

The importance of Webster's words can be measured by the impact that his dictionary had. It became, in effect, the standard for the correct spelling of words for the American variant of the English language. His unequivocal goal was to differentiate Americans from their former sovereigns. Webster's fervent anti-British sentiment and orthographic innovations waned as his dictionaries began selling in Britain (Baron 1990: 47). Apparently the lure of profits from the eastern side of the Atlantic tempered his revolutionary and anti-British zeal. In any case, the American version of the language, both in its spoken and written forms would differentiate the two communities.

AMERICAN IDENTITY AND NON-ANGLOPHONES

If the English language, as spoken in North America, distinguished the British from their American cousins, it also separated the colonists from non-English speakers. As numerous writers have mentioned, North America was never a linguistically homogeneous continent. The pre-Columbian era gave rise to a myriad of indigenous languages, some of which are still spoken today. Additionally there were other European languages with which these early American colonists came into regular contact. For example, the city of New York had a significant Dutch enclave. But the rival linguistic community that would encourage the incorporation of the English language into the American identity was German.[8] While there were German immigrants in many colonies, their largest settlement was in Pennsylvania. Their presence in that colony was so large that Benjamin Franklin once asked: "Why should *Pennsylvania*, founded by the *English*, become a Colony of *Aliens*, who will shortly be so numerous as to Germanize us instead of our Anglifying them?" (Dinnerstein, Nichols, & Reimers 1979: 23) [emphasis in the original].

Franklin's statement attests to the fact that concerns over other languages are nothing new in the United States. In fact Baron (1990), whose work made significant advances into the study of American identity and language, argued that

52   *Language, Elites, and the State*

the English-first or English-only movements of today can trace their political lineage all the way back to the eighteenth century:

The English-first movement in America was reinforced by the political identification of the American language with Americanism, but it began locally at least a generation before the establishment of the United States, as a defensive reaction to German immigration in Pennsylvania, and it continues unabated in areas with large non-English-speaking populations. Many English-speaking Americans in the eighteenth century, as now, reacted to nonanglophones with suspicion, if not outright fear and intolerance of those considered racially inferior to the Anglo-Saxon stock. (Baron 1990: 64)

A pattern of low tolerance for languages other than English began with German in the eighteenth century, but this pattern of linguistic animosity was repeated with succeeding waves of immigration in the nineteenth and twentieth centuries. The first order of business is to explain why the British and their American successor state allowed Germans to settle their North American colonies. Simply put, they were needed; British and later American immigration policies were swayed by practical considerations, despite misgivings about the arrival of these outsiders (Steinberg 1981: 10-11). Englishmen and their Celtic minorities were not migrating to the American colonies fast enough or in sufficient numbers to meet the demands of the growing colonial economy. Labor shortages in the eighteenth century motivated the Crown to restrain the mass departures of Englishmen, particularly skilled artisans (Steinberg 1981: 10). For the most part, the few British who were allowed to settle in the American colonies without any restrictions were paupers, vagrants, and convicts (Steinberg 1981: 11). This economic need opened the door to large-scale, non-British immigration both before and after the independence of the United States.

The first German families, led by Francis Pastorious, were encouraged to settle in the American colonies by William Penn in 1683 (Dinnerstein, Nichols, & Reimers 1979: 21). They were promised personal freedom and assured that the government would not interfere in the practice of their religion. Freedom to practice their faith without state entanglements was an extremely important enticement since a significant portion of these newcomers were so-called sect Germans: Amish, Mennonites, Moravians, and Dunkers (Dinnerstein, Nichols, & Reimers 1979: 22). They were pacifists and on many issues, particularly those involving the use of the military, tended to side with the Quakers. This would have a profound effect on the future Commonwealth of Pennsylvania as Germans would comprise a third of its population by the 1760s (Dinnerstein, Nichols, & Reimers 1979: 21). This large-scale immigration increased contact between English and German speakers. But in and of itself this contact did not create political tensions.

German-English antagonism grew as community leaders struggled with the issue of territorial expansion. Westward expansion served the dual purpose of increasing the wealth of colonial elites while simultaneously acting as a social safety valve. Some colonial elites looked to the western territories for farming, timber, trapping, and other commercial endeavors. Also, providing the poor with their own land would furnish them with economic opportunities (Carlson 1987: 3) and bolster loyalty to the regime that gave them this property and new livelihoods. The parceling out of western lands served as valued selective benefits that would cement elite-mass ties in society.[9] Carlson (1987: 3), referring to one of the Founding Fathers of the American Republic, said that "[Benjamin] Franklin's projected new society depended on an expanding frontier to provide the poor with economic opportunity."[10]

The clash between these two groups of colonists over expansion crystallized in the 1740s. Pennsylvania's colonial legislature, dominated by Quakers, turned down the call to fight alongside His Majesty's troops against the French and their Native American allies (Dinnerstein, Nichols, & Reimers 1979: 22). When legislative action proved fruitless, Franklin and his supporters sought to form their own militia and even solicited support from German colonists. However, these German colonists refused to fight (Van Doren 1947: 39). Since they declined to support the struggle against France, many English colonists began to question the loyalties and reliability of these pacifists (Dinnerstein, Nichols, & Reimers 1979: 22). It is rather ironic that Franklin, one of the founders of the new American government, would implicate others in a charge of disloyalty to the British Crown. In his anger Franklin not only accused the Germans of disloyalty to the Crown but also contributed to a trend of stereotyping non-English speakers by belittling their intelligence. The diffusion of such an elite-sponsored stereotype served as a good indicator of the popular acceptance of either the hegemonic order or counter-hegemonic order. Ignoring the peasant backgrounds of most British settlers in North America, Franklin said:

Those [Germans] who come hither are generally the most stupid of their own nation, and as ignorance is often attended with credulity, when knavery would mislead it; and with suspicion when honesty would set it right; and as few of the English understand the German language, and so cannot address them either from the press or the pulpit, 'tis almost impossible to remove any prejudices they may entertain. (in Van Doren 1947: 38)

He was but one who promoted this popular trend. One of his contemporaries, William Smith, the first provost of the Philadelphia College, Academy and Charitable School (the forerunner of the University of Pennsylvania) also assumed that ignorance of English proved low intelligence (Baron 1990: 67).

Franklin's comments regarding German intellectual prowess are rather ironic. Yes, in a letter written in 1753, Franklin wrote that few German children knew English (in Van Doren 1947: 38); however, he also noted in the same document that Germans were voracious readers. Germans imported large numbers of books, and of the six printing houses in Pennsylvania, two were completely German, two were completely English, and the other two were mixed (in Van Doren 1947: 38). Comparing the two communities, this parity in printing facilities is a rather remarkable statistic, given that Germans were a linguistic minority in the colony. Additionally, this high rate of literacy preceded the era of large-scale publicly funded education. So, were they "stupid" because of the language they spoke or because of the stances they took against him? Baron's (1990: 87) research indicated that when English-speaking politicians, even in the eighteenth century, knew the language of a given community they were more than willing to use it in an attempt to appeal to an ethnic bloc. This explains why the Continental Congress printed many documents, from proceedings to the Articles of Confederation, in German (Baron 1990: 87).[11]

A sizable portion of the German leaders objected to their participation in armed conflicts for religious reasons. Their language facilitated communication with their people. Simultaneously it impeded American elite communication with ordinary German speakers. German elites, with their relatively large number of printing houses or through the pulpit, could easily communicate with their masses. On the other hand, it would have been difficult for Franklin and his supporters to challenge this message without knowing German themselves. As the previous chapter noted, those most likely to be bilingual are subordinate elites. In this case that applied to German elites. Thus, the English-speaking American elites would generally have to employ German elites to communicate with the German masses.

The growth of a German community, one with its own set of elites, posed a direct threat to the power of the English-speaking elites of that time. The expansionist projects of various leaders were compromised. As Steinberg (1981: 12) put it: "Predictably, as immigration grew in volume and complexity, xenophobia developed into a full-fledged ideology and political Involvement." Again, we go back to the words of Benjamin Franklin:

They begin of late to make all their bonds, and other legal instruments in their own language, which (though, I think, it ought not to be) are allowed good in our courts, where the German business so increases, that there is continued need of interpreters: and, I suppose, in a few years, they will also be necessary in the Assembly to tell one half of our legislators what the other half say. In short, unless the stream of their importation could be turned from this to other colonies, as you very judiciously propose, they will soon so out number us, that all the advantages we have, will, in my opinion, be not able to preserve our language, and even our government will become precarious. (in Van Doren 1947: 39)

As the German-speaking community increased in number, it would have a greater need for teachers, lawyers, politicians, and other highly skilled individuals. These individuals would enlarge the ranks of German-speaking elites, not English-speaking ones. This put the American elites of that time in a bind. On the one hand they needed the labor and skills that these non-British immigrants provided. On the other hand their continued obedience to rival leaders posed a threat to their grand designs. Franklin, whose previous statements had verbally attacked Germans, also admitted that the country needed them. In one of his letters from 1753, he wrote: "I say, I am not against the admission of Germans in general, for they have their virtues;—their industry and frugality is exemplary. They are excellent husbandmen; and contribute greatly to the improvement of a country" (in Van Doren 1947: 40).

This situation created an interesting dilemma. The duality of American immigration patterns, needing immigrants yet resenting them, may help explain why Americanism shied away from openly defining itself on the basis of language or other cultural attributes, although they were omnipresent. In the first place the most important divide was between Americans and the British, and this division was not based on a distinct language. The overthrow of the British regime is one of the preeminent components in the American myth. There was a difference of dialect, but not one of language. American resentment toward British rule could be swathed theoretically in terms of philosophical principles but could not easily be articulated on the basis of differing cultures. When one is in the process of breaking from another's rule, there are rarely any incentives to expound commonalties of any kind.

Additionally, success on the battlefield against London's government required the participation, or at a minimum the complacency, of the Germans. Alienating Germans at that crucial juncture could have been detrimental to the revolutionary movement. Furthermore, estranging Germans could have a negative impact on those Europeans contemplating settling in the United States. They were fleeing economic and social problems at home. They were not eager to move to a country where they would be met with hostility or resentment. American English-speaking elites still needed the labor and skills these immigrants provided.

These conflicting needs were reconciled in a two-step approach. In step one, European immigrants would be invited to settle. The price they paid was to reconcile themselves with a low-group status. A social status overseas would not automatically transfer to this side of the Atlantic. However, that was a status they could escape by following step two—assimilating culturally and linguistically.[12] Assimilation was rewarded with social acceptance.[13] At that point one ceased to be a foreigner and became a hyphenated American. On the other hand, those who chose, for whatever reason, not to change their ways were branded with the stigma of a low social standing and accused of being un-American. The outsider status, while real, was not insurmountable, particularly for the bilingual children of immigrants. For most immigrants the American compact offered them greater social mobility than that found in a more socially rigid Europe.

Americanization demanded linguistic assimilation. The problem was how to carry this out. Most immigrants, even today, tend to live in ethnic enclaves. As Laponce (1987) noted, territorial concentration acts to preserve languages. In some cases the urban ethnic ghettoes were large enough that one could work, reside, and socially interact without leaving the confines of the neighborhood or city sector. Were Americanization to succeed it would have to penetrate deep inside the linguistically distinct enclaves. The solution to this problem was a mass-based and publicly funded educational system.

PUBLIC SCHOOLS AND STATEHOOD

The notion of using schools as vehicles for cultural assimilation in the United States came as early as the seventeenth century. A new language was to accompany a new faith as clerics from the period advocated the assimilation of Native Americans (Carlson 1987: 3). Let there be no question about the ultimate goal of this policy. It was the complete substitution of one culture and its accompanying language for another. As Noah Webster put it in 1789: "It must be considered further, that the English is the common root or stock from which our national language will be derived. All others will gradually waste away—and within a century and a half, North America will be peopled with a hundred millions of men, *all speaking the same language*" (in Crawford 1992: 34) [emphasis in the original]. Assimilation was the goal and schools were the means to achieve this. In time this would require a large bureaucracy to implement the policy. This bureaucracy would naturally be filled with English speakers, thus adding to the prestige and economic potency of Anglophones. In the twentieth century American pedagogical policy would have a profound effect on the development of Puerto Rican ethnic identity.

At the outset it should be made very clear that this policy of assimilation was aimed primarily at European immigrants. Non-white immigrants, especially blacks, were excluded from this process.

Immigrants were disparaged for their cultural peculiarities, and the implied message was, 'You will become like us whether you want to or not.' When it came to racial minorities, however, the unspoken dictum was 'No matter how much like us you are, you will remain apart.' Thus, at the same time that the nation pursued a policy aimed at the rapid assimilation of recent arrivals from Europe, it segregated the racial minorities who, by virtue of their much longer history in American society, had already come to share much of the dominant culture. (Steinberg 1981: 42)

The first attempts at assimilating other Europeans were aimed at Germans. Leaders from the English-speaking community organized a "Society for the Propagating of Christian Knowledge among the Germans" for this purpose (Dinnerstein, Nichols, & Reimers 1979: 23).[14] It was hoped that their free tuition would entice parents to send their children. Naturally, German leaders realized what their underlying purpose was and objected to these schools. However, the definition of "Americanism" based on cultural attributes meant that those who did not acquire them were, invariably, "un-American." "The concept of Americanism as an act of *choice*—the decision to learn English, to apply for citizenship—and a choice of specific beliefs, acts and modes of behaviour implied the corresponding concept of 'un-Americanism' " (Hobsbawm 1983b: 280) [emphasis in the original].

In time, compulsory public elementary and secondary schools, operating with English as the language of instruction, would succeed in linguistically assimilating the vast majority of German Americans. As Steinberg (1981: 54) put it: "More than any other single factor, the public school undermined the capacity of immigrant groups to transmit their native cultures to their American-born children." The need to prove one's loyalty to the United States became more acute for this linguistic minority during the two world wars.[15] During times of conflict in particular, maintenance of other languages is seen by society at large as virtually treasonous. Thus, this language policy would be carried into the new territories in the western part of the continent.

The United States grew demographically thanks in large measure to prolonged immigration. The country also expanded territorially by annexing lands west of the Appalachians. Throughout the eighteenth and nineteenth centuries, the United States pursued its quest to become a transcontinental power. Once the property of the U.S. government, Congress would have the final word on the status of the new territories.[16] As far as the continental territories were concerned, the eventual goal was statehood. Under the Northwest Ordinance of 1787, a territory would be appointed a governor by the president,[17] to be followed by the election of a territorial legislature, and the eventual granting of statehood itself (Leibowitz 1989: 6). Though this statute only applied to a limited number of territorial possessions,[18] it became the basic blueprint for subsequent statehood admitees.

The federal constitution gave Congress full authority over the territories; it also granted the federal legislature the power to admit new states.[19] Most territorial settlements were comprised of citizens from the established states who moved west. "The territorial populations were to be composed of the friends, relatives and acquaintances of the States' populations and their representatives and senators so that when Statehood was to come to this new geographical area it was in the context of a reunion of the Stateside family" (Leibowitz 1989: 8). Thus, the United States, while annexing new parcels of land in the west, was essentially incorporating Americans who had left the established states. The statehood pattern established in the last decade of the eighteenth and first two decades of the nineteenth centuries did not foresee the absorption of new peoples into the Union. As native peoples were confined to reservations, they did not upset this preset formula.[20]

This model was challenged for the first time with Louisiana's petition for statehood in the early nineteenth century. White settlement came long before Thomas Jefferson procured it from France. Native Americans could be, and would be, ignored by the dominant society so long as they were pacified and confined to their respective reservations. However, white settlers were not as easy to ignore. These settlers came with their own language and culture.

Germans now voluntarily left their countries of origin to come to the United States. Thus many, including Franklin and Webster, felt that Germans had an obligation to conform to their new society. Louisiana's situation was rather dif-

ferent. In this case the thousands of French speakers in the territory did not deliberately move to the United States. They settled in the French territory of Or-
leans only to find that the borders around them changed. Regardless of the circumstances of their arrival, the issue of German immigration set a precedent for
future dealings with non-English-speaking peoples. To be American meant to
speak English.

Congress accepted Louisiana's petition for statehood in 1812 under the pro-
viso that English become the new state's official language. Both legislative debates and judicial proceedings had to be conducted in English (Serrano & Gorrín
1979: 524). Louisianans did have a distinct legal code that they wanted to maintain even under statehood. Congress agreed that they could keep French Civil
Law, so long as judicial proceedings were conducted in the English language.
Moynihan summed up this contradictory policy as follows: "Louisiana, for example, might and did retain the *Code Napoléon*, but trials were to be in English.
This position may seem arbitrary, but it is defensible. *E Pluribus unum*"
(Moynihan 1993: 74) [emphasis in the original]. In the end geography and mi-
gration would transform Louisiana, making it an English-majority state. Its co-
terminous frontiers with other Anglophone states facilitated the migration of
English speakers. The extension of public education, in English, would also
"Americanize" the French-speaking inhabitants of the state in a few generations.

As the fate of future immigrants followed the German precedent, Louisiana,
in time, became the model for the admission of territories with large non-
English-speaking populations. Linguistic assimilation at the individual level
would also apply to the collective level. Oklahoma's and New Mexico's admission into the Union early in the twentieth century was predicated on establishing
English as the language of instruction in these territories' public schools
(Comptroller General 1980: 13-14). In the case of Arizona, Congress required
that the new state's executive and legislators speak, read, and write English
(Serrano & Gorrín 1979: 524). As was the case with Louisiana these states were
located in continental North America, a condition that facilitated the unimpeded
flow of English-speaking migrants from other states.

Some observers point to Hawaii as an exception. After all, no one questions
the heterogeneous nature of this society as it is the only state in the Union without a white majority. At one level one can say that appearances can be deceiving.
There is no doubt that Hawaii is culturally a very mixed society; however, there
is also no question that it is also an overwhelmingly English-speaking society.
Long before this archipelago became a part of the United States, British and
American missionaries flocked to the Kingdom of Hawaii in search of converts
to Christianity (Lind 1967: 87). They were largely responsible for establishing
the first western-style schools where English would be introduced. Public
schools followed suit with the inclusion of English-medium schools into the
system in 1854 (Reid 1941: 169). By 1894 English was already the primary medium of instruction on the islands (Comptroller General 1980: 36). Long before
the *Stars and Stripes* flew over Honolulu's royal palace, English was already

entrenched as the medium for conducting trade, diplomacy, and the affairs of state (Lind 1967: 87). In time migration from overseas and from the U.S. mainland would relegate the status of Native Hawaiians to that of an ethnic and a linguistic minority in their own homeland.

While there is no law stating that Congress cannot admit non-Anglophone entities into the Union, it has never done so: "In two centuries, the United States Congress has admitted thirty-seven new states to the original union of thirteen. But always a stated or unstated condition was that English be the official language" (Moynihan 1993: 73). The prior cases (Louisiana, Oklahoma, New Mexico, and Arizona) clearly confirm Senator Moynihan's synopsis of congressional attitudes toward non-English-speaking entities. Precedent does not guarantee an end result, but it does set a clear pattern.

There is but one government study that casts a doubt on this general line of thinking, and that is the report of the United States-Puerto Rico Commission on the Status of Puerto Rico, issued in 1966. It was organized by the Johnson administration less than two decades after the ratification of Puerto Rico's 1952 Commonwealth Constitution with the intent of studying possible status alternatives for the island. The three alternatives the Commission explored were: continued commonwealth status, outright independence, and the incorporation of the island into the federal Union via statehood. A question of some concern was the possible admission of this culturally distinct Caribbean territory into the Union as the fifty-first state. Holding up Hawaii as a case in point, the Commission wrote: "The experience with Hawaii, although so very different in many important ways, attests to the capacity of the U.S. citizens and the union of States to develop full Statehood with cultural diversity and without territorial contiguity" (U.S.-Puerto Rico Commission 1966: 15). A second question that arose was congressional reaction to the possible admission of a non-English-speaking state. James Rowe, the report's chairman, wrote: "Statehood would necessarily involve a cultural and language accommodation to the rest of the federated States of the Union. The Commission does not see this as an insurmountable barrier, nor does this require the surrender of the Spanish language nor the abandonment of a rich cultural heritage" (US-Puerto Rico Commission 1966: 15).

On the surface one could infer that the commission's findings rejected Senator Moynihan's conclusions on this matter. However, Leibowitz (1989:75) noted that this 1966 report, written at the heart of the civil rights era, most likely underestimated the special accommodations needed to accept a non-English-speaking territory into the American Union. Leibowitz's view on this matter has been supported by succeeding federal reports on the implications of admitting a non-English-speaking territory into the Union. One published by the General Accounting Office in the early 1980s was much less confident about congressional openness toward linguistic accommodation in statehood petitions.

Like many controversies surrounding the status debate, the language question will depend upon future decisions by Puerto Rico and the Congress. These determinations will likely involve weighing conflicting emotional opinions and assessing varied considerations, including Puerto Rico's unique circumstances, past statehood admissions, and the United States' as well as other nations' actions to accommodate linguistic minorities. (Comptroller General 1981: 89)

This statement masks in subtle language the difficulty Congress would have in opening its doors to the inclusion of a non-English-speaking state. The earlier statements by both Moynihan and Leibowitz more directly point to the importance of language when it comes to the statehood process since this political status grants full partnership to a territory.[21] While Congress could admit any territory, including a non-Anglophone one, into the Union, it historically has avoided doing so unless the federal possession agreed to restrictions on the use of languages other than English.

THE ENGLISH LANGUAGE AND AMERICAN IDENTITY

Early in the history of the United States, the country's populace was defined, partially, on the basis of language. The colonists spoke a dialect that separated them from their British-born counterparts. The British used this trait as evidence of the inferiority of colonists, thus justifying the lower social standing. Language also separated the English-speaking majority from the other language groups, especially the Germans. Debates over the westward territorial expansion of the British colonies highlighted the potential that a rival elite had in opposing a major military and political undertaking. To protect their position in society, elites premised loyalty to the new country on the acquisition of the English language, in addition to other things. The dominant group in society defined itself on the basis of language, relegating non-Anglophones to the status of outsiders.

The definition of the dominant group in society became hegemonic when no mainstream political actors dared challenge this notion openly. While there are discussions as to the appropriate role of languages other than English in the United States today, there is still no question that to be an American requires one to learn the language. Applications for naturalization are still judged partially on familiarity with the language. Elite status in society additionally requires the speaking of standard American English. For the popular classes their fluency in English gives them a higher social standing than that of immigrants. The cycle, which began early in the country's history, would repeat itself as the descendants of immigrants would look down upon subsequent waves of newcomers.

All this was imposed on individuals. The same standards applied at the collective level, which was apparent when territories with large non-English-speaking populations petitioned for statehood. Full membership in the American political family required a territory to be English speaking. If not, its application for statehood rested on its commitment to restricting the use of the "other" language and promoting the use of English. The most common means of doing so was by way of the public school system.

The following chapter will explore the nexus between language and identity in Canada. Here a socioeconomic hierarchy also emerged—one based partially on the basis of language. In Canada, as in the United States, the English language and its speakers would be rewarded with preference. Unlike in the United States, the identity of Canada's dominant society would not develop out of conflicts with those who spoke German, but with French. And unlike the Germans of Pennsylvania, the French of Canada preceded the English settlement of North America. In time, the French would demand parity in social status and resources.

NOTES

1. One of the exceptions was the assignment of metropolitan elites to the colonies to serve as colonial administrators and officers. But they were not always permanent settlers. After their tours of duty many returned either to the motherland or to another colonial outpost.

2. For more details on this process, see Lafaye's (1976) work on colonial Mexico.

3. Voting in Britain during the eighteenth and even part of the nineteenth centuries was restricted to property-owning males. This political tradition was preserved early in the history of the United States where the original states adopted franchise laws that restricted participation on the basis of land or wealth.

4. One of the few exceptions to this pattern was the Bible, one of the only books that would have been seen in many non-elite Protestant homes. However, those who owned a copy in all likelihood read the King James Version. As such, this translation did not vary with the changes in language use.

5. Bourhis (1984: 3) referred to this maneuver as *corpus* language planning—changing a language's orthography, lexicon, and grammar. This is opposed to *status* language planning, which is the result of altering the social functions a language performs.

6. Language academies, for example in Spain and France, are the most blatant examples and the most bureaucratized framework for elite standardization of languages.

7. In 1780 Adams, inspired by the language academies of Europe, proposed that Congress establish an institution to be entitled "the American Academy for refining, improving, and ascertaining the English language" (in Crawford 1992: 32).

8. The British conquest of New France would bring English speakers into direct contact with French speakers. However, this linguistic contact would have a greater impact on the development of Canadian identity as opposed to American identity.

9. The United States offers a rare example of large-scale distribution of selective benefits. Usually selective benefits, because of their scarcity and high value, are handed out to small numbers of individuals. But in the case of the United States, land (at the expense of Native Americans) was so abundant that American elites could offer parcels to large numbers of the populace and in so doing cement mass loyalties to the post-1776 order.

10. Of course, this exchange was founded on the dispossession of North America's "First Nations" which would lose their ancestral lands (save for a few minuscule reservations) and the livelihoods they derived from them.

11. Some of these same documents were also translated into French, in an attempt to appeal to the Canadiens (Baron 1990: 87).

12. One might also want to add a step three: naturalization. Interestingly enough, one of the requirements for attaining U.S. citizenship, in addition to a certain degree of familiarity with U.S. history, is knowledge of the English language.

13. As Steinberg (1981: 42) noted, this compact was limited to whites. Initially, it was also limited to Protestants. Catholics and Jews, though European, were excluded from the full force of this social agreement. Regarding Jews, the persistence of anti-Semitism in the United States casts serious doubts on whether they have ever been completely accepted in American society. On the question of Catholics, Moynihan (1993: 31) wrote that anti-Catholic attitudes, and fear of the papacy, in nineteenth-century America were as powerful as abolitionism. The acceptance of Catholics took decades. It was not until the 1950s, argued O'Brien, that Catholics were fully accepted. He suggested that Senator McCarthy and his "witch hunts" were responsible for moving the address of the "Antichrist" from the Vatican to the Kremlin (O'Brien 1988: 36). At that point the unofficial American religion became "pan-Christian," as opposed to "pan-Protestant" (O'Brien 1988: 38).

14. The title of this organization is rather ironic, given that many German-speaking immigrants came to the United States to freely practice their Christian faith.

15. Anti-German sentiments were so strong during the two world wars that some communities burned their German-language books. Of course, this did not compare to the anti-Japanese sentiments during World War II that resulted in the deportation of thousands of Japanese Americans to concentration camps.

16. "The Congress shall have Power to dispose of and make all needful Rules and Regulations respecting the Territory or other Property belonging to the United States" (U.S. Constitution, Art. 4, Sec. 3, cl. 2).

17. Like all presidential appointments, the nomination of the territorial governor designee had to be confirmed by the U.S. Senate (U.S. Constitution, Art. 2, Sec. 2, cl. 2).

18. The vast majority of entities admitted into the Union were former federal territories. There were a couple of notable exceptions. Texas was a separate country prior to statehood and West Virginia was partitioned from a previously existing state, the Commonwealth of Virginia, during the Civil War. Hawaii was a territory at the time of its inclusion as a state. But, before becoming an American possession, it was an internationally recognized sovereign country. It was a republic in the 1890s and prior to that a monarchy.

19. U.S. Constitution, Art. 4, Sec. 3, cl. 1.

20. An example of their peripheralization from American society was ingrained in the federal Constitution, which did not count native or aboriginal peoples residing in reservations ("Indians not taxed") in the census used to distribute seats in the House of Representatives (U. S. Constitution, Art. 1, Sec. 2, cl. 3).

21. In addition to concerns over the issue of language and Puerto Rican statehood, Stepan suggested that Congress has also been concerned about admitting a territory with an active separatist movement. For this reason he labeled a hypothetical Puerto Rican state an "American Quebec" with potential for violence as high as "Ulster" (Stepan 1983: 268). William Webster, director of the F.B.I. and C.I.A. under the Reagan administration, went even further by warning Congress that Puerto Rico could become the "Achilles' heel" of the United States (Millán & Cabán 1987: 7).

5

Canada and the King's English

The previous chapter indicated that North America's colonial society was far from unanimous in supporting the 1776 Revolution. By the early 1780s the Loyalist-Republican rift coincided with a rough North-South divide. This pattern gelled with the exodus of thousands of monarchists from the southern colonies to the northern maritime colonies and the territories of the former New France. This collection of British possessions in the northeastern corner of the North American continent constituted the origins of what later became the Canadian Confederation. In the words of Lipset (1990: 1), if the United States was the country of the revolution, then Canada epitomized the counter-revolution. The leaders of the United States sought to counter British rule politically and socially, thus establishing a rival order in North America—a counter-hegemony. Their dialect, thanks to Webster's work, would make them distinct from the British; it also distinguished Americans from non-English speakers. To the north their counterparts labored to preserve the *status quo*—the hegemonic order.[1] As a result, those loyal to the Crown in North America did not focus on distinguishing themselves from the British linguistically. Though language would not develop into a distinguishing sociopolitical marker between Britain and Canada, it would serve to set apart Canada's two dominant linguistic communities: the English and the French.

The traditional deference of Canadians toward Britain did not connote blind obedience to the Crown. It did, however, signal a philosophical disagreement with their southern cousins regarding the appropriate path to instituting change. Canada's leadership promoted gradual change over its more radical variant.

It has been said that the binding force of the United States of America was the idea of liberty, and certainly none of the relevant constitutional documents let us forget it. By comparison, the Canadian nation seems founded on the common sense of empirical politicians who had wanted to establish some law and order over a disjointed half continent. (Trudeau 1968: 197)

The partition of Anglo-North America initiated the development of a distinct Canadian identity—one separate from its southern neighbor despite the multiplicity of shared objective cultural attributes, norms, and institutions. Outside of juridico-legal definitions culminating with citizenship, many have difficulty defining what it is to be an American. The same may be said of what it is to be a Canadian. In fact, some have argued that defining *Canadianness* is even more problematic. Part of this difficulty may lie in the fact that this identity arose in juxtaposition to an American one, which itself was not always clearly defined except in philosophical terms. As Lipset (1990: 42) noted the question of national identity remains "the quintessential Canadian issue." The first step toward a definition of Canadian identity is to outline what it is *not*. As was stated in the second chapter, there is no "us" unless there is also a "them." In this context the "others" were Americans.

To justify separate national existence, Canadians have deprecated American values and institutions, mainly those seen as derived from an excessive emphasis on competition, which they once identified as an outgrowth of mass democracy and equalitarianism but which in recent years are explained by their intellectuals as endemic in the hegemonic capitalist values and institutions. (Lipset 1990: 53)

Whereas the United States adopted many of the symbols of Republican Rome, Canada embraced those of monarchical Europe; the separation of church and state to the south was countered with strong church-state cooperation to the north; and the limits on the powers of the American state contrasted with the activist role of the government in Canadian society (Berton 1987; Lipset 1990).

But they do share some common experiences. One of the most readily acknowledged of these is the dramatic impact of large-scale immigration. Policymakers in both Washington and London (later Ottawa) used newcomers as both a source of needed labor and agents in the settlement of the continent. Immigrants were also extremely valuable in fortifying, over time, the dominant position of English speakers in North America as their progeny linguistically assimilated. Yet at the same time, perhaps more than any other single factor, the successive arrival of one wave of immigrants after another has deferred the crystallization of both American and Canadian identities. After all, ethnic and national identities need the dissemination of a common ancestry myth. Such a myth is difficult to solidify if the group parameters are constantly in flux as is the case with immigrant societies embracing newcomers. As was stated in the second chapter, the point is not that ethnic group members *are* related, but rather that they *believe* that they pertain to an immense extended family. This is a characteristic they feel makes their identity "natural." Interestingly, continuous immigration hampers this process by presenting example after example of individuals who either were born abroad or whose proximate antecedents came from elsewhere.[2]

Immigration may be a common experience for both countries, however, their interpretations of these experiences and their official immigrant myths vary considerably. The American "melting pot" theory advanced the ideal of culturally assimilating its European arrivals. As noted in the previous chapter, acquiring the English language was used as a litmus test of patriotism. Ironically this theory espoused a collective identity in a country that supposedly lauds individuality.[3] This is but one of many contradictions found in American society, keeping in mind that every society houses inherently contradictory attitudes. On the other hand the supposedly collectively oriented Canada proclaims that its society upholds the "mosaic" model whereby cultural diversity is preserved (Lipset 1990: 172). Despite these divergent proposals most European immigrants to North America have assimilated linguistically.[4] Also despite attempts at preserving non-English vernaculars, the grandchildren of these newcomers almost always became Anglophones. Immigrants may have preserved bits and pieces of their former cultural milieu but usually not their vernacular. The overwhelming power of the English language in North America is such that few groups avoid losing their former languages.

The American Revolution thus created English Canada (Dufour 1990: 44); but, Canada already had a French portion. This community was already going by the name *Canadien* before the start of London's rule. "At the side of the young Yankee giant, Canada would be born—already old and looking towards the past—of the improbable marriage between the Canadiens of the Sun King and the Americans who wanted to remain under the King of England. The leftovers of two empires!" (Dufour 1990: 45). Loyalist and English North America came to grips with living under the same roof with the French settlements along the St. Lawrence River. It was under French rule that its white inhabitants were known as *Canadiens*. The English speakers north of the Great Lakes went by the name of "the British" until the separate English and French colonies were politically wed in 1840 (Dufour 1990: 25).

Here is perhaps the greatest difference between the two English-speaking societies of North America. As was discussed in the previous chapter, American identity tended to reject non-Anglophones. They remained as outsiders until they were linguistically assimilated—a process that normally took a couple of generations. On the other hand, Canadian society would be defined, from the start, on the basis of two languages. American monolingualism contrasted with Canadian bilingualism. However, this was not a marriage of equals. New France was conquered and joined to Britain's North American empire by force. Thus, in the construction project that was Canadian society, its French inhabitants would be relegated a role as "junior partners." Their secondary social status would be reinforced by their lower rank in the country's economic order. As in the United States, Canadian society would develop a clear social hierarchy based on language whereby English speakers commanded the top positions, leaving non-Anglophones with what remained. The difference is that the French were Canadian. In fact, after the country's indigenous population, the French were the first Canadians.

THE BRITISH CROWN AND THE ENGLISH-FRENCH DIVIDE

The English-French divide in Canada emerged with the British conquest of New France in 1763. It was distinguished on the basis of religion, language, and other objective cultural attributes. In time these attributes, interpreted both positively and negatively, would form the basis of group stereotypes. The prevalence of stereotypes are indicative of the popular acceptance of certain traits as characteristic of a collective entity. Examples of French stereotypes, from the British perspective, were recorded in one of the most noted government reports in the nineteenth century—the Durham Report of 1839. In his report to Westminster, Lord Durham (1905: 17) praised the French as a people for being "mild and kindly, frugal, industrious, and honest, very sociable, cheerful and hospitable, and distinguished for a courtesy and real politeness, which pervades every class of society." He also reproached them for their attachment to traditions and traditional authority structures. Durham said of the French: "They clung to ancient prejudices, ancient customs, and ancient laws, not from any strong sense of their beneficial effects, but with the unreasoning tenacity of an uneducated and unprogressive people" (Durham 1905: 17).

The negative attributes of the French contrast to Durham's more complimentary appraisal of the English community in Canada (Durham 1905: 14-15). When comparing early English Canadian attitudes toward the French with early American feelings toward the Germans, one finds the common thread of demeaning the "other" on the presumed basis of a lower intelligence. An inferior level of intelligence or education on the part of one's adversaries naturally implies the opposite for one's own group. Such stereotypes made by society's dominant group were meant to animate not only its elite, but also its lower-class members. The presumed veracity of such a popular notion meant that the Anglophone masses could hold their heads up high for at least they were superior to the "others." Such views, which reflect on the group as a whole and not just its elites, helped to institutionalize a cultural hierarchy at the popular level.

Durham (1905: viii) observed that the two communities in Canada were "filled with jealousy and bitterness." They regularly belittled each other (Durham 1905: 23). The chasm between them was so wide that Durham referred to the two as separate "nations" and distinct "races" (Durham 1905: 8-9). What Durham failed to note was the role played by the British state in fomenting the divide between the English and the French in Canada. While these two groups were distinguished from the start of British rule, the main dividing line in the eighteenth century was religious, not linguistic.[5] Protestant Britain exported its numerous anti-Catholic laws to its new Canadian colony with the 1763 Royal Proclamation (Sheppard 1971: 22). Holding public office and authorization to join various professions required oaths against popery (Sheppard 1971: 22). In an effort to cut the Canadiens off from their spiritual leaders, British authorities advised their governor in Canada to deny entry into the colony to the new Catholic prelate (Dufour 1990: 32). By cutting Canadiens off from the Catholic church and offering them incentives to convert, the Proclamation promoted their assimilation (Trudeau 1968: 162). It appears that eighteenth-century British policy in Canada paralleled American policy of inclusion/exclusion based on assimilation.

The man enforcing this policy was James Murray, the colony's first governor. According to one account he personally favored the assimilation of the Canadiens. He not only thought this process was unavoidable, but it was also in their best interest (Dufour 1990: 28-29). Interestingly, despite Britain's clear position of dominance and pro-assimilation attitudes among many high-ranking officials in Canada, there were some who advocated a more benign rule. Governor Murray, ironically, was one of those individuals. In fact, while Murray supported the idea of assimilating the Canadiens, he simultaneously refused to enforce many of the harsher provisions of the 1763 Proclamation (Sheppard 1971: 22). The government had the anti-Catholic provisions declared nonapplicable to the French Canadians in 1765 (Dufour 1990: 33), and they were formally removed with the passage of the Quebec Act in 1774 (Sheppard 1971: 34-35).[6] Britain would not resurrect the issue of cultural assimilation until the 1837 Revolt (Durham 1905: 216).

Murray's attitudes may seem contradictory on the surface, but they were in fact quite logical. Personal desires for assimilation were apparently tempered by the realities of governance. Britain's assimilationist policies were seen as a declaration of war against the Roman church. Removing the French government was a relatively simple matter since most administrators and soldiers were concentrated in Canada's few cities. The state's absence throughout much of its Canadian colony contrasted with the Church's penetration of French colonial society. Catholic priests lived in cities, towns, and villages. In some communities they represented the only formal authority figures. Thus the Catholic church, well entrenched at the grass roots, could mobilize resistance to London's legates.

Lord Durham noted in the 1830s, over half a century after the British conquest of New France, that the Canadiens still had a strong deference toward their leaders. He blightingly referred to the French as "[a]n utterly uneducated and singularly inert population, implicitly obeying leaders who ruled them by the influence of a blind confidence and narrow national prejudices" (Durham 1905: 14). Interestingly, he mocked the French for their deference toward their leaders while at the same time noting that this esteem was beneficial to maintaining British rule in the colony (Durham 1905: 11, 43). Even after the arrival of British troops, not every town had a government official but usually there was at least one priest. In this sense the Church had a very dispersed and efficient means of communication, something that the Crown lacked at that time.

As Laitin (1986) noted with the Yorubas of Nigeria, the British learned the value of power-sharing agreements with local elites. "Colonial experience elsewhere taught [the British] that it was more effective to co-opt and utilize indigenous authority structures rather than trying to dismantle and impose alien systems of authority on colonized people" (Nevitte 1985: 341). There were two potential partners in this process, the Church and the *seigneurs* (the French Canadian landed aristocracy). McRoberts (1979: 301) noted that British accommodationist policies benefited both groups of local elites in terms of their leadership in French Canadian society. However, Dufour (1990: 35) countered that the *seigneurs* were never the leaders of the Canadiens, even under French rule. Their disconnection from the masses disqualified them from the stewardship of the French in Canada. The same could not be said of the Church:

Another reason for the strength of the Church in Quebec is that, in contrast to some Catholic countries, the clergy has never been set off from the mass of the people by being recruited from any one particular class. ... Unlike France, where the higher clergy, even after the Revolution of 1789, came largely from the aristocracy and the upper middle class, the clergy in Quebec has always come from all walks of life. (Quinn 1979: 11)

As a result the Catholic church logically became "the Conqueror's only go-between" (Dufour 1990: 35). This mediator role would safeguard the Church's capacity as protector of French Canada until well into the twentieth century. A Catholic French Canada guaranteed a prominent role for its clergy. In exchange the Church played an active role in procuring the loyalty of its flock, or at least its neutrality, to the British Crown.[7] This cooperation proved extremely valuable to Great Britain during the American Revolution, the War of 1812, and the 1837 Rebellion (Woodcock 1989: 158). The benefits the Church received through this power-sharing arrangement were akin to those received by the Yoruba chiefs in colonial Nigeria (Laitin 1986). In both cases British colonial policies would have an immense impact on the nexus between the colonial populations and their respective local leaders. The division of power between the Catholic church and the British government would lay the foundations for what Lijphart (1968) would later refer to as a consociational or power-sharing arrangement based on elite accommodation and ethnic elite distribution of material benefits.

THE ESTABLISHMENT OF A LINGUISTIC HIERARCHY

The flight of thousands of Loyalists to Canada during the American Revolution inexorably altered the demographic standing of the two linguistic communities in Canada. The new settlement patterns created large English-speaking enclaves north of Lakes Erie and Ontario and the southern shores of the St. Lawrence River. In response to demands for popular government, the Crown divided the Canadian colony in order to provide the Loyalists with a majority in the western portion, which later became Ontario (Durham 1905: v). The French would retain a majority in the eastern half—Lower Canada, the future province of Quebec (Sheppard 1971: 43).[8]

To the victor goes the spoils, and the benefits from the conquest went to the King's English-speaking subjects. The British of Canada would enjoy the privileges of governance both in terms of employment in the public sector and increased economic opportunities in the private sectors. Business that used to be channeled through France was now diverted to Great Britain, a change that promised greater profits for the colony's English-speaking elites. "Now that the colony was linked to Great Britain rather than France, furs had to be sold on the British market and consumer goods had to be purchased there as well. Inevitably, British residents of the colony were better able than were the French Canadians to link up with buyers and suppliers in Great Britain" (McRoberts 1984: 72). The same applied to the public sector. There choice jobs were given on a priority basis to Anglophones over their Francophone counterparts.

Even in Lower Canada, the future province of Quebec, the English residents held tremendous power (McRoberts 1984: 73). Lower Canada was the only British colony in North America where French speakers would remain a majority. This demographic status proved critical to the survival of a linguistically distinct local elite—one that catered its services to the local community and derived its principal benefits from it. These conditions proved adequate for the continuation of a small elite, founded on lawyers, small merchants, physicians, and clerics, but not captains of industry (Durham 1905: 19). That role befell Quebec's English minority. Even within colonial elite circles, the French constituted the bottom rungs of the ladder. In the words of Hechter (1975), a "Cultural Division of Labor" emerged in Lower Canada with English over French, Protestant over Catholic. It was the emergence of this cultural division of labor that fueled the division between English and French in Canada (Durham 1905: 48-49).

Confined to the borders of Lower Canada, French elites were determined to protect their sole remaining bastion. As much as possible they attempted to safeguard their colony. One instrument they were not shy about using was the colonial legislature (Durham 1905: 65). The local political system was used to establish patronage and also to sabotage English settlement and business opportunities in the colony. As the bulk of the French masses were resigned to working primarily in the agricultural sector and light industries, they needed relatively little in terms of large-scale public capital expenditures. On the other hand the economic well-being of the British in Canada, especially in the great port of Montreal, needed a large infrastructure that could only be provided with public monies. Withholding or restricting the flow of these investments would constrain English economic opportunities in Lower Canada. Lord Durham (1905: 31-32) noted that the French-dominated legislature refused to increase local taxes or shift budgetary priorities to fund public works. The French Assembly frequently passed "temporary" laws or statutes with fixed terms, a move requiring their constant reapproval (Durham 1905: 61). In order to expedite bills of their choosing, the colonial legislature's majority would at times disassemble after passing a bill. Their withdrawal from the legislative chamber denied the assembly the necessary quorum to proceed with a debate, thus obliging the London-appointed governor to accept the bill as it was (Durham 1905: 62).

These moves were meant to hinder Anglophone penetration of the Quebec economy. Legislative actions also soured the expansion of English settlements. Early in the nineteenth century, Anglophone leaders exerted tremendous pressure on the colonial legislature to establish a unitary publicly funded English-language school system (Levine 1990: 27). Such an institution could be used to culturally assimilate Lower Canada's youth, taking educational matters outside the bounds of the traditional pedagogues—Catholic clerics. A widespread educational system in this language also served to make Anglophone settlement of the colony a more attractive alternative. These potential consequences were not overlooked by the French majority which subsequently passed amendments to the original educational statute that effectively relegated these schools to the colony's English enclaves (Levine 1990: 27-28). The British of Lower Canada assumed that since the Union Jack flew over Quebec City, that the colony was theirs to do with as they wished (Durham 1905: 213).

The frustration felt by the colony's English residents led some to contemplate rebelling against the Crown. Angry English colonists assumed they had a right to expand their economic and political penetration of Lower Canada despite their minority status in this territory. Their resentment of the French for their ability to thwart English Canadian designs on Lower Canada strongly resembled the apprehension Franklin expressed about the Germans in Pennsylvania. In both cases two sets of elites, one Anglophone and one non-Anglophone, were locked in political combat. As Canada's English tried to use the Assembly of Lower Canada to further their economic strength so did Franklin's Pennsylvania Legislature when it tried to amass a militia to defeat the French and their aboriginal allies who threatened white expansion toward the West. In their anger English elites in both Pennsylvania and Lower Canada resorted to verbal attacks and ridicule in an attempt to belittle their non-English-speaking allies. The point of this tactic was to give the English-speaking masses a reason to reject the "other" as they were "less educated" or "inferior" in some way. In this way English-speaking elites raised the social standing of those with whom they shared the common bond of language.

Westward expansion in the United States diminished as a divisive issue between the English and German communities. That policy's implementation became the responsibility of a new federal government dominated by English speakers. Anglophones represented a larger proportion of the U.S. population than they did a percentage of the population of Pennsylvania. Demographic changes were reflected with a greater share of legislative seats and its resultant political power.

Changing policy by dislocating responsibilities from one level of government to another was not a tactic ignored by the English merchants of Lower Canada. If the Crown did not defend their interests, the English of Lower Canada might have to do it themselves. Lord Durham (1905: 41) noted that some leaders of

Lower Canada insisted that the colony must be "*English*, at the expense, if necessary, of not being *British*" [emphasis in the original]. Referring to the English of Lower Canada, he observed that some of His Majesty's subjects, the children and grandchildren of Britain's Loyalists, were considering an alliance with the English-speaking majority of the United States in order to get their way:

Without abandoning their attachment to their mother country, they have begun, as men in a state of uncertainty are apt to do, to calculate the probable consequences of a separation, if it should unfortunately occur, and be followed by an incorporation with the United States. . . . [t]hey believe that the influx of American emigration would speedily place the English race in a majority; they talk frequently and loudly of what has occurred in Louisiana, where, by means which they utterly misrepresent, the end nevertheless of securing an English predominance over a French population, has undoubtedly been attained. (Durham 1905: 42)

The incompatibility of French Canadian and English Canadian designs on the colony led to an increase in political instability, culminating in the French rebellions of 1837 and 1838 (Levine 1990: 28).

In the end Durham was charged with recommending a solution to the crisis in British North America. His remedy was the creation of a unitary legislature—a Union of the two Canadas (Durham 1905: 227). Thus, Lord Durham's report served as the "inspiration" for the 1840 Union (Martin 1972: 42). This was the first step toward establishing the larger Canadian Confederation of 1867. In such a scheme the French of Upper and Lower Canada would instantaneously be transformed into a minority, thus diminishing their political power. The Union was intended to put Canada's French "at the mercy of an English majority" (Clift 1982: 60). Additionally, Durham (1905: 227) presumed that English immigration to Canada would add to Anglophone political strength. His hope was that as a minority the French "would abandon their vain hopes of nationality" (Durham 1905: 227).[9] In this new combined legislature Anglophones hoped that they would reap the rewards of a majoritarian status.

Since the reasoning behind the Union was to crush Francophone resistance to British rule and open the flood gates to the expansion of Anglophone power, it was only logical that the unitary legislature employ only one language. Thus, a result of the Union of the two Canadas was the elimination of French as a medium of legislative debate (Sheppard 1971: 55). While French was dislodged as medium of legislative debate, it was still used in judicial proceedings (Sheppard 1971: 58). Nonetheless, the unilingual provisions of the Union bill passed by the British Parliament were intended to promote the Anglicization of the French population (Sheppard 197 1: 56). While assimilation may have been the goal it was rarely stated straightforwardly: "No doubt many English Canadians have looked forward to the eventual absorption of the French within a vast English-speaking throng, but most have avoided talking openly about 'assimilation' " (Forbes 1994: 89).

While the Union succeeded in preventing the French from breaking free of British rule, it did not prevail in assimilating them. After 1840 the goal of the French parliamentarians focused on cultural survival (Clift 1982: 60). They were able to accomplish this by taking advantage of divisions within the larger English-speaking community. Lack of Anglophone consensus in the legislature meant that the French would play the role of "king-maker" and determine which English faction or party would attain a parliamentary majority. Taking full advantage of their critical role in the Assembly, Canada's French politicians engendered a consociational system that prevailed for over a century (Levine 1990: 29-30). As parliamentary king-makers they were effective in lobbying the British government to eliminate Section 41 of the Act of Union, the segment of the Union law restricting the use of French in legislative debates, less than a decade after the original statute was promulgated (Sheppard 1971: 58). Starting in 1849 all official government texts were published in both English and French (Sheppard 1971: 59). The founding of *de facto* bilingualism in the united Canadian legislature shows how quickly French political elites were able to defeat the purpose of the Union Act itself (Morton 1972: 42). In the long run they succeed in preserving a French-majority enclave in Quebec, but despite massive migration to the western territories they failed to expand the boundaries of French Canada. Despite the beginnings of official bilingualism, English was still the stronger of the two languages.

THE FRENCH LANGUAGE WEST OF ONTARIO

The expansion of Canada's boundaries left open the question of what language would predominate in those western territories. French Canadians, with an extremely high birthrate, migrated from Quebec and northern Ontario in large numbers and established settlements west of the Ontario border. Their birthrate was so high that assimilation in much of the eighteenth and nineteenth centuries favored the French as they overwhelmed many English-speaking communities in eastern Canada (Joy 1972: 31). English Canadian policy-makers were obliged to deal with a cohesive minority that responded to their particular elite—an elite that was able to thwart the intent of the Union Act in only a few years. Allowing the French language to flourish in other parts of Canada would only strengthen this rival elite. The first territory to test Canada's linguistic dilemma was Manitoba, which was initially created as a homeland for the country's Métis population (Dufour 1990: 68).[10] French-speaking Métis had been colonizing Canada's western territories throughout the nineteenth century. The 1870 act that made it a province guaranteed the French and English languages an equal footing and provided for the establishment of separate Protestant and Catholic school systems (Robertson 1971: 68). The two phenomena were closely linked. Catholic clerics promoted the French language in Canada not to protect the French culture, *per se*, but to erect a barrier between the faithful and "wrong" ideas. "Language and religion were closely allied, and the maintenance of the French language was not only an instrument of racial separatism, but also a barrier against the subversive ideas of Protestantism or of modern secular thought" (McInnis 1969: 427). In the same vein, attacking the French language was a way of attacking French elites. Since the establishment of the Union in 1840 and following the Confederation in 1867, the spearhead of the French elite in Canada was the Catholic church.

Beginning in the 1890s some Conservative members of Parliament began attacking the bilingual educational policies of Manitoba. Encouraged by the rhetoric of one such Tory parliamentarian in Ottawa, D'Alton McCarthy, the Manitoba provincial legislature repealed French language instruction and petitioned the federal government to grant the province the autonomy to decide educational matters for itself (Robertson 1971: 68-69). This created in the province, contrary to federal guarantees, a unilingual school system (Sheppard 1971: 79-80). One scholar suggested that McCarthy's attacks on French-language instruction in the West may have been strongly motivated by a fear that the Catholic church, in particular the Jesuit order, was attempting to expand its power and influence in the country (Wade 1968: 423-425).

In the end the Privy Council in London held that Manitoba's government could abolish bilingual education despite the 1870 federal law, but Ottawa had the power to override such a provincial statute (McInnis 1969: 432). Ironically, it was a French executive, Prime Minister Wilfrid Laurier, who refused to overturn Manitoba's law on the grounds that such a measure could isolate Quebec (McInnis: 1969: 431-432). By promoting provincial autonomy he could defend the French majority in Quebec at the expense of the French minority in Manitoba (Robertson 1971: 69). At the same time the prime minister helped to establish a unilingual precedent for future provinces.

Sheppard's study of federal and provincial legislation demonstrated a clear pattern in the provinces to the west of Manitoba. In Alberta and Saskatchewan no law specifically proscribes the use of French; but neither is there any explicit protection of the language in schools, the legislature, or courts (Sheppard 1971: 88). The same general rule applies in British Columbia where the supremacy of English does not seem to have been questioned (Sheppard 1971: 92). Despite large-scale Francophone migration to the western provinces, it was clear by the end of the nineteenth century that the "French Fact" would be limited to eastern and central Canada (Dufour 1990: 68). This assessment was confirmed by Joy's (1972) often cited demographic study that indicated that Francophones outside Quebec and the French regions of neighboring Ontario and New Brunswick are linguistically assimilating at a very high rate. By the end of the nineteenth century, English, the language of the dominant society in Canada, was extended from one part of the country to the other, restricting its rival to only one primary enclave—Quebec. As a result, Canada's two largest linguistic communities were separated into separate enclaves. Linguistic partition facilitated the economic and political ascension of English Canadians at the expense of their French-speaking compatriots.

THE ENGLISH FACT IN NORTH AMERICA

Though they took divergent paths, both the United States and Canada arrived at the same point. English became and remained the dominant language throughout the continent save for a few enclaves. In the case of the United States, American identity itself was partially defined on the basis of the English language. American elites began to define their group's boundaries on the basis of language when German-speaking elites threatened to hamper their economic interests. The English language, and hence, English speakers, were seen as having a higher station in society than non-English speakers.

However, American identity emerged in contrast to a British one, which may explain why the linguistic factor, while implicit in American identity, is not explicit. For immigrants its acquisition was seen as evidence of loyalty to the country and its ideals. In order to be American, newcomers had to accept the hegemonic order that situated English above other languages. When it came to incorporating territories into the American Union, there was an understanding, sometimes explicit, that English would dominate in state governments and in the classroom—the ultimate assimilator. It was accepted as the *de facto* language of the country, and its status was not questioned. Any accommodations the U.S. federal government made to non-English languages was temporary and accepted as an "exception" to the rule rather than a change in it.

In contrast Canadian society was from the beginning a bilingual one. However, it was an unequal partnership. As in the United States, the English language and its speakers did acquire a higher social status. The link between high social standing and fluency in Britain's vernacular was promoted most vigorously by Quebec's English-speaking minority who sought to weaken French power by combining the colonial governments of Quebec and Ontario. In time Canada's Anglophone elites succeeded in designating their western expanses, as the United States had done earlier, English-dominant zones. However, the power of the country's French-speaking minority meant that it took English-speaking elites longer than their American counterparts to consolidate their grip on Canadian society. Thus, Ottawa was obliged to accommodate non-English speakers to a greater extent and for a longer period of time than did their American counterparts. It was only in the late nineteenth century that Anglophone political actors could challenge the presumed equality of the two languages west of the Ontario border. In the end both Ottawa and Washington succeeded in making English the dominant language of the North American continent.

NOTES

1. Many of the same processes that changed American English, such as the incorporation of indigenous words, also affected speech in Canada. Whereas Americans resisted Britain's linguistic hegemony, Canadians embraced it. In the contemporary Canadian popular press one may see either American or British spellings; however, the British standard still predominates in official publications.

2. This would not apply to immigrants if they arrived from what society considered either the "mother country" or from a traditional immigration source. Since the national myth already made room for people from these places, the assimilation process and the passage of ethnic inclusion proceed at a much faster rate.

3. This expectation of assimilation did not apply to American slaves. Though it was an institution begun under British suzerainty, Canada's collective identity would be free of the stain of slavery, an issue that continues to instill resentment in the United States.

4. The position of the English language in Canada is strengthened by the economic status of English in the United States and in the global economy. As Laponce (1987: 59) noted, this language's strength in Canada is such that it is subduing all other languages. Global and continental economic conditions heavily favor the acquisition of English even when the Canadian government does not actively push it.

5. Sheppard's (1971: 10) examination of Canadian language laws noted that neither the Quebec nor Montreal Articles of Capitulation make references to the status to be accorded to the French language under British rule.

6. Interestingly, the British compromise with the Catholic church on behalf of the French population protected their freedom of religion and also preserved the borders of New France (thus restricting the American colonists from settling the Ohio valley), fueling American colonial resentment toward the Crown and stimulating the passions that led to the 1776 Revolution (Dufour 1990: 43). Thus, not only did the American Revolution create English Canada, French Canada served as a catalyst, in the American Revolution. While the French may have performed a pivotal role as an unintended revolutionary catalyst their location on the "Canadian" side of the border prevented French Canadians from becoming a significant factor in the development of a distinctly American identity.

7. One of the tactics used by the Roman Catholic church in Canada to prevent large-scale French Canadian assistance to the American Revolution was to threaten the Canadiens with denial of the sacraments if they aided the rebellion (Dufour 1990: 43).

8. Lord Durham, the author of the noteworthy government report that bears his name, referred to the partition of Canada into English and French components as "unwise" and incomplete since a large English-speaking community would remain in portions of Lower Canada (Durham 1905: 47).

9. Durham (1905: 229) further proposed that a legislative union of British North America beyond these two provinces would go even further toward securing Anglophone loyalty in the colonies.

10. Since the 1700s the Métis, of mixed European (primarily French) and aboriginal ancestry, viewed theirs as a distinctive culture—separate from other indigenous or European peoples (Giraud 1986: 319-320).

6

The Evolution of Puerto Rican Identity and Nationalism

As one of the last remaining Spanish colonies in the Americas, Puerto Rico was formally ceded to the United States in the Treaty of Paris. U.S. interest in this Caribbean island was triggered by its potential as a market for American goods and its proven value as a strategic site (Maldonado-Denis 1972: 56; Pedreira 1978: 43).[1] This bilateral accord ended the Spanish-American War of 1898 and opened a new chapter in American history as the country expanded its sphere of influence beyond continental North America. The treaty not only agreed to Cuba's independence but it also ceded to the United States the islands of Puerto Rico, Guam, and the Philippines. The construction of military bases on all of these islands, coupled with the military outposts established in the newly created Republic of Panama and in the former Hawaiian Republic, marked the emergence of the United States as a Pan-American power and foresaw its impending emergence as a global force.

American administrators, institutions, and economic policies replaced European ones in Puerto Rico. Just as Spanish officials assumed their inherent superiority over creoles, so did their American counterparts accept as common sense the natural preeminence of American institutions and cultural norms, including their language. In time American society would also influence insular social trends. Interestingly, these social influences rather than diluting a sense of Puerto Rican identity actually strengthened it. As Morris (1995: 152) noted: "Far from destroying Puerto Rico's national identity, the import of U.S. culture has strengthened the sense of Puerto Ricanness by providing a counterexample of what Puerto Ricanness is not." American rule did not, however, inaugurate the beginnings of a distinctive Puerto Rican identity.

Recognition of a distinctive Puerto Rican personality emerged while the island was still a colony of the Spanish Crown.[2] While dating a collective consciousness is far from a precise science, one noted historian postulated that it emerged sometime between the late eighteenth and the early nineteenth centuries

(Picó 1986: 115). Pedreira (1978: 118) dated the emergence sometime in the nineteenth century.[3] Maldonado-Denis (1976: 36) concurred with their general assessments, placing the origins of Puerto Rican nationalism, the political mani-festation of such a collective identity, at the beginning of the nineteenth century. These suppositions would situate the genesis of a distinctive Puerto Rican iden-tity at the dawn of the nationalist era.[4] The emergence of a new identity that set the local populace apart from peninsular Spaniards arose on the island with the increased concentration of economic resources, political clout, and social privi-leges in the hands of Spain's European-born subjects over those born in the Americas. The Puerto Rican case paralleled earlier ones in continental Latin America.

In Latin America, the Spanish Crown implemented a policy of promoting European-born Spaniards over those born in the Americas (Anderson, B. 1983: 58). Thus, the origins of a distinctive Puerto Rican identity paralleled those of a Mexican identity among the country's creole population as described by Lafaye (1976). In Puerto Rico the emergence of a distinctive identity can be traced to the social distancing of peninsular Spaniards from local creoles (Pedreira 1978: 119). This sense of rejection was particularly acute among native-born creoles who were increasingly rejected by their peninsular cohorts and relegated to a second-class status (Maldonado-Denis 1972: 22). Spain's cultural hegemony in Puerto Rico, as in the rest of its Latin American empire, ranked peninsular Spaniards over creoles. Referring to the Spanish government in Puerto Rico, Jiménez noted: "The regime's preference for peninsular employees weighed heavily on the shoulders of the creole professionals who, deprived of schools and institutions of higher learning in Puerto Rico, were forced to spend their few resources abroad in search of an education, only to return home where they would be deprived of jobs" (Jiménez 1993: 39). Such a discriminatory policy was felt more acutely by local elites toward the middle of the nineteenth cen-tury—a period where competition for positions of power and privilege was made more critical by the arrival of large numbers of Iberian-born immigrants (Jiménez 1993: 13-14). As political and ecclesiastical authority were concen-trated in the hands of these *peninsulares*, so was economic power. Trade and credit were dominated by Iberian-born Spaniards and other European-born im-migrants (Maldonado-Denis 1976: 37; Jiménez 1993: 18).

Throughout the nineteenth century Puerto Rican creole elites responded to this attitude with the genesis of a counter-hegemonic regime. By way of this counter-hegemonic order, insular elites attempted to convince the masses that they were no longer a Spanish subset but their own unique entity. One historian posited that in contrast to most of the new creole nationalisms and ethnic identi-ties in continental Latin America during the early nineteenth century, the one in Puerto Rico embraced peasant norms early on (Scarano 1996: 1401-1402).[5] In time this distinctiveness in terms of identity would manifest itself in the political realm with calls for greater local autonomy. Demands for home rule emerged as islanders increasingly felt alienated from their peninsular cohorts. The first political manifestations of Puerto Rican nationalism appeared in the form of an autonomist movement in the nineteenth century. This autonomist segment of society was composed primarily of the local insular elite: professionals, small farmers and ranchers, native industrialists, and merchants (Maldonado-Denis 1972: 23). However, the event that is most often touted by contemporary nationalists as the benchmark of the struggle for self-determination was the unsuccessful rebellion against the Spanish State—the *Grito de Lares*, or Lares Uprising, of 1868.[6]

SCHOLARLY ATTEMPTS TO DEFINE PUERTO RICANS

Acknowledging the existence of group boundaries implies understanding where to draw the line between one collectivity and another. Drawing an analogy to cartography, this means that we should know where the frontier lies so that we can readily determine what falls on each side of the border. This is not such a simple task when determining ethnic boundaries. Group demarcation often implies enumerating the characteristics that define the group to exclude those who do not share those traits.

For over a century most islanders would emphatically agree that Puerto Ricans existed as a distinct people. Puerto Ricans, in particular elites, saw themselves as a distinct people prior to the arrival of American troops in 1898 (del Rosario 1969: 31). However describing the traits of a Puerto Rican is another matter entirely. A superficial examination of a random group of islanders shows a vast range of physical attributes. These traits have been used in other societies to indicate membership in distinctive groups, including (but not limited to) skin color. Some Puerto Ricans would be classified as white, others as black, but the vast majority are racially mixed to varying degrees. One consequence of this mixture is that in terms of place names, foods, music, legends, spiritual/religious beliefs, and other frequently enumerated characteristics of group identity, that which is "Puerto Rican" derived from the Spaniard, the African, and the indigenous Taíno peoples. In addition, the creation of a large diaspora community on the U.S. mainland and the island's status as one of Washington's dependencies has complicated this debate over identity by asking what role American culture and society play in Puerto Rican identity. Scholars have debated which of these places represents the "true source" of Puerto Rican culture. Thus, defining Puerto Ricanness on the basis of objective traits is a rather arduous process involving a great deal of debate. Out of various scholars who have attempted to provide such a definition, three stand out: Pedreira, González, and Flores.

Of these three Pedreira was the first to make the attempt in the 1930s. His essay, written three decades into U.S. rule, attempted to specify what Puerto Ricans were. The task was encumbered by the heterogeneity of insular society. Four centuries of Spanish rule had virtually eradicated the indigenous Taínos. As a result of this genocide, Spaniards and the African slaves they imported would form the earliest foundations of Puerto Rican society. To these two cornerstones of Puerto Rican society, one must add a sprinkling of dozens of others, primarily non-Spanish Europeans who chose to relocate to this Caribbean colony. As Pedreira described it, the first three centuries of Spanish rule constituted Puerto Rico's "nursing" or "suckling" phase, followed by a "crawling" phase in the nineteenth century that constituted the first steps in the evolution of local culture (Pedreira 1978: 119). He viewed Puerto Rico as an immature and rather fragile society:

We believe, honestly, that there exists a disintegrated Puerto Rican soul, dispersed, in power, brilliantly fragmented like a painful puzzle that has never enjoyed its completeness. We began to create it in the last century of our history, but unforeseen disasters of political destiny hindered us to prolong until today the ship's course.[7] (Pedreira 1978: 118) [author's translation]

This torpid analysis of his own people would not be universally accepted by other observers of Puerto Rican society. Subsequently other writers would attack Pedreira for viewing his own people in this manner (Flores 1993: 18).

The essence of that identity, Pedreira (1978: 6) insisted, is Puerto Rico's "Hispanic" nature and heritage. The Puerto Rican creole and peasant are principally descended from "pure Spaniards" who learned to adjust to the rigors of a tropical climate (Pedreira 1978: 29). This Iberian element established Puerto Rican society, which was later mixed with other groups, including non-Europeans. In fact, he argued that this "fusion" led to our collective "confusion" (Pedreira 1978: 27). Pedreira made no apologies for his belief in the superiority of the European over the African (Pedreira 1978: 28).[8] However, Africans were not his only target. His essay also lamented the arrival of American troops, who brought with them Protestantism and popular democracy, which he felt undermined Puerto Rico's Catholic and monarchical past; a high culture was sacrificed in order to make way for technological progress (Pedreira 1978: 75).[9] Nonetheless, for Pedreira (1978: 44) Puerto Ricans were neither "Continentals" nor Antilleans, but "*insulares*," or insular people. For Pedreira a Spanish heritage combined with an insular character made Puerto Ricans unique.

Pedreira's interpretation of Puerto Rican society and identity was later challenged by González. Whereas Pedreira only embraced Puerto Rico's Spanish heritage, González (1993: 9-11) began his analysis with non-European Puerto Ricans. Puerto Rican culture, for him, was a "Four Storied Country" founded on African slaves and their descendants. White immigrants in the first couple of centuries of Puerto Rican colonial history were "unstable," often migrating to more economically prosperous Spanish territories in the Americas (González 1993: 10). This left black and mulatto Puerto Ricans as the backbone of insular society. Africans were forcibly transported to Puerto Rico to work as slaves in the agricultural sector of the insular economy. As this was concentrated primarily on the coasts and lowlands, this was the true birthplace of Puerto Rican culture, according to González, as opposed to the interior highlands—the land of the *jíbaro*, or mountain peasant. Upon this first layer were added a large wave of European and Latin American[10] immigrants in the nineteenth century (González 1993: 12). On top of these two stories would be added a third—a twentieth-century urban and professional class—and a fourth—a managerial class that emerged in the 1940s (González 1993: 15, 27).

Flores, the last of the three essayists, attempted to build on the contributions made by González. Pedreira moved the locus of Puerto Rican culture from Iberia to the highlands of Puerto Rico. However, in so doing he subsumed Puerto Ricans to an inferior position vis-à-vis Spaniards and other Europeans. González attacked Pedreira for his Eurocentrism—a move that Flores praised. González relocated the heart and soul of Puerto Rican culture from the creole-dominated mountains of the classical *jíbaro* to the African and mixed Afro-European coasts. For González the roots of Puerto Rican identity were to be found in popular culture and not the norms of local elites—a principle that Flores lauded (Flores 1993: 62).

As Flores noted, González was not the first author to exalt the African and Afro-Antillean components of Puerto Rican culture. However, González was the first to give it full "analytical articulation" (Flores 1993: 63). African rhythms were behind more popular forms of music such as *plena* and *bomba* as opposed to the European origins of *danzas*, he argued (Flores 1993: 85). González "added" the European elements of Puerto Rican culture onto an African-based foundation. Flores, on the other hand, fused them.[11] "It is not the popular, African component in itself that goes to define the 'real' Puerto Rican culture, but its interplay with the non-African, elite and folkloric components" (Flores 1993: 98). In addition to amalgamating African and European elements, Flores also added the Taíno component—Puerto Rico's pre-Columbian inhabitants. González tended to dismiss the importance of the Taíno myth in the formation of contemporary Puerto Rican society since these aboriginal peoples were virtually annihilated by Spanish colonizers early in the sixteenth century. Their importance is such that Flores argued that the Taínos should be considered another floor in González's metaphorical four-storied Puerto Rican identity, if not, at least, the culture's "basement" (Flores 1993: 66).[12] Taíno words and place names are still used and many of the plants they cultivated are still consumed. Perhaps more important than these objective traits is that the Taínos, representing the first Puerto Ricans, metaphysically anchor the contemporary inhabitants of their island in the Caribbean as opposed to Europe.

Perhaps Flores's greatest contribution to the analysis of Puerto Rican identity is his break with the tradition of locating the center of this culture in the Caribbean. He drew the parameters of Puerto Rican culture as a bimodal map in which the two dominant enclaves, one on the island itself and the other on the U.S. mainland (primarily in the greater New York City metropolitan area), together constituted the realm of the Puerto Rican. Building upon González's metaphor, the *Nuyorican*,[13] or mainland Puerto Rican, constituted the "attic" in the multi-layered edifice that is Puerto Rican identity (Flores 1993: 66). He criticized

González for omitting this significant contingent of the Puerto Rican family (Flores 1993: 67). "Under the present conditions of transportation and communication, Puerto Rico is part of New York, and like it or not, New York is present in Puerto Rico" (Flores 1993: 103). The constant flow of people from the mainland U.S. to Puerto Rico and back again has, according to Flores's interpretation, forever linked these two regions and has inexorably influenced the Puerto Rican people.

Each of these three writers tried to capture the essence of Puerto Rican culture by focusing on different traits. The main problem encountered, particularly by the last two authors, was in providing a list of the fundamental objective elements in Puerto Rican identity in a century when this group was in a state of constant political, social, economic, and geographical flux. The political manifestations of a distinctive Puerto Rican identity began under Spanish rule with the first movements for local autonomy from Madrid. Defining Puerto Ricans had to account for the distinctiveness of this identity vis-à-vis both Spaniards and Americans. The attempt of these three scholars at cultural objectification was intended, in a way, to "prove" the nationhood of a people and define it on the basis of a select group of traits (Handler 1988). None of the three attempted to provide an exhaustive list of these characteristics. "The cultural traits by which an ethnic group defines itself never comprise the totality of the observable culture but are only a combination of some characteristics that the actors ascribe to themselves and consider relevant" (Roosens 1989: 12). Roosens's analysis applies to both the dominant groups in society, whether in Spain or the United States, as well as its subalterns, as is the case here with Puerto Rico. Dominant groups attempt to establish a cultural hegemony that will be based on those cultural traits that harmonize with their interests (Maldonado-Denis 1972: 25). Elites within subordinate groups may attempt to challenge this state of affairs with a counter-hegemonic order. Has a counter-hegemonic order been established in contemporary Puerto Rico? If so, what traits does it highlight? The following section will focus on one trait that has been mentioned with uncommon frequency—the Spanish language.

PUERTO RICAN SELF-DEFINITION

Each one of the three writers—Pedreira, González, and Flores—attempted to capture the essence of what a Puerto Rican is and was, focusing on a different constellation of cultural traits. Those are the traits highlighted by a small set of scholars. But how do Puerto Ricans define themselves? Out of the six million or so Puerto Ricans today, around 60 percent reside on the island of Puerto Rico itself. Most of the remainder live in the continental United States. Do they define *Puertorriqueñidad*, or Puerto Ricanness, in the same way? What about the various political actors and parties within Puerto Rico? Research has shown a rather remarkable consistency among these groups, starting off with group definitions, by noting the language of most Puerto Ricans.

One of the first divisions that is frequently made is between Puerto Ricans who live on the island and their family members residing in the United States. As Ginorio's (1987: 201) study indicated, many insular Puerto Ricans label their ethnic brethren on the U.S. mainland as *Nuyoricans*. A similar conclusion was reached by Zentella (1990: 89), whose research indicated that despite sharing many objective cultural traits such as food and music, mainland Puerto Ricans often saw themselves as distinct from their insular brethren who they referred to as *los regulares*.[14] Mainland Puerto Ricans are often caught in a terminological no-man's land where Anglophone Americans refer to them as "Puerto Ricans" and their brethren on the island of Puerto Rico refer to them as "*Nuyoricans*."

The most frequently touted distinction between the two groups was linguistic. Whereas the vast majority of insular Puerto Ricans speak Spanish[15] many mainland born Puerto Ricans are either English-dominant bilinguals or speakers of *Spanglish*, a blend of Spanish and English.[16] The rejection of *Nuyoricans* is based primarily on this linguistic differential (Morris 1995: 125).

On the one hand, our defense of Puerto Rico's Hispanic-American heritage made us ill-at-ease with those of our brothers in the United States who through no fault of their own spoke a kind of garbled Spanish. For too long we had a kind of conditioned reflex approach concerning Spanish as a tool in the resistance to colonialism, and many times we were turned away by what we considered—wrongly, we now realize—a less-than honest effort to speak our vernacular correctly. (Maldonado-Denis 1972: 318)

Yet, despite this rejection from islanders, most of their mainland brethren still demonstrate a desire to maintain what little Spanish they preserve. This attitude is true even among the young who often know extremely little Spanish (Flores 1993: 167). Though mainland Puerto Ricans are acquiring English, Flores asserted that they are not "abandoning their native Spanish" (Flores 1993: 158). He stated that it is important to realize that "[l]anguage, then, is the necessary terrain on which Latinos negotiate value and attempt to reshape the institutions through which it is distributed. This is not to say Latino identity is reduced to its linguistic dimensions" (Flores 1993: 204).[17]

Mainland Puerto Ricans differ from most European immigrants to the United States in that they can return to their country of origin with relative ease as a result of Puerto Rico's status as a U.S. territory. But this juridico-political status has a significant impact on culture. Whereas most immigrants to the United States would pass through a bilingual phase on their way toward becoming monolingual Anglophones, mainland Puerto Ricans seem to have achieved a quasi-permanent state of bilingualism (Flores 1993: 166). On the one hand they are compelled to learn English in order to function in the larger American society; but on the other they are obliged to keep at least some Spanish in order to communicate with family and friends who are often monolingual Hispanophones. Either they or members of their families may go back to the island at some point. In addition, their communities are constantly receiving new monolingual Spanish-speaking neighbors. These factors simultaneously "replenish the presence and influence of Spanish in all aspects of social life" and hinder the usually overwhelming assimilative forces imposed on newcomers to the United States (Flores 1993: 166). Even where Spanish is not spoken, it is seen as a symbol uniting Latinos, including Puerto Ricans. This point was reemphasized by Jean Franco: "Both in Latin America and the United States, Puerto Rico stands for something which cannot be assimilated. It is island and continent, a colony and a nation, a community bound by a language that some Puerto Ricans do not speak" (Franco in Flores 1993: 9).

One of the first major empirical studies on political party and party leader perspectives on Puerto Rican identity and culture was recently conducted by Nancy Morris. Her study (Morris 1995: 82), based primarily on interviews with Puerto Rican party leaders and focus groups, concluded: "The most consistently cited element of Puerto Ricanness was the Spanish language, which was mentioned in every focus group and by all interviewees." Her findings reinforced the assertion made in a congressional study that "all status participants, intensely proud of their Puerto Rican heritage, are adamant about preserving and enhancing the island's culture and Spanish language" (Comptroller General 1981: ii). This is true even for the less nationalistic parties that even acknowledge that the American and Puerto Rican cultures embrace different symbols and cultural traits while the parties promote stronger ties with the United States:

Puerto Rican political leaders of all parties were clear about the central symbols of their culture and their relationship to them and equally aware of corresponding and potentially competing symbols from the United States. They did not disagree about the value and uniqueness of Puerto Ricanness, as expressed through key symbols that they explicitly recognized as such. Rather, disagreements arouse out of differing evaluations of whether those symbols could withstand pressure from competing symbols. In part, the debate over Puerto Rico's status is itself about the potential displacement of symbols of Puerto Ricanness. (Morris 1995: 151)

Out of all the various objective cultural traits or markers pointed to as essential to Puerto Rican identity, language plays a paramount role. This connection between identity and language crosses the island's tumultuous partisan lines. Puerto Rico's political panorama is dominated by three political parties that distinguish themselves on the basis of their preferred status for the island. Supporters of a sovereign Puerto Rico usually support the Partido Independentista Puertorriqueño (PIP).[18] Limited autonomy is the official platform of the Partido Popular Democrático (PPD),[19] and the island's incorporation into the American Union as a member state is the goal of the Partido Nuevo Progresista (PNP).[20] Viewed in terms of allegiance to the center or the periphery, the separatist PIP is the most nationalistic of the island's three major parties, and the PNP, as the official advocate of permanent incorporation into the American Union, is the least nationalistic.

Support for the Spanish language by separatists should not be surprising as they constitute the most nationalistic of all political sectors. After all, they claim that this Caribbean island should break its formal political ties to the United States on the basis of a distinctive culture, which they feel is often threatened by American popular culture. Maldonado-Denis (1972: 229) proclaimed with a bit of pride that Spanish was still being spoken in Puerto Rico "despite seventy years of concerted effort to undermine the very foundations of our national identity." However, strong support for defending the Spanish language among supporters of Puerto Rican statehood is more surprising as this is the most pro-U.S. political movement on the island.[21] "Although statehood party [PNP] members were the least likely of the respondents to rank Spanish as an element of highest importance to their conception of Puerto Rico, neither did they dismiss the language" (Morris 1995: 82). Furthermore, statehood supporters in her study were willing to make accommodations to the English language, a communicative medium spoken by a minority of insular Puerto Ricans, but were not disposed to discard Spanish (Morris 1995: 145). The current statehood movement formally rejects the idea of cultural assimilation (Meléndez 1993: 9). Interestingly, even within the most pro-American political sector, one finds leaders who have a strong sense of identification with the Puerto Rican cultural collective identity and its various cultural traits.[22] If one assumes that political actors are rational actors and take public stances on issues in order to maximize their electoral appeal than one must logically infer that transpartisan support for this vernacular is based on its endorsement at the popular level.

This was not always the case. The PNP, founded in 1967, is the latest in a series of pro-statehood parties in twentieth-century Puerto Rico. Some of these parties and their leaders openly promoted cultural assimilation while others advocated adding English to Puerto Ricans' linguistic repertoire. The first pro-statehood party, which emerged in 1899, the Partido Republicano (Republican party), promoted the idea of spreading public education throughout the island, using English as the medium of communication, not Spanish (Bothwell 1979a: 261).[23] Educational policy in twentieth-century Puerto Rico became a litmus test of a political actor's commitment to either promoting English, Spanish, or some compromise strategy entailing bilingual instruction. By the late 1960s the new PNP gravitated away from promoting English in the classroom as the medium of instruction and toward a policy of Spanish-language instruction, though it would continue to encourage the learning of English as a second language (Bothwell 1979b: 915).

What could have caused the most pro-American partisan segments of Puerto Rican society to gravitate from promoting English in the classroom to Spanish? Morris's study indicated that it was pedagogical policy itself and the battle over the language of classroom instruction.

The power of Spanish as a defining element of Puerto Ricanness was evidenced by respondents' repeated references to the attempt by the United States to impose English as the language of instruction in schools, an issue that continued to resonate forty-two years after Spanish was reinstated as the school language. The language controversy was described, with greater or lesser historical accuracy, even by respondents who were born after the issue was resolved. (Morris 1995: 144)

Spanish was not only the Puerto Rican vernacular, it was also the cultural trait American officials used to block the ascent of well-educated Puerto Ricans within the territorial bureaucracy—one of the few channels for upward mobility early in the twentieth century.

CULTURALIST AND RATIONAL CHOICE EXPECTATIONS

What might explain this change of linguistic emphasis among the strongest supporters of Puerto Rico's incorporation into the United States? The Culturalist perspective (see chapter 2) would attribute this phenomenon to language itself. As Laponce (1984: 91) argued, languages inherently reject others, and need a geographic niche if they are to survive in the long-run. He held that linguistic contact itself was responsible for social tensions. People are inherently unilingual, though capable of learning more than one language. In order to survive languages must occupy a geographic niche or a language with a more tenacious social, economic, and political standing will displace it (Laponce 1987: 3-4).

From the viewpoint of this theoretical school, Puerto Rico's attachment to its language is explainable in terms of a perceived threat coming from English, the dominant metropolitan idiom. However, this was not the case in Puerto Rico. Due to the island's relatively small size, great distance from the North American mainland, and high population density, it never received large numbers of Anglophone immigrants—unlike the territories in the western parts of the United States (Barreto 1995a: 101-105). There was no significant increase in English-speaking migration to Puerto Rico from the 1930s through the very early 1950s—a period that marked the electoral highpoint of nationalist parties (both separatist and autonomist) and a dramatic increase in nationalist inspired violence (Barreto 1995b).

The rational choice school, as per Hechter's model, has a serious problem explaining Puerto Rican nationalism in terms of support from various social sectors. His analysis posited that a cultural division of labor could trigger nationalism. Clearly Puerto Rican nationalists in the first half of the twentieth century—the period of greatest nationalist activism on the island—argued against the excesses of American capitalism and the vicious exploitation of Puerto Ricans found in the agricultural sector. However, his model cannot explain why Puerto Rican nationalism, particularly its separatist strain, finds its strongest base of support not from the exploited masses but from intellectuals. In addition, many of the poorest Puerto Ricans tend to support the *status quo*, and an even larger percentage strongly support permanent union with the United States via statehood. These nationalist and antinationalist bases of support are the opposite of what Hechter's model would expect.

An alternative explanation is offered by the Gramscian school of thought (Gramsci 1971; Laitin 1986). Language became the primary symbol around which Puerto Ricans would veil their identity vis-à-vis Americans. It is not the only cultural element that distinguishes Americans and Puerto Ricans. Nonetheless it was selected and then highlighted because language was the issue that threatened the future of a newly emergent elite in Puerto Rico. This elite group was a new cadre of local bureaucrats, primarily public school teachers, whose livelihoods were threatened by the U.S. federal government's policy of Americanization. Under this policy, implemented in the first half of the twentieth century, Americans were given priority over Puerto Ricans when it came to jobs in the territorial bureaucracy. In addition, the positions held by Puerto Ricans in the continually growing local government were in constant jeopardy due to a series of administrations that threatened to fire those bureaucrats found to be deficient in their knowledge of English. Again, this policy was aimed primarily at the growing army of public school teachers who were issued the directive to linguistically assimilate the island's school teachers. The Americanization policy affected those in the government along with those who wanted to get into it, and the government was one of the major employers of educated Puerto Ricans. As geographically dispersed street-level bureaucrats, they were at an advantageous position. Teachers, as the purveyors of knowledge at the local level, were members of the local intelligentsia and thus possessed a high social standing among islanders. At the same time their distribution in every city, town, and village facilitated the dissemination of their collective grievances. If their upward mobility and their very tenure were threatened so would those of future generations aspiring to join the ranks of the new elite. This was a message that non-elite parents could not ignore. Increased nationalism was one of the unanticipated side effects of the policy of Americanization.

AMERICANIZATION IN PUERTO RICO

As stated in chapter 4 the policy of *Americanization* originated on the U.S. mainland as a response to the growing numbers of non-Anglophone immigrants from Europe (Steinberg 1981: 42). Assimilation on the part of newcomers was generally interpreted as a sign that one desired to embrace American ideals and institutions (Hobsbawm 1983b: 280). And the institution primarily responsible for this was the public school system, which would target their efforts at children who were naturally more malleable than their parents (Steinberg 1981: 54). Following the Spanish-American War this policy, originally targeted at immigrants, was extended to the culturally diverse overseas American periphery.

One of the two individuals primarily responsible for the implementation of this policy was the territory's governor. Less than a year after the signing of the Treaty of Paris, Puerto Rico's presidentially appointed governor, General Guy Henry, published a government circular requiring local teachers to learn English. In order to accelerate the Americanization policy, the new Puerto Rican government established a preference for Anglophone teachers from the U.S. mainland (Negrón 1975: 10). The other bureaucrat charged with enforcing this directive was the territory's education commissioner. Unlike most territorial education commissioners, the one in Puerto Rico would be appointed directly by the U.S. president until the establishment of the Commonwealth constitution of 1952.[24] Negrón's detailed study of educational policy in Puerto Rico in the first decades of U.S. rule showed how the intensity of the Americanization policy, along with the zeal of its implementors, varied from one administration to another. Nonetheless, the goal was always the substitution of one set of cultural traits for another.

American administrators during this period were not only following the directives of their superiors but were also attempting to implement the recommendations of a linguistic policy charted by government commissions. In the case of Puerto Rico the two most noted were the Carroll and the Insular commissions (García 1976: 57). President McKinley's secretary of war, Elihu Root, sent to Puerto Rico a committee made up three Americans to study the general state of insular affairs (Bothwell 1971: 34). In the words of one noted authority, the report issued by the Insular Commission was extremely "superficial" and frivolous (Bothwell 1971: 34). One of its recommendations was the abolition of all Spanish laws. Recognizing the few resources Spain had invested in the Puerto Rican public education, the Insular Commission endorsed the creation of a widely distributed public school system to be manned by American teachers (Bothwell 1971: 34).

Following the Insular Commission's report, President McKinley designated his own commission to provide a more thorough analysis of the Puerto Rican state of affairs. This second commission was headed by Dr. Henry Carroll. Unlike Britain's Durham Report on the situation in Canada, the Carroll Commission was not the result of a looming crisis. Yet, like its British counterpart, it did provide policy-makers both with an image of this new society that in time would manifest itself in the form of stereotypes and also with a set of guidelines for the future course of the colony. In both the British report from the 1830s and the American report written six decades later, the assumption was that the metropolitan sovereign inherently knew what was best for its culturally distinct subjects.

The Carroll Report laid the groundwork for American policy toward Puerto Rico, offered the American leadership its first detailed look at its newly acquired dependents, and, in keeping with its larger plans, made appropriate recommendations. One of the first steps in this process was to assess the local population— a process that contributed to the generation of ethnic stereotypes. Stereotypes about the "other" serve several interrelated purposes. One, they "confirm" the distinction between "us" and "them." In the case of negative stereotypes, they corroborate the inherent superiority (if only a moral one) of "our group" over the "other," thus reinforcing the basic assumptions that lift the cultural hegemonic order to the level of common sense as it applies to both elites and masses. Additionally, the inclusion of some positive remarks about the "other," though many may consider them pejorative, attest to the dominant society's inherent "good nature" and beneficence. In the case of the Carroll Commission, the enumerated stereotypes would confirm the superiority of Americans over Puerto Ricans and the inherent generosity of the new American overlords since their subsequent moves, aimed at the cultural assimilation of the islanders, were carried out with the best of intentions.

Carroll's report described the local populace as "kindly, hospitable, polite people" who were "cheerful in disposition" (Carroll 1975: 36). They were a "courteous" lot whose disposition made them good neighbors (Carroll 1975: 36). In terms of their lifestyles, they were fond of music and also of cockfighting (Carroll 1975: 36-37). He also classified islanders, as did Pedreira three decades later, as possessing a "habit of obedience" or submissiveness (Carroll 1975: 57). These were the kind of traits that were valuable to a new territorial overseer, concerned with the potential for rebellion and thus the costs of governance. Thus the report concluded that Puerto Ricans "seem to have few customs or prejudices which would prevent them from becoming good American citizens" (Carroll 1975: 58). All of these comments were, from the perspective of the American administration, positive images of the local populace and a sign of the good nature of the local population and of the good intentions of the U.S. authorities.

Like the earlier Insular Commission, the Carroll Commission noted the high rate of illiteracy. However, Carroll did not believe that education, in and of itself, was a hindrance to good citizenship. A better test of citizenship was examining moral conduct. "Education and experience, although too high a value can hardly be set upon them, do not necessarily make good citizens. Men may be well educated and yet be bad morally. Moral conduct is the first and most indispensable qualification for good citizenship" (Carroll 1975: 57). Carroll's questioning of local behavior was meant to be a negative reflection on the whole of Puerto Rican society.

The fact that so many of them enter into marital relations without the sanction of state or church is, of course, a serious reflection upon their social morality. Half or more of their children are illegitimate. From this stigma they can not escape. But too much to their discredit may be easily inferred from this scandalous state of affairs. (Carroll 1975: 57)

In other words while Puerto Ricans were morally deficient, there was hope for them. Their otherwise good nature and passivity would make them acceptable candidates for amalgamation into the larger American Empire. As Carroll remarked: "The customs and usages and language of a people are not like old vestments, which may be laid aside at command, but become a part of their life, and are very dear to them. They will learn our customs and usages, in so far as they are better than their own, as they learn our language" (Carroll 1975: 58-59). From his perspective the implementation of this policy would require the full weight of the island's public school system. One of his recommendations to President McKinley was that the territorial government provide for a universal and compulsory public school system whereby English would be employed as the language of instruction (Carroll 1975: 65).

The Commission acknowledged the importance of linguistically assimilating the new territory and recommended implementing this policy, which would require that the majority of the island's teachers be Americans, and that they conduct their classes in the English language (García 1976: 59). In this way the United States was assuming that it could transport to Puerto Rico the same policies that were effective in culturally amalgamating immigrants. However, assimilation did have one major barrier to overcome—the island's separatists.

Supporters of independence for Puerto Rico were deemed "disloyal" United States citizens, and were kept out of teaching posts by the commissioner of education, and out of government posts by the governor, both United States appointees. Citizenship brought with it continuing pressure to adopt United States ways and the English language, which in turn brought continued counter-pressure to return to Spanish in the schools. (Morris 1996: 20)

Given that the direct target of this policy was school teachers, it should not be surprising that they were among the first to organize pressure groups and petition the territorial legislature for changes in educational policy. Strict enforcement of the Americanization policy put teachers' positions in jeopardy. A 1905 school law mandated English-language exams for teachers. Failing the exam would require the instructor to be reevaluated three months later. A second failure would result in a teacher's suspension, and a suspension of two years would annul a teacher's license (Negrón 1975: 100). The intensity of the Americanization policy fluctuated from administration to administration, but the stated goal was always culturo-linguistic assimilation. Where possible the Education Department would hire Americans as school teachers and pay them more than their Puerto Rican counterparts (Negrón 1975: 55). However, the distance from the U.S. mainland, the difficult working conditions at a time when schools were in the process of being constructed, and the relatively low salaries all contributed to a scarcity of teachers that could only be satisfied by hiring locals despite the goals of the Americanization policy (Negrón 1975: 39).

Teachers began lobbying the territorial legislature early in the century for changes in the Americanization policy. In 1912 the General Assembly of the Teachers Association approved a resolution favoring the use of Spanish as the medium of instruction in local public schools (García 1976: 99). Only a year later the Union of Puerto Rico, one of the largest political parties in the first decades of American suzerainty, proposed a bill in the local legislature to change the medium of instruction to Spanish (García 1976: 86).[25] The Union of Puerto Rico was responding to the rise of a new segment of the electorate that had a vested interest in changing pedagogical policies. This group constituted a new elite and the Union's policies were aimed at capturing this valuable constituency.

For teachers a change in language laws would safeguard their positions in the government and make the recruitment of teachers from the U.S. mainland unnecessary. Instruction in Spanish would protect teachers' livelihoods and hence their social status, which derived from their vocations. These new elites had a choice over which cultural elements they could attempt to incorporate into the counter-hegemonic order. Language was a resource over which pedagogues had a near monopoly. As noted in chapter 3 elites in the dominant society have little incentive to learn the idiom of subaltern groups. Thus, there was little incentive for American administrators to learn Spanish. This is not the case with peripheral elites who need the dominant group's language in order to communicate outside their ethnic enclave. This process makes peripheral elites go-betweens, linking dominant elites with peripheral masses, which only adds to their social status in the periphery. Ethnic Puerto Ricans in the territorial bureaucracy succeeded in highlighting the Spanish language as a distinguishing trait vis-à-vis Americans. But this achievement could not have taken place had the U.S. government in Puerto Rico not created a clear distinction and hierarchy relegating Puerto Ricans to a lower social and economic status on the basis (at least partially) of their language.

Clearly a vigorous pursuit of cultural assimilation worked to the detriment of ethnic Puerto Ricans in the local bureaucracy. This, however, does not explain how these new elites were able to convince the masses that theirs was a just cause that had repercussions for the entire populace. The glue that would bind Puerto Rico's new elites and masses was provided by the territorial administration itself. One rather resolute supporter of the Americanization policy was Juan Huyke, education secretary in the 1920s. His policies followed those of his predecessors in pressuring teachers to improve their English-language skills. Where he differed from earlier education secretaries was in the issuance of new regulations that would mandate high school students to take and pass an examination in "oral English." Failure to pass this test would deny students their diplomas and hence their opportunity to advance economically and socially (Negrón 1975: 190-191). This directive, along with other discriminatory policies, would make it easier for teachers to convince the public that language policies not only adversely affected their own rank and file, but also threatened the general public.

Almost a century after this policy was first articulated, Spanish is still the vernacular of the vast majority of Puerto Ricans. Despite the assiduous intentions of the American administrators in Puerto Rico, their assimilationist policy failed. Assimilation tends to occur as an unanticipated consequence of other social phenomenon and rarely succeeds as a calculated policy. As Conner noted: "Programmed assimilation appears to produce an opposite effect. Assimilation is apparently most apt to be achieved as an accidental by-product, not by design" (Conner 1994: 139). In the case of immigrant societies such as those in the United States, assimilation as a design was largely successful in transforming the acquired cultural properties of whole groups of newcomers. Such a transformation was due to a monopoly of the educational system. School lessons conducted in a new language were reinforced by the larger community outside of the traditional ethnic enclave. Immigrants to the United States found that interactions with the larger society had to be conducted in English. In addition it was also a needed skill in terms of upward mobility. However, in the case of Puerto Rico, the lessons taught, in particular the teaching of the English language, were performed by those who were not totally fluent in the language. Even in those cases where a teacher was fluent in English, that idiom was not reinforced anywhere in ordinary Puerto Rican life in the first half century of American rule.

Throughout the first half of the twentieth century, the Teachers Association grew in importance and political clout as its membership increased. Ironically this increase in the group's size was an unanticipated byproduct of the push to implement the government's Americanization policy. The Teachers Association continued to advocate Spanish-language instruction from the 1910s (Negrón 1975: 160) to the 1930s (García 1976: 100-101). It was in the 1930s that nationalism of both moderate and radical varieties emerged as a significant political force in Puerto Rican politics (Maldonado-Denis 1972: 308-309). This was the period in which teachers and other new elites pushed for changes in the political structure of Puerto Rican society. A few joined the ranks of the militant and separatist *Partido Nacionalista* (Nationalist party) in the 1930s and 1940s. However, the bulk gravitated toward the more moderate nationalist party, the *Partido Popular Democrático* (PPD), which dominated Puerto Rican electoral politics from the 1940s through the 1960s.[26] Maldonado-Denis said:

Its main base of support came from the peasantry, although after 1944 it managed to count upon other significant sectors of the Puerto Rican population, such as the working class, the intellectuals, and the professional middle class. In a sense, it may be said that the PPD attempted to steal the thunder and the lightning from the Nationalist party, whose program for basic social reforms was frequently clouded by its elitist approach to politics and by its repeated emphasis upon the solution of the problem of colonialism as the *sine qua non* for the solution of all other problems. But the men who were to hold sway within the Popular Democratic party after the consolidation of its power base were not the nationalists and socialists within its fold, but rather the pragmatic, technocratically oriented liberals who naturally would put 'economic development' within an unaltered colonial framework. (Maldonado-Denis 1972: 310) [emphasis in the original]

Regardless of the political party they choose to support, Puerto Rican intellectuals have been among the most important members of the island's nationalist movements—both the autonomist and especially the separatist movements (Maldonado-Denis 1972: 178).

THE SPANISH LANGUAGE AND PUERTO RICAN IDENTITY

The introduction of an American educational system did not, in and of itself, subsume Puerto Rican identity within an American one. To the contrary, it fortified the growing sense of Puerto Rico as a distinctive culture and subsequently flamed a growing nationalist movement precisely because it threatened the livelihoods of a growing cadre of up-and-coming elites. The growing numbers of low- and medium-level bureaucrats were constantly threatened throughout various administrations with the termination of their employment due to their lack of fluency in English. This was particularly true of school teachers—one of the largest and most dispersed groups of street-level bureaucrats in early twentieth-century Puerto Rico. Even in those cases where a Puerto Rican bureaucrat was fluent in English, a clear hierarchy was entrenched that ranked American over Puerto Rican—and thus the upward mobility of islanders was also hampered.

The elite status of these bureaucrats, especially teachers, did not derive from a domination over the Puerto Rican economy. Their power as a new elite came from a monopoly of a valued social resource. In this case that was knowledge. Education eventually led to a degree with which one could obtain professional employment. This gave teachers, as a collective, a great degree of power and influence over Puerto Rican society just as it gives pedagogues influence in all societies. Their strategic location at the grassroots gives pedagogues the ability to convey their message directly to the next generation of leaders and followers. However, in order to convert ethnic passions into a fully blown nationalist movement of either the autonomist or the more radical separatist variety, the elite must be able to create a bond with the masses. Americanization's implementation facilitated this task for local teachers by threatening to deny diplomas to students who did not demonstrate a mastery of English. In this way teachers could not only claim that this policy hurt their particular group, but it also hurt every individual who aspired to obtain a diploma—the ticket to upward mobility.

Puerto Rico's new elites, who constituted González's third story, had an array of cultural traits from which to attempt to build a counter-hegemonic order to challenge the cultural hegemony imposed by the United States. They could have chosen religion, music, food, folklore, or any one of a number of traits. After all, group boundaries are established by a select group of cultural characteristics and never by the entire constellation of possible traits. They chose Spanish—the vernacular. Here was a cultural trait that they controlled and provided them with a high status within the peripheral society as the bilingual intermediaries with the outside world. Puerto Rico's new elites attempted to transform their cultural milieu from one of a low-status group within the larger American realm to a high-status group within the confines of a small Puerto Rican nation. This was the benefit that the new elites were willing to share with the masses. But this relationship was cemented only when they were able to convince the population as a whole of the "common sense" of the group's distinction based on this trait—a move made easier by the harshness of the Americanization policy. The next chapter will explore many of the same processes that affected the development of a distinctive Québécois identity and its ties to the French language.

NOTES

1. Research conducted by various scholars noted U.S. interest in acquiring Puerto Rico long before the 1898 Spanish-American War (Anderson, C. 1984: 71; Picó 1986: 221). Among the first American leaders to express such an interest was John Adams in 1783 (Azize 1984: 77).

2. Since a significant part of Puerto Rico's population was comprised of relatively recent immigrants from Europe and Latin America in the nineteenth century, González (1993: 15) argued, contrary to the stance of many scholars, that Puerto Rico at the dawn of the twentieth century could be described as a society "on the way to nationhood" but not a full-blown nation. In this sense he agreed with Pedreira (1978), who emphasized the immaturity of Puerto Rican society at this time in history rather than its national character.

3. While Pedreira acknowledged the emergence of a distinctive Puerto Rican identity in the nineteenth century, he clearly subsumed it within a Spanish one. In terms of identity he argued that nineteenth-century Puerto Ricans were a part of the Spanish family, a subset within the larger Spanish whole, and that they never gave up their "Puerto Rican Spanishness" despite the activities of a "handful of separatists" (Pedreira 1978: 73).

4. To reiterate an important point, many scholars suggested that nationalism emerged in Europe around the latter part of the eighteenth or the outset of the nineteenth century. See chapter 2.

5. These early links helped to crystallize the *jíbaro*, or highland peasant, as the paramount archetype of the ethnic Puerto Rican (Scarano 1996: 1404). This elite attempt at promoting the *jíbaro* as the paradigmatic Puerto Rican was severely criticized by González (1993), who alternately advanced the coastal black population as the foundation of Puerto Rican society.

6. This uprising was named after the western Puerto Rican town of Lares where the revolt began.

7. Original: "Nosostros creemos, honradamente, que existe el alma puertorriqueña disgregada, dispersa, en potencia, luminosamente fragmentada como un rompecabezas doloroso que no ha gozado nunca de su integralidad. La hemos empezado a crear en el último siglo de nuestra historia, pero azares del destino político nos impidieron prolongar hasta hoy el mismo derrotero" (Pedreira 1978: 18).

8. Interestingly, while he disparaged islanders of African ancestry, he did laud their contributions to popular music (Pedreira 1978: 136-138).

9. As Flores (1993: 41-45) described in detail, Pedreira was heavily influenced by the elitist framework established by Ortega y Gasset (1960).

10. As many American Loyalists fled to Canada with the 1776 Revolution, so did monarchists in Latin America flee to Puerto Rico and Cuba, Spain's remaining colonial bastions in the hemisphere.

11. Flores and González debated the influence of African culture on Puerto Rican popular culture, especially dance and music. However, when it came to language, its impact on the Puerto Rican vernacular was relatively minor, argued del Rosario (1969: 13), especially in comparison to the large number of words and place names from the aboriginal Taínos that are still in use on the island.

12. Del Rosario (1969: 7) went so far as to argue that the true foundation of Puerto Rican culture was not Spanish at all, but indigenous.

13. The term *Nuyorican* is an amalgam of "New York" and "Puerto Rican." Though not all ethnic Puerto Ricans on the U.S. mainland live in New York City, or even New

York State, this diaspora formed such a large enclave as to be permanently associated with the mainland Puerto Rican experience. Hence, even Chicago- or Hartford-born ethnic Puerto Ricans are often labeled *Nuyoricans*.

14. Literally "the regular ones."

15. Many have frequently pointed to the large number of English words in the Puerto Rican variant of Spanish. Such remarks are often made with the intent of classifying this dialect as inferior to those found in Spain or other parts of Latin America. However, del Rosario (1960: 7) pointed out that Anglicisms are not the exclusive purview of Puerto Ricans within the Hispanophone world, and many of them have been formally adopted into the language's lexicon (del Rosario 1969: 18-19).

16. The 1990 U.S. federal census in Puerto Rico reported that 98 percent of the island's population spoke Spanish (U.S. Dept. of Commerce 1993: 70).

17. Though Flores's essay represents one of the key works on Puerto Rican culture, he is not the first to draw the connection between language and Latino identity. Earlier Delgado boldly argued that the key to preserving Puerto Rican culture was the preservation of the Spanish language (in García 1976: 22).

18. Puerto Rican Independence party. This party has no formal ties to any U.S. mainland political party but is affiliated with the International Socialist.

19. Popular Democratic party. While it is a separate institution, the PPD has some connections with the Democratic party in the United States.

20. New Progressive party. The PNP has connections with both the Republican and Democratic parties in the United States; however, historically its ties with the Republican party have been much stronger than those with the mainland Democrats.

21. Referring to the island's major political parties, Frambes-Buxeda (1980: 178n) contended that the pro-commonwealth PPD and the pro-statehood PNP discuss cultural issues more than the separatist PIP since separatists are viewed inherently as "more Puerto Rican" than their more pro-U.S. partisan counterparts.

22. A very surprising finding in Morris's study was that most of the statehood supporters she interviewed, the majority of whom were party leaders and activists, did not feel any identification with the United States at all (Morris 1995: 125).

23. Promoting the English language via public education was a long-term pro-statehood concern reiterated in Partido Republicano platforms in 1902 (Bothwell 1979a: 278), in 1906 (Bothwell 1979a: 296), in 1920 (Bothwell 1979a: 374), and in 1923 (Bothwell 1979a: 414). Such a policy was also promoted by its pro-statehood successor, the Partido Unión Republicano (Republican Union party), in its 1936 platform (Bothwell 1979a: 578). The Partido Estadista Republicano (Statehood Republican party) in 1948 likewise supported public education in English (Bothwell 1979a: 677) and again in 1956 (Bothwell 1979b: 773).

24. The education commissioners in the U.S. overseas territories were selected by various means. In Alaska they were chosen by the Territorial Board of Education whose members were appointed by the governor (Reid 1941: 35). In both Hawaii (Reid 1941: 175) and the Panama Canal Zone (Reid 1941: 414), they were appointed by their respective governors. In Guam (Reid 1941: 319) and American Samoa (Reid 1941: 362), they were naval chaplains. And in the Virgin Islands they were appointed by the secretary of the interior upon the recommendation of the governor (Reid 1941: 463). But only in Puerto Rico were they appointed directly by the U.S. president (Reid 1941: 231-232).

25. The Union of Puerto Rico, under the leadership of José de Diego, was the first Puerto Rican political party under American rule to accept independence from the United States as an acceptable status alternative (Maldonado-Denis 1972: 93-94; Bothwell

1979a: 340). The first officially separatist party was the Independence party, founded in 1912 (Maldonado-Denis 1972: 97-98).

26. While the Popular Democratic party (PPD) is today regarded as an autonomist party, it had in its infancy a strong separatist component. In this sense the PPD was, early in its history, a nationalist coalition uniting separatists with autonomists. Separatists were encouraged to stay in the party in the late 1930s and early 1940s by the party's leader and founder, Luis Muñoz Marín. At that time one of his most frequently cited slogans was "*la independencia está a la vuelta de la esquina*" ("independence is just around the corner"). The PPD's most staunch separatists, members of the party's Pro-Independence Congress, were expelled in 1946. This former PPD faction became the *Partido Independentista Puertorriqueño* (PIP—Puerto Rican Independence party).

7

Quebec's Distinct Society and Nationalism

When comparing any two societies, one can easily overlook the similarities and common patterns in their historical evolutions by dwelling on their multiple differences. The point of comparison, particularly with regard to ethnic and nationalist movements, is to look beyond a group's particular cultural traits and to examine the processes that politicized these traits and created these movements to begin with. It is in this light that our attention will move from the Caribbean to continental North America. Despite their vast social, political, economic, and historical differences, both Puerto Rico and Quebec underwent certain parallel processes that gave rise to their respective nationalist movements and their current focus on language as one of the highest-ranking group traits.

Both Puerto Rico and Quebec were formally joined to the United States and Great Britain, respectively, by way of peace treaties that consecrated military conquests. Puerto Rico became a possession of the United States, a country that already embraced a notion of group identity based on acquiring fluency in the English language and viewing other language speakers as a potential threat. This cultural hegemony resulted in a clear hierarchy of English speakers over all others. In contrast Quebec became a member of a political union in 1867 that tacitly embraced a policy of bilingualism. A British policy of forced cultural assimilation in the late eighteenth and the early nineteenth centuries gave way to cultural and linguistic accommodation. The Dominion of Canada was organized as a bilingual entity as opposed to its monolingual cousin to the south. In time English speakers north of the United States would acquire a "Canadian" identity that would separate them from other British subjects in the Anglo-Irish Isles. However, that definition of Canadianness, as far as Anglophones were concerned, assumed a "common sense" hierarchy of Anglophone over Francophone. In both Canada and the United States, the English language became the dominant medium of government affairs, commerce, and social interactions at the highest levels. This relegated a lower status to other languages and to their speakers.

Like Puerto Rico, the inhabitants of Quebec embraced a common identity prior to the switch in sovereignty. The French-speaking settlers along the St. Lawrence River used the label *Canadien* to identify themselves as early as the seventeenth century (McRoberts 1984: 55). This term differentiated French settlers from neighboring British colonists as well as dividing them from their European-born Francophone brethren. Dufour (1990: 41) noted that not long after the British conquest of New France, the local population began using such expressions as *nous* (us) and *patrie* (homeland) to refer to themselves and to their place of residence. Such terms are indicative of a collective consciousness that separated the "us" from the "them"—the first steps in ethno-genesis (see chapter 2).

However, this identity did not manifest itself politically until the advent of British rule. It was not until the Union Jack flew over Quebec and Montreal that the French-speaking community and its leaders asked for certain political rights and a degree of local autonomy. Timing may explain why defining Puerto Rican identity was much more problematic than its Québécois counterpart. Those writing about Puerto Rican identity had to differentiate this racially heterogeneous Caribbean population[1] from both Spaniards and Americans since the first clamorings for political autonomy manifested themselves while the island was still governed by Madrid. In contrast, analyses of Québécois identity are rarely obliged to differentiate the *Canadien* from the metropolitan French since the Francophone struggle for political rights started under British rule rather than the French *ancien régime*.

EARLY FRENCH CANADIAN IDENTITY

The *habitants* developed a distinctive identity based upon a rather short list of cultural attributes. British policies going back to the mid-eighteenth century encouraged a social division of English versus French. Early in Britain's tenure over Canada, its Francophone communities feared not only state efforts aimed at cultural assimilation but also worried about forced mass expulsion.[2] Uneasiness over Britain's plans in its new colonies north of the Great Lakes and along the St. Lawrence River sewed the seeds of distrust between the two communities and promoted a strong sense of social and ethnic differentiation. Later the difference between these communities would be defined on the basis of a small list of traits.

One who spoke about this identity at the turn of the twentieth century was Henri Bourassa, who was described as "the most prominent spokesman of French Canadian resentment" (Levitt 1970: 8). Referring to the English of Canada, he distinguished them on the basis of their country of origin, vernacular, Protestant faith, and their legal system (Bourassa in Levitt 1970: 103). These fundamental tenets of French identity (a presumed racial/biological difference, the French language, and the Roman Catholic faith) continued to dominate Quebec society through the 1950s. That decade marked the final years of the Duplessis administration in the Province of Quebec. It was said that: "[h]is

[Duplessis's] rather moderate nationalism had taken the form of an unshakeable opposition to any idea or trend which might threaten the historical trinity of *la foi, la langue, la race*—faith, language, and race—on which French cultural survival had long been said to depend" (Clift 1982: 3) [emphasis in the original].

Their use of the term "race" paralleled that employed by Lord Durham in his report to Westminster on the state of British North America six decades earlier (see chapter 5). By using the word in this way both authors tried to elevate cultural differences between the two groups to the level of genetic differentiae. It was clear to Bourassa that the discerning group characteristics implied a distinctive social hierarchy in Canadian society that maintained a higher position for the English over their French counterparts.[3] This social hierarchy was based upon the economic standing of Canada's Anglophone population vis-à-vis the French.

If the most influential and most enlightened of the two races tried to have more to do with each other and got to know each other better, our national future would not be so precarious. . . . Moreover, our neighbors would discover that we were not the inferior race that a great number of them scorned with such naive arrogance. (Bourassa in Levitt 1970: 105)

Bourassa felt indignant about the way his people were portrayed in Canadian society at large. This image was etched in society at the level of a cultural stereotype that bolstered even the social ranking of Anglophone blue-collar workers above their Francophone counterparts. As Latouche argued, the impact of this stereotype is still felt today:

The picture Lord Durham gave of the French-Canadians led to a whole series of stereotypes, which still have a place of honour in the imagination of a good number of English-Canadians and which even get around in Quebec: a charming, joyous folk, little given to education or the economy, emotional and drawn to the things of the spirit. (Latouche 1986: 75)

Bourassa warned English Canadians in 1912 that this kind of attitude threatened the very survival of their binational and bilingual Confederation: "[I]f the Canadian constitution is to last, if the Canadian Confederation is to be maintained, the narrow-mindedness towards minorities which manifests itself more and more in the English provinces must disappear, and there must be a return to the initial spirit of the alliance" (Bourassa in Levitt 1970: 132).

Referring to the cultural traits themselves, Bourassa listed ancestral homeland, religion, legal system, and customs. The ancestors of the modern-day French of Canada did, of course, come from France. In the same vein the original Anglophone Canadians emigrated either directly from the Anglo-Irish Isles or were British Loyalists who emigrated from the southern colonies during the American Revolution. Differing countries of origin were responsible for distinctive legal systems; British Common Law was employed in English Canada as was French Civil Law in Quebec. However, Bourassa's account omitted any mention of the non-French who were assimilated into French Canadian culture. In the nineteenth century there were immigrants from Ireland and Great Britain who became French speaking. In his often cited demographic study of Canada, Joy wrote: "During the late 18th Century and well into the 19th, assimilation in Canada tended to be in the other direction as French expansion engulfed many small colonies of Irish, Scottish and English origin and as French-Canadian families welcomed into their homes the orphans of Irish immigrants" (Joy 1972: 31). As it turned out his claim of French Canadian uniqueness, based on country of origin and thus common blood or ancestry, cannot be substantiated by objectively assessing the historical record. Nonetheless, the myth of a shared country of origin and common ancestry does persist. To repeat a point from the second chapter, "you can partially forget what you know if others do not notice or do not mind" (Roosens 1989: 161).

Following the ancestral points of origin, Bourassa mentioned what were perhaps the two most touted differences between the English and the French in Canada: language and religion. These differences did not, he argued, thwart the possibility of cooperation between the groups or a continued political union with English Canada (Bourassa in Levitt 1970: 107). The medium of communication shared by French Canadians made them, in Bourassa's eyes, a separate people since it influenced their spiritual-psychological makeup. "In effect, it is language which gives the spiritual works of a race that indelible stamp which gives it all its value, just as the art of a race has no real value unless the works which it inspires reflect the particular genius of the race" (Bourassa in Levitt 1970: 134). A loss of language as a result of assimilation was a signal that the death of a people was imminent.

[t]he day a race ceases to express its thought and its sentiments in its language, in that language which has grown with it and which took form with its ethnic temperament, it is lost as a race. The preservation of its language is absolutely necessary to the preservation of the race, of its genius, its character and its temperament. (Bourassa in Levitt 1970: 134)

If the two groups in question were divided on the basis of language, then it was the responsibility of a few French Canadians to learn English. This task he relegated to the upper echelons of French Canadian society. Bourassa did not feel that it was either necessary or "desirable" for the French masses to learn English (in Levitt 1970: 105). He also felt that elites in Canada's English-speaking community also shared this responsibility (Bourassa in Levitt 1970: 105). Bourassa's belief in the intellectual superiority of elites over the masses and in their guiding role in society echoed the sentiments of his Puerto Rican counterpart Pedreira in his analysis of Puerto Rican identity early in the twentieth century. Elites had a vital role in protecting the culture of French Canadians and in serving as the bilingual intermediaries between the two communities—a duty that would assure the elevated status of well-educated Francophones within their community.

Another major cultural element that set French Canadians apart was their Catholic faith. In the eyes of French Canadian nationalists of the 1950s and earlier, these two aspects of their society were intimately intertwined. Rioux (1971: 29) argued that in fact religion was a more significant social barrier between the French and English communities than was language in the nineteenth century. Catholicism, as a key feature defining Canada's second-largest linguistic group, was wholeheartedly endorsed by clerics in order to preserve their influence (McInnis 1969: 427). Referring to French Canadian identity in the eighteenth century, Dufour agreed with Rioux, stating that "Catholicism was the hard core of the Canadien identity" (Dufour 1990: 36).[4] Quinn's (1979: 3) interpretation of Québécois political culture extended this principle well into the twentieth century.[5] Bourassa's writings from early in the twentieth century seemed to confirm Dufour's and Quinn's assessment. Maintaining strong ties with the institutional Church was not only valuable for spiritual reasons but also for nationalistic ones (Bourassa in Levitt 1970: 126). Bourassa attributed the preservation of culture to strong ties with its faith when he said: "In all times and in all countries the Church gives lead to the traditions, the language, the national aspirations of the peoples who obey its laws" (Bourassa in Levitt 1970: 125). The Church was important to French Canadian society but it was an institution that did not belong to any one culture (Bourassa in Levitt 1970: 125). As the *universal* Church, Roman Catholicism belonged to many nations.

Finally, in addition to these three frequently mentioned elements in French Canadian identity (faith, language, and race), Bourassa's writings added a fourth—geography. Bourassa's vision of a French Canadian nation spanned beyond the provincial boundaries of Quebec and included all of Canada (Bourassa in Levitt 1970: 107). His French Canadian nation included hundreds of thousands of Francophones in New Brunswick, Ontario, Manitoba, and other Canadian provinces. Bourassa's interpretation of French-Canadian reality inexorably linked the fate of Quebec's Francophone majority with that of the Francophone minorities in other provinces. "The French people of Quebec, a minority in the whole of Confederation, have neither more nor fewer rights to their ethnic preservation than the French minority in each of the English provinces" (Bourassa in Levitt 1970: 157). In sum Bourassa's nation was a pan-Canadian community founded on a myth of common ancestry ("race"), a shared language (French), and one faith (Roman Catholicism). This vision of French Canada was altered within the provincial boundaries of Quebec and gave way to a new conceptualization of what the Québécois was.

CONTEMPORARY QUÉBÉCOIS IDENTITY

The previous definition of a French Canadian underwent a significant change in the 1960s as a result of the social upheaval known as the *Révolution Tran-*

quille—the Quiet Revolution. The traditionally rural Quebec became urbanized, the economic reliance on the agricultural segments of its economy gave way to a greater reliance on industry, and the traditionally preeminent role given to religion and its clergy in the past waned as it became a much more secular society (Cook 1986: 86).

This new definition of Quebec society is observable in *Quebec in a New World* (Chodos 1994), a document drafted by the nationalist Parti Québécois (PQ). In it the PQ defined the Québécois culture in the following manner: "Our culture is defined by a shared language, a shared history and heritage, and shared values and institutions. It is through our culture that we shape our life together, our forms of solidarity and our common projects" (Chodos 1994: 15).

Quebec, the largest Francophone enclave in North America could still be distinguished on the basis of its language (French), heritage (country of ancestral origin and folk traditions), and institutions (French Civil Law). It is rather interesting to note that this definition parallels Bourassa's definition from earlier in the twentieth century to a remarkable degree, with one major exception. This PQ document omits any mention of the role of Catholicism in Québécois identity. With the new nationalism of the post 1950s era, a novel definition emerged. "Culture was defined essentially in terms of language with no reference to the former role of Catholicism as an important ingredient of French-Canadian culture" (Quinn 1979: 247). Even the staunch federalist Pierre Trudeau acknowledged the view that Quebec represented a "distinct society" and that the basis of this uniqueness was its language and civil law tradition (Johnston 1990: 73). The Parti Québécois raised the status of the French language even further when it stated that: "[t]he French language is the cornerstone of Quebec's cultural identity. It is and will remain the official language of Quebec. It is and will remain the preferred instrument for integrating newcomers into Quebec society" (Chodos 1994: 37). The exalted role of language in defining Québécois culture, particularly as it manifests itself politically by calling for greater autonomy or even secession, is a far cry from previous periods where language was only one group characteristic out of several. As Mallea (1984: 225) noted protecting the French language has become the focus of Quebec's political culture.

In addition to a redefinition of the cultural traits that went into the making of a Québécois, there was an alteration in the geographical boundaries of Canada's Francophone "nation." There were still large Francophone pockets outside of Quebec, particularly in New Brunswick (north and east) and northern Ontario. However, the new nationalism was a Quebec-centric one. French nationalists in Quebec focused on distancing this province from the others in the Confederation to a significant degree. As Levine (1990: 44) observed: "[T]he Quebec state would replace the church as the locus of Francophone power" French Canadian nationalists relied more on the Quebec provincial government for legal remedies—a tactic facilitated by its status as the only Francophone majority province in Canada. However, in turning "inward" and relying more on the Quebec provincial government, French nationalists in Quebec began to curtail their traditional role as the protector of Francophone minorities throughout all of Canada.

The diminishing attention to protecting French Canadian communities outside Quebec was more easily justified with the publication of demographic data that illustrated the high rates of linguistic assimilation of members of these Francophone communities (especially the young) to the English language and the exodus of Quebec Anglophones from the province (Joy 1972: 4-5). With the passage of time, the linguistic frontiers were coinciding more with provincial boundaries. These demographic patterns observed in the early 1970s were confirmed a couple of decades later (Kaplan 1994: 60). What the two nationalist visions, traditional and modern alike, maintained was the focus on language as a key cultural marker (Cook 1986: 82).

Narrowing the geographic focus of French Canadian politics made it easier to contemplate Quebec's separation from the Canadian Confederation. Bourassa, in 1902, referred to the establishment of a separate French Canadian country as a "dream" for now and a plan for the distant future. This is a far cry from the current platform of the Parti Québécois, which calls for the province's "sovereignty" (Chodos 1994: 17). In sum the dominant mode of French Canadian nationalism that developed in the post-1950s era was both Quebec-centered in terms of geography and lingual-centric with regard to objective cultural traits that defined group boundaries. Speaking French became a more accurate barometer of Québécoisness than did French ancestry or adherents to Catholicism's tenets. Why did French Canadian nationalism change and in the process become, primarily, a Québécois nationalism? Differing theoretical schools have attempted to answer this question.

CULTURALIST AND RATIONAL CHOICE VIEWPOINTS

Foremost among scholars who have used a culturalist approach to explain the rise of Québécois nationalism since the 1960s is Laponce, who suggested that this phenomenon was the result of increased linguistic contact. He argued that people innately think, and thus identify, with one particular language. While bilingualism may be a common phenomenon, it is "abnormal" in that it runs counter to our unilingual nature (Laponce 1987: 3). As innate unilinguals people tend to reject languages other than their particular vernacular. "The spatial dynamics of a language lead it normally . . . to occupy a geographical niche that is exclusively its own: languages reject other languages" (Laponce 1984: 91).

From this perspective Laponce argued that the rise in modern Québécois nationalism was a direct result of increased contact between French and English speakers in Quebec.[6] The 1960s marked a period of heightened industrialization whereby Quebec society became increasingly urban. Migrants from overwhelmingly Francophone communities in rural Quebec came into more frequent and more intense contact with Anglophones (Laponce 1980). Rural migrants in an urban setting dominated by the English language were disadvantaged in terms of employment and diminished in terms of social standing. With increased linguistic contact Québécois nationalism grew in intensity from a largely autonomist movement to a more separatist one. Thus, Laponce attributed the more ardent strains of Québécois nationalism, especially its more separatist undertones, to the incompatibility of the two languages in the same geographic space. This contact was particularly intense in the city of Montreal where the two linguistic communities battled for social, political, and economic control.[7]

If Laponce's argument, that linguistic contact fueled a more intense French nationalism is true, then the reverse should be true. A reduction in linguistic contact should reduce ethnic tensions, assuming that the groups in question define themselves at least partially on a linguistic basis. Such a linguistic separation did take place in Quebec during the late 1970s. With the victory of the separatist Parti Québécois in 1976, many Anglophones decided to leave the province. Between 1976 and 1981 Quebec witnessed a net loss of over 100,000 Anglophones (Harrison & Marmen 1994: 56-57).[8] While support for any political party fluctuates over time, the separatist Parti Québécois consistently garnered over 40 percent of the vote in provincial elections from 1976 through 1994 (Barreto 1995a: 120). Quebec nationalists also acquired an electoral option at the federal level with the organization of the Bloc Québécois. In the fall of 1995 a record 49.4 percent of Quebec's population voted in favor of the province's sovereignty (Wilson-Smith 1995: 14). This steady support for a sovereigntist party and the separatist option in a recent referendum run counter to Laponce's culturalist argument.

On the other hand the rational choice perspective also has problems explaining Québécois nationalism. The cultural-division-of-labor argument would expect a high degree of nationalism in Quebec to result from an Anglophone-imposed linguistic caste system that relegated Francophones to a lower economic standing. At the same time an equalization of economic opportunities for Francophones should diminish nationalistic tensions. Various studies have demonstrated a strong association between support for separatism and a higher level of education (Hamilton & Pinard 1976: 6; Hamilton & Pinard 1982: 222; Pinard & Hamilton 1984: 32). This is the social segment most apt to feel frustrated as a result of a cultural division of labor that denied them a social and economic ascent commensurate with their educational background. However, the one major exception to this general pattern is a lower level of support for separatism within the managerial sector of the economy (Hamilton & Pinard 1976: 17; Pinard & Hamilton 1984: 32). This sector shows a greater propensity than other well-educated Francophone Quebecers to support stronger ties with the other provinces. Coleman (1984: 143) explained that the Francization goals of various pieces of provincial language legislation, in particular the famous Bill 101, were most successful in opening up middle-management positions within Quebec's private sector. Levine (1990: 220) argued that by the early 1980s "this new Francophone business class clearly displaced the state-centered new middle class as the dominant group in Quebec society."

As Coleman (1984: 139) noted, Quebec's language laws to a large degree succeeded in opening up the provincial economy to French speakers at mid-level managerial positions; but it has not had much success beyond that point. If this is the case, then one would expect elevated levels of nationalist support among mid-level managers who would be the individuals most likely to take advantage of openings at the upper levels. Yet, the studies from Hamilton and Pinard noted that nationalistic sentiments, in particular support for separatism, are lower for this group than other well-educated Francophones. We are presented with an interesting paradox. Those well-educated Francophones who no longer experience a cultural division of labor are more nationalistic than those (middle-level managers) who still do. In sum both the culturalist and the rational choice schools have serious difficulties explaining the rise of Québécois nationalism in the last half of the twentieth century.

OLD ELITES: THE RISE OF THE CLERISY

One of the results of the change in sovereignty from France to Great Britain was a change in economic patterns. It was previously mentioned that raw materials that used to be channeled from the ports of Quebec and Montreal to metropolitan France were now being sent to English ports. The old French business elites, whose livelihoods depended on these commercial ventures with France, were accordingly displaced by English ones. Many French businessmen who decided not to leave Canada moved into the agricultural sectors of the local economy.[9] But even here they would face competition from English entrepreneurs who invested in Canadian timber and agriculture (Durham 1905: 21). Their lack of opportunities in the business world were matched by restrictions to careers in the new public administration (Clift 1982: 57).

While the business elites who catered to the metropolitan French market diminished in influence and power with the loss of their commercial ties, a new French Canadian business elite emerged in its place. This new elite arose from the ranks of the *habitants* and was composed primarily of well-educated professionals who serviced the Francophone community, such as physicians and lawyers (Rioux 1971: 45). Durham's report, issued in the late 1830s, described a colonial society that was establishing an ethnic caste system whereby secular French Canadian elites were prevented from ascending the socioeconomic ladder. In their positions of power and prestige, he observed, many English civil servants in Canada looked down upon the populace they were serving:

The circumstances of the early colonial administration excluded the native from power, and vested all offices of trust and emolument in the hands of strangers of English origin. The highest posts in the law were confided to the same class of persons. The functionaries of the civil government, together with the officers of the army, composed a kind of privileged class, occupying the first place in the community, excluding the higher class of the natives from society, as well as from the government of their own country. (Durham 1905: 20)

The findings in this report explain the resentment that this new elite harbored against the British state. However, this group would also develop an antagonistic relationship with their own Church—the state's partner in French Canada. In reference to nineteenth-century nationalism in Lower Canada, Clift wrote:

The rise of nationalism coincided with that of a new class of educated professionals who assumed political leadership in the towns and in the countryside and who eventually came to dominate the Assembly. It displaced the older class of seigneurs and even managed to undermine seriously the influence of the Catholic clergy on the political and social views of the population. (Clift 1982: 56)

The pact between the British government and the Roman Catholic church in Canada bartered deference for the English Crown in exchange for the Church's virtual monopoly over social and spiritual affairs in French Canada. Britain's deal with the Church of Rome did not make provisions for sharing power with any other social sectors. Restricted by this accord Lower Canada's new elite would resent both the Church and the British state for their lack of upward mobility. As the quote from Lord Durham's report noted, the ranks of the French Canadian professional corps were already saturated at this time with little chance for upward mobility despite a citizen's formal training. The rise of this new secular elite was a serious challenge to the Church's authority as some members of this new bourgeoisie embraced notions that were associated with revolutionary France: democracy, liberalism and anticlericalism (Rioux 1971: 45). They would challenge the state by demanding greater political autonomy.

Social groups finding themselves in this type of situation tend to direct their resentment and frustration against the dominant power. . . . These groups sustain their self-esteem by glorifying tradition and the historical past. They put forward ideological systems which maximize their own role in society and they press for the kind of change that will make them into the new dominant power. It was this model which the educated class of lawyers, notaries, and doctors followed during the decisive period at the beginning of the nineteenth century and expressed through their political arm, the Parti Patriote.[10] (Clift 1982: 58)

Prevented from exercising power through the administrative organs of the colonial state, French Canadian elites would wield power through the one institution that they did control—the Assembly of Lower Canada. In an effort to exert greater power and influence, the Patriotes would hold up key legislation until such time as they received, in return, major concessions from the colonial governor. English property owners in Lower Canada complained vehemently about a colonial legislature that refused to pass bills aimed at facilitating the transfer of real property (Durham 1905: 21). British investors in Canada also grumbled that this legislature was slow in authorizing public works projects such as the roads, bridges, and ports that they relied upon. The underlying motivation behind this fiscal conservatism was not so much concern over the public treasure as it was to prevent or retard publicly financed projects that ultimately served English elites in Canada by improving the value of their properties and facilitating their penetration of the Canadian market.

Frustration fueled demands for greater autonomy—a proposition that the Crown was unwilling to entertain in the nineteenth century. When French secular elites could not extract their demands from the state, they turned to popular appeals. They were responsible for triggering the politics of nationalism in Quebec. Lower Canada's corps of professionals were in an advantageous situation. Their dissemination throughout French Canada gave them access to large numbers of ordinary citizens. To that one must add that their educational background (in many cases the mere fact that they were literate at all) gave them a significant degree of respect and status in the eyes of ordinary French Canadians. Durham observed the nexus these elites, whom he labeled "demagogues," were forging with the French Canadian masses in the hopes of pressuring the British state for political reforms (Durham 1905: 19). Their message of political autonomy and anticlericalism would, if successful, have the effect of siphoning both the power of the state and that of the Church. Thus in the 1830s the Catholic bishop of Montreal began criticizing the Patriotes and Papineau in the hopes of countering their popular appeal (Rioux 1971: 45-46).

While the colony's new bourgeoisie wanted to mobilize mass support for their cause, they were not eager to share power. One noted Québécois nationalist commented:

The Patriots, the petty bourgeois led by Papineau, had not wanted a popular revolution. In mobilizing the people they had only sought to bring pressure on the English in order to obtain for themselves, for their class—and not for the Habitants—a new division of power which would bring them certain additional revenues and a greater share in the economic advantages of the system. Thus, they demanded control of the trade in wheat and domestic consumer goods in Lower Canada. They wanted to participate in the financial activities which had up to that time been reserved for the English and to take back from them the rights which they declared had long been their due. But they did not want to overturn the system or to drive the English out. They demanded nothing more than a redistribution of privileges between themselves and the English. (Vallières 1971: 27)

While this nationalist movement was elite led and designed to suit their needs, it is, nonetheless, extremely important to recall that they would not have been able to energize the French Canadian masses were it not for Britain's official and unofficial discriminatory policies toward the French. It was the rejection of this peripheral elite by society's dominant sectors that laid the foundations for what would become a nationalist movement.

In the end the British authorities crushed Papineau and his Patriotes rebellion in 1837. The Crown's response was to strip these French secular elites of their political power by taking from under their feet the one institution they dominated—the Assembly of Lower Canada. Upon the recommendation of Lord Durham, the colonial legislatures of the two Canadas, Upper and Lower, today's Ontario and Quebec, were fused into one lawmaking body in 1840.

What Durham advised the English of Canada to do was not to attack the *Canadiens* but to stop behaving as a minority—which they were, statistically, at the time—and to turn themselves into the political and economic majority of the country. The linguistic and demographic majorities would follow inevitably. In short, what Durham recommended was that the English should create the Canadian nation and take possession of it. (Latouche 1986: 76) [emphasis in the original]

Lower Canada's Anglophone minority would now merge with the Anglophone majority in Upper Canada. By way of this constitutional engineering project, the French of Canada were stripped of their majoritarian status in Quebec and their base of political power.

With the union of the two Canadas, one of two sets of French Canadian elites was removed from the political landscape. Thoughts of establishing a sovereign French polity in North America gave way to preoccupation over cultural survival, which was exacerbated by pressures to linguistically and culturally Anglicize and as a result of mass migrations of French Canadians to the United States in search of employment (Rioux 1971: 55). Clerics, the Crown's postconquest partner in co-governing Canada, were left standing as the dominant elites of the colony. Not long after the 1830s, the Catholic clergy acquired control over social and cultural institutions in what would become Quebec (Clift 1982: 63). Antagonisms between the postconquest bourgeoisie of French Canada and the Church were sufficiently short lived to have little lasting impact on mass attitudes toward the clergy (Clift 1982: 65).

After the rebellion's failure, the French-Canadian elites sank gradually into a religious messianism—conservative and anti-state. It was at this time, and not, as is often believed, during the French regime or the Conquest, that the French-Canadian 'Church Triumphant,' which would play a major political role until 1960, was born. In 1840, the credibility of the Church was at its zenith. The other elites had failed miserably. Only the Church could say: 'I told you so.' (Dufour 1990: 66)

Safeguarding its influence over French Canadian society, the Church strongly encouraged an attachment to their language, their faith, and the one place where those two cultural elements met—the local parish. As Dufour noted, the French Canadian identity that the Church fostered during the nineteenth century was rather conservative. The preservation of such an identity was facilitated by the relative isolation of the French Canadian population in the rural expanses of Canada. Rural living isolated the populace from outside influences and simultaneously preserved the parish priest's role as perhaps the most important notable at the grass-roots level. Thus it should not be surprising that the Church's attitude toward industrialization and urbanization was rather hostile, opting instead to encourage a "return-to-the-land" movement (Vallières 1971: 28-29).

Sacerdotal admonitions kept many of the masses on the farm and engaged in agriculture. But some were destined for a different life. Their training was the purview of the Church as well. It ran the so-called classical colleges that produced a well-educated body of French Canadians (Clift 1982: 9). However, their numbers were relatively small and their training was limited to a few professions, which tended to keep French Canadians from working at the upper levels of management in industry and commerce.

It should also be pointed out that the Church always held that higher education was for the *élite* rather than the masses and that it had to be built around the hard core of classical studies. Thus, it was an educational system better suited to turning out priests, doctors, lawyers, and other professional people, lather than the accountants, engineers, and technicians required by an industrial society. (Quinn 1979: 13) [emphasis in the original]

Such an arrangement left English Canadians in charge of the Canadian economy, including its Quebec branch, through Confederation in 1867 up until the 1960s when this order was severely questioned.

THE RISE OF A NEW ELITE

Over the years scholars have continually associated the more militant forms of Québécois nationalism with the industrialization and urbanization that occurred in the second half of the twentieth century. French nationalists who espoused cultural autonomy for French Canada in the first half of the twentieth century were increasingly advocating "sovereignty" by the second half of the century. Interestingly, Quebec began large-scale industrialization after World War I, and by the 1930s this was a primarily industrial province (Quinn 1979: 31-33). Industrialization would significantly alter the relationship between the two linguistic communities in the province. At least within the agricultural sectors of the economy, many Francophones were self-employed. However, in industrial Quebec the French were usually relegated the lowest positions. Industrial Quebec established a very clear linguistic division of labor whereby Anglophone entrepreneurs dominated a largely Francophone work force (McRoberts 1984: 72). Until the mid-1970s Anglophone businesses (both English Canadian and American) controlled over 78 percent of the province's manufacturing (Coleman 1984: 131-132).

The French nationalism that developed in the first half of the twentieth century was quite conscious of its subordinate role in industrial Quebec, and its adherents resented their ethnic status as "hewers of wood and drawers of water" (Quinn 1979: 38). Their principal political vehicle, the Union Nationale, would promote cultural autonomy for Quebec while it formally scorned industrialization (Quinn 1979: 77-78). The French nationalism that flowered after the 1950s sought to mobilize the Quebec state to remedy that imbalance.

Industrialization brought many changes to Quebec, but it did not directly alter the basic tenets of French Canadian identity. The Francophone majority of

Quebec was still defined in terms of Catholicism and the French language. Québécois identity changed with the rise of a new highly educated elite who discarded the traditional connection with Catholicism and embraced a more tenacious connection with the French language. This change occurred without the adoption of a new theology to replace Roman Catholicism. The new nationalists sought to emphasize the cultural elements that they "controlled" rather than ones, such as religion, that they did not.

New elites emerged as a result of the efforts of the Lesage administration to expand colleges and universities (Levine 1990: 163). The policies of this Quebec premier, elected in 1960, were directly responsible for the social upheaval known as the Quiet Revolution.[11] This was a period in which Quebec sought economic *rattrapage*, or "catching-up" with the rest of North America (Coleman 1984: 133). Among his educational reforms was the establishment of an education ministry, a multicampus University of Quebec system, and a new set of postsecondary colleges (Rawkins 1984: 92).[12] These institutions, in particular the new Ministry of Education, would stay outside the control of the Catholic church. As Church-led universities emphasized classical studies and the training of physicians and lawyers, the new secularly based system added programs in business, the natural sciences, and the applied sciences to its curriculum.[13]

Despite the training of a new cadre of university-educated professionals eager to enter the work force, a significant proportion of them found barriers to their upward mobility. English was still the language of commerce in Quebec. The vast majority of upper-level managers and captains of industry came from the province's Anglophone minority. Francophone access to managerial and professional positions (outside of medicine and the law) had been less of an issue in the early decades of Quebec's industrialization as there were relatively few French speakers qualified for these positions. Majoring in the social sciences may qualify one for the magisterial trade but not for designing industrial equipment. It became an issue with the availability of French-speaking professionals who wanted to put their degrees to use and enter the middle class.

Studies showed that even with comparable levels of formal education, Anglophones were still selected over their Francophone counterparts (McRoberts 1979: 305). If they were hired at all French speakers were often given positions for which they were overqualified and thus underpaid in relation to their training. Industry in Quebec refused to absorb these new professionals. This left the Quebec government. Quebec provincial premiers embarked on a policy of state expansion of multiple social programs, the educational system, and even acquiring formerly private businesses—in particular Hydro-Quebec (Levine 1990: 46-47). Within the provincial bureaucracy speaking French was not a hindrance to upward mobility. Quebec was undergoing a "bureaucratic revolution" (Quinn 1979: 194), and in this revolution the state was seen as the solution to social and cultural problems and not just a mere observer (Vallières 1971: 32). In time, the Quebec provincial government would become as influential in the daily lives of the Québécois as was previously the case with the Church.

By turning its back on classical liberalism, which for a brief period had seemed to be taking hold, Quebec reverted to a type of social control and leadership which were largely patterned on the role which the Catholic clergy had taken on during the 100-year period between Confederation and the Quiet Revolution. From the early 1960s on, the historical role of the clergy was assumed by a new elite: the state bureaucracy. (Clift 1982: 28)

With a greater reliance on the Quebec provincial government, the staunchest defender of Francophone interests, French identity began to change. People began distinguishing Quebec from French Canada (Rioux 1971: 113). French Canada became a vision of the past, a vast geographic expanse with no unifying political institutions save for the Canadian federal government. "French Canadians" would have to struggle with the Anglophone-dominated federal legislature in order to procure government assistance. On the other hand within Quebec Francophones found an activist state anxious to promote their social and economic ascent.

The Church's former bastion of power, the provincial educational system, was now in the hands of secular bureaucrats who had no interest in incorporating Catholicism into their vision of Quebec. With the rise of a new secular elite, "[c]ulture was defined essentially in terms of language with no reference to the former role of Catholicism as an important ingredient of French-Canadian culture" (Quinn 1979: 247). This new Quebec-centered French nationalism was also less apprehensive than its predecessors to call for separation from the Canadian Confederation (Williams 1984: 209).

QUÉBÉCOIS IDENTITY AND THE FRENCH LANGUAGE

The defeat of Quebec's early-nineteenth-century bourgeoisie left Roman Catholic clerics as the strongest voices in French Canadian society. They succeeded, with the blessings of the British government, in establishing a counter-hegemonic order in Canada. The idea that Canada was also British was directly challenged by the Church, which pushed a binational definition of Canada. The Catholic church's counter-hegemony (within the Confederation) became hegemonic within the confines of French Canada. It became hegemonic at the point where no major Francophone leader dared to challenge the "common sense" enumeration of French Canadian cultural elements that highlighted religion and language.

Both high-ranking clerics and local parish priests promoted a French Canadian identity that benefited the interests of the Church. That identity focused on a common language and faith. Concerns over the influence of contradictory ideas, such as Protestantism and liberalism, led clerics to exalt rural living over the corruptive influences found in the cities. It was in rural communities that clerics were left standing, virtually unopposed, as the dominant elites at the local level. The Church's interest in proselytizing throughout the country meant that its French nationalism was a pan-Canadian nationalism. As a pan-Canadian identity this older variant of French nationalism could not, inherently, support the establishment of an independent Francophone homeland.

The *status quo* was challenged in the 1960s by a newly emerging elite who also sought to redefine what it was to be French in Canada. The French Canadian label in Quebec, during this decade, was replaced by the new nationalist tag of *Québécois*. Such a redefinition, in terms of geography, was necessary due to the reliance on the provincial government, the only French-majority government in Canada, to redress concerns over perceived inequalities. This new elite, comprised primarily of well-educated urbanites also reconstituted the elements that went into the construction of the Quebecer. They countered the Church's definition of a French Canadian with their own. In time this more linguistically centered and secular identity became accepted as a "common sense" definition of what it was to be a Quebecer.

The new Québécois was essentially a French speaker who lived within the territorial limits of the Province of Quebec. Adherence to the tenets of Roman Catholicism were no longer considered an integral part of what it was to be Québécois. This new elite had no interest in defining their culture on the basis of elements that advantaged another elite—in this case clerics. After all, their frustrated social and economic ascendancy was not due to their religion but to their language. This was not an issue as long as relatively few Francophones had the necessary skills to compete for highly prized professional positions in government and industry. However, the dissemination of a business- and technologically centered university educational system only augmented the number of well-educated Francophones who were denied access to positions for which they were qualified. After the Quebec government absorbed as many of these young professionals as it could, by expanding the parameters and services provided by its ministries, it turned to enacting legislation to open the doors of private firms. Laws that purport to protect cultures reflect attempts by established elites to further entrench a hegemonic order in the center. However, the ascent of a new elite in the periphery who endeavors to establish a counter-hegemonic order will often be reflected by new legislation from substate political units that protects and promotes those cultural elements it deems are critical to defining group parameters.

NOTES

1. The myth that all of today's Francophone Québécois were descendants of the original French settlers of the St. Lawrence facilitated the consolidation of a collective identity. France was clearly the "ancestral land." In contrast, the racial heterogeneity of Puerto Ricans made classifying Spain as the "ancestral land" an issue of controversy and debate (see chapter 6) since a significant portion of Puerto Rico's population could trace at least part of its ancestry to Africa.

2. The French-speaking communities of Upper and Lower Canada were aware that the British government expelled thousands of French speakers from what are today the Ca-

nadian maritime provinces (Sheppard 1971: 6). A significant portion of these Acadian refugees settled in France's Louisiana territory where in time they became the *Cajuns*.

3. In his discussion of apportioning loyalties, Bourassa made it clear that French Canadians owed fidelity to their French Canadian nation, to Canada at large, and to the United Kingdom (Bourassa in Levitt 1970: 103-104). By referring to Canada and Britain separately, Bourassa, by implication, differentiated the English of Britain from the English of Canada (Bourassa in Levitt 1970: 105).

4. It is interesting to note in terms of comparison, that Roman Catholicism did not play a vital role in shaping Puerto Rican identity vis-à-vis Americans. Catholicism was, and remains, the religion of the vast majority of Puerto Ricans. This stands in contrast to the various Protestant sects that predominate in most of the United States. Yet this religious difference did not translate into a rallying cry for Puerto Rican nationalists. Part of the explanation lies in the fact that the vast majority of Catholic clerics and virtually all the high-ranking Church officials were recruited from Spain as opposed to Puerto Rico throughout the four centuries of Spanish dominion over Puerto Rico. Institutionally the Church did not take on the role of "protector" of the masses or the local culture as it did in Quebec. Thus, this practice denied the institutional church a vital nexus to the bulk of the population. On the other hand the Catholic church in Quebec recruited its priests and its Catholic hierarchy locally, thus establishing Church-mass links (Quinn 1979: 11) that manifested themselves with the incorporation of religion into French Canadian identity.

5. In addition to noting the importance of Catholicism in Québécois politics, Quinn (1979: 3) also added to this list of cultural attributes, in a less than flattering manner, his view that the French Canadian demonstrated a "lack of democratic convictions and of an adequate understanding of parliamentary government in spite of his association with democratic institutions."

6. His controversial argument that linguistic conflict is a direct consequence of linguistic contact has not gone unchallenged. Some of his harshest critics have gone to the extreme of accusing Laponce of "pleading the cause of linguistic apartheid" (Pattanayak & Bayer 1987: 261).

7. In addition to the established Anglophone community, French Quebecers also came into increased contact with immigrants from abroad who were increasingly sending their children to English-medium schools, where as future Anglophones they would generally gravitate more toward the province's numerically inferior, but economically superior, English-speaking minority.

8. The single largest block of these Anglophone Quebecers left for Ontario and more specifically the Greater Toronto Metropolitan area (Harrison & Marmen 1995: 56-57).

9. Rioux (1971: 34) noted that many twentieth-century historians misinterpreted this change of vocations on the part of French business elites as a move to avoid cultural assimilation by the British when in fact this transition was motivated more by economic necessity than ideological commitments.

10. Patriote leader Louis-Joseph Papineau was himself a lawyer (Schull 1971: 12).

11. It is rather ironic that Lesage's policies helped trigger the Quiet Revolution when in fact his Liberal party was "resolutely antinationalist" (Clift 1982: 18). His party associated nationalism with the previous Duplessis regime, which Liberals viewed as extremely conservative. By initiating key reforms, especially in education, he denied the Catholic church (a strong defender of Duplessis and his Union Nationale party) one of its bases of support. However, the reforms also created a large pool of highly educated Francophones who found the doorways to upward mobility shut on account of their language.

12. These were the CEGEPS, or the Colleges d'Enseignennent General et Professionel (Rawkins 1981: 92).

13. Rawkins's (1984: 92) analysis pointed out the success these new institutions had in transforming the educational profile of Quebec by noting that most engineering degrees awarded before the mid-1950s were issued by Anglophone universities; by the 1970s the majority of degrees in the applied sciences were being issued by Francophone institutions of higher learning.

8

Defending Spanish in Puerto Rico's Territorial Government

When analyzing lawmaking, in general, an inordinate amount of attention is focused on legislatures at the highest levels. After all, state constitutions usually give these bodies the greatest degree of latitude in passing laws over the entire breadth of the country, and in many cases their superior rank to lower-level legislatures means they can often override local laws and ordinances. Such a focus is more defensible when looking at a highly centralized polity where relatively few policy-making decisions are exercised by local lawmakers. However, this approach is much less sensible when examining federal and confederal systems that inherently devolve significant policy-making decisions to local levels of government. Local governments in these less-centralized polities not only exercise a wide latitude of decision-making, but they are also often the catalysts for new initiatives at the federal level.

Both the American and Canadian political systems contend with a constellation of responsibilities that are divided between the federal and "state"/provincial levels of government. The "state" governments in the United States and their provincial counterparts in Canada represent the fundamental constituent components of their respective regimes. The relatively simple pyramidal structure of federal systems distributing powers from their highest level to their subordinate correlative systems is complicated by the existence of territorial governments, which are also subordinate to the government centers in Washington and Ottawa but do not enjoy all of the privileges and responsibilities bestowed to their "state" or provincial cohorts. These territorial administrations, while peripheral to the goings-on in their respective federal capitals, are still parts of their respective federal systems. This chapter will examine lawmaking in the U.S. territory of Puerto Rico with a particular focus on its language laws. The following chapter will examine the role played by Quebec's provincial legislature in language protection and promotion.

The legislatures in both San Juan and Quebec City have been the sites of ongoing battles over the appropriateness and extent to which they should protect the Spanish and French languages, respectively. In the Puerto Rican case the language issue resurfaced as recently as the early 1990s after lying dormant for decades. On the other hand, the Quebec provincial legislature have been debating and passing language laws since the late 1960s. Local language laws in both of these cases reflect an acknowledgment of the hegemonic nature of the English language in North America. Additionally these laws clearly define the local populace on the basis of another medium of communication, thus attempting to set up a local counter-hegemonic order. Discussions, arguments, and impassioned speeches in these assemblies focus on how far they should go in protecting that alternative language. Naturally, legislative latitudes are restricted by both their respective federal statutes and judicial interpretations of their constitutions.

Subfederal governments are frequently targeted for legislating cultural issues because of their unique status as minority/majority enclaves. Ethnic minorities are often territorially concentrated, whether at the state's geographical periphery or in urban pockets. As a result, subfederal political units are often the only ones where minorities enjoy a majoritarian standing. This is certainly the case for Hispanophones in the United States and Francophones in Canada. The only Spanish-speaking majority enclave within the American federal system is the Commonwealth of Puerto Rico. In Canada Quebec is the only French-majority province in the Confederation. Thus state minorities almost always find a more receptive audience with substate legislators than with their federal counterparts to legislation in general and cultural issues in particular.[1] This was the goal of educators as they sought to protect and promote the Spanish vernacular in Puerto Rican public schools in the first half of the twentieth century.

THE IMPOSITION OF OFFICIAL BILINGUALISM

Not long after the arrival of American troops on Puerto Rican soil, the new administration recognized that the island's people were culturally different and that these differences would be responsible for peripheralizing Puerto Rico within the U.S. federal system.[2] Despite the fact that the island's residents would not be considered equals to those living on the U.S. mainland, the American governors of Puerto Rico would still pursue a policy of assimilation (see chapter 6). Toward this end the U.S. Congress assigned Puerto Rico a tentative constitution, or "organic act."[3] The Foraker Act of 1900 gave Puerto Rico a "civilian" regime with an elected lower house of the legislature. However, both the territorial executive and the members of the territorial Supreme Court were appointed by the U.S. president along with the upper house of the legislature.[4] As a result the Foraker regime in Puerto Rico guaranteed American domination of the executive[5] and judicial branches of the local government, in addition to a significant standing in the legislature. Formal bilingualism, as enshrined in the 1902

Official Languages Act, was one of the legacies of this American-dominated government.

The Official Languages Act[6] declared both English and Spanish as the official languages of the Puerto Rican government. Either one of the two idioms could be used in any court,[7] government office, or office of any governmental department (García 1976: 82).[8] In theory the two languages were equal in the eyes of the Puerto Rican government. Where necessary translations were made from either language to the other. Strictly speaking this law only affected the local bureaucracy and did not make any statements that the two were now the languages of the *people*. Yet, one must keep in mind that this piece of legislation accompanied the federal government's policy of cultural assimilation, aimed at the public schools.

The theoretical parity of the two languages that this law anointed was violated only three years after its passing in 1902. The American-dominated Puerto Rican Supreme Court had the opportunity to rule on the equality of the two languages in a 1905 divorce case. Before the court was a dispute involving, among other issues, a discrepancy between the English and Spanish versions of the relevant section of the Civil Code. The Official Languages Act said clearly that the two languages were equal; however, it did not make any provisions for inconsistencies in the translation of a statute from one language to the other. Justice Wolf of the territorial Supreme Court resolved the matter by stating that "[t]here can be no doubt that the English text, which was signed by the Governor, is the law which must govern."[9] This ruling made the 1902 law, in effect, a merely symbolic piece of legislation. Supposedly the two idioms were equal, but when a conflict between the two arose, English, the language of the colonial administration on the island, would outrank Spanish, the language of the local population.

This judicial ruling served as an example of the "dual-policy" the United States pursued in Puerto Rico in the first half of the twentieth century. On the one hand the federal government pointed to the 1902 law as evidence of its intent to treat islanders' culture on par with the dominant Anglophone culture of North America. They argued that this law embraced locals rather than rejected them. On the other hand the same government, by way of the U.S. Supreme Court decision *Downes v. Bidwell*, made a clear distinction between the culturally distinct territories acquired in the aftermath of the Spanish-American War. Americans were set apart from Puerto Ricans and the reason, according to Justice White, was the cultural and racial composition of the insular populace. Additionally, the 1905 Puerto Rican Supreme Court decision entrenched within the insular bureaucracy a hierarchy of English over Spanish. And the Americanization policy, the last hymn in the requiem for formal equality between the two languages and cultures, endorsed the ideal of substituting the new metropolitan language for the local one as it was considered the superior idiom. Various American-appointed governors in the first half of the twentieth century vetoed subsequent attempts by the Puerto Rican legislature to do away with the Americanization policy and to promote Spanish as the medium of instruction (García

1976; Delgado 1991). In sum the policies of the federal government, judicial rulings combined with legislative action, served as evidence of attempts by representatives of the U.S. government to establish theirs as the hegemonic culture and language of Puerto Rico.

Statutes that attempt to legislate cultural matters can be purely symbolic. Yet, symbolism ends at the point where the legislative action promotes one group ahead of another. The promotion of a collectivity on the basis of a shared cultural trait inevitably restricts the mobility of "others," risks promoting their ire, and facilitates their mobilization as they now share a common good. This was the consequence of the Americanization policy pushed by various U.S. administrators in the first half of the twentieth century. This policy continually threatened the tenure of Puerto Ricans within the territorial bureaucracy, especially public school teachers. Promoting the English language in the classroom meant that Americans had priority over locals when it came to magisterial positions and when hired they received higher salaries than their insular counterparts. Thus, not surprisingly, teachers were at the forefront of abolishing the Americanization policy and promoting their language—Spanish—as the medium of instruction in public schools.[10] As García (1976: 108) put it, the Teachers Association of Puerto Rico was at the "vanguard" of the struggle for the Spanish language.

The controversy ended when Luis Muñoz Marín, the first elected governor of Puerto Rico, abolished the Americanization policy by way of an executive order in 1949 (García 1976: 109). Governor Muñoz's education commissioner, Mariano Villaronga, signed a departmental directive initiating a policy of Spanish-language instruction. With that directive language ceased to be a major issue in Puerto Rican political life until the 1990s. Once in place there were no significant efforts to reinforce the directive by incorporating its contents, in the form of a statute by the Puerto Rican legislature. What was an extremely controversial political issue faded in the 1950s despite the fast that the 1902 Official Languages Act remained on the books until 1991. With no numerically significant Anglophone settler communities in Puerto Rico,[11] teachers and other bureaucrats could assume that their positions were now secure.

In the aftermath of elected Puerto Rican governments, the position of Spanish in Puerto Rico strengthened at both the municipal and commonwealth levels of government.[12] Still, the concurrent industrialization of the insular economy, resulting from greater investment from, and closer trade ties to, the U.S. mainland, meant that English was now a more vital resource in terms of advancement in the private sector. While the very highest levels within multinational corporations in Puerto Rico are occupied by Americans, the vast majority of middle-management positions are held by bilingual Puerto Ricans, many of whom received their university education in the United States. The greater need for proficiency in the English language did not result in a nationalistic backlash in the last half of the twentieth century in Puerto Rico. As compared to the first half of the century, Puerto Ricans were not threatened with replacement by Americans

in the private sector even when fluency in English was required. The Spanish/
English debate in Puerto Rico did not resurface again until the early 1990s.

REVIVING THE LANGUAGE DEBATE IN THE 1990s

Like the mythological phoenix that arose, from the ashes the moribund language debate came back with a vengeance. Héctor López Galarza, a member of
the pro-commonwealth PPD in the territorial House of Representatives, presented Bill 417 in March of 1989 with the intent of overturning the 1902 Official
Languages Act (Delgado 1991: 587). The House of Representatives held hear-
ings on the matter throughout the spring, summer, and fall of 1990; the Senate
did not take up the matter until early 1991 (Delgado 1991: 587). Finally, on
April 5, 1991, House Bill 417, with the support of legislators from the pro-
commonwealth PPD and the separatist PIP, became a law and Spanish became
the only official language of Puerto Rico.[13]

The 1991 language law, disparagingly referred to as "Spanish Only" by its
detractors,[14] declared that Spanish would henceforth be the official language of
all branches of the Puerto Rican government, its agencies, and departments. The
English language would no longer have an "official" status within the Commonwealth administration. As this was a statute from a territorial legislature, it did
not make, nor did it attempt to affect, the operations of the U.S. federal government in Puerto Rico, which still operated exclusively in the English language.
Interestingly enough, this law did allow the executive branch to use "another
language" if it were necessary for carrying on its work.[15] While there is no mention of this "other" idiom, it clearly refers to English. Additionally, Bill 417
clearly stated that it did not in any way trample on the rights of individuals to use
any language of their choosing.[16] Individuals could still speak, write, and adver-
tise in any language they preferred.

One must keep in mind that with the advent of elected executives in Puerto
Rico, the executive branch had been effectively Hispanicized since the late
1940s. At that time the full membership of the insular legislature was also
elected.[17] The Puerto Rican Supreme Court ruled in 1965 that Spanish was the
sole language of the Puerto Rican judiciary.[18] With a Hispanophone majority in
every municipal government in Puerto Rico, there was no argument that Spanish
was the *de facto* language of all of the administrative units subordinate to the
Commonwealth government. Again, this law would have no effect on the Anglophones living within the confines of military bases as these are federal properties. It is true that this law formally abolished the Official Languages Act of
1902. However, with no government enforcing an Americanization policy any
longer, that statute was largely forgotten. In sum Bill 417 merely codified the
linguistic *status quo* and nothing more.

Nonetheless, the bill was lauded vociferously by many members of the
Puerto Rican intellectual community. A noted scholar praised the intent behind
this statute. He said: "There is no doubt, that the axis of Puerto Rican culture is

the Spanish language. In this lovely language we elaborate all of the expressions that typify us as a national collective" (Delgado 1991: 603) [author's translation].[19] More surprisingly was the praise the law received from the separatist Partido Socialista Puertorriqueño (PSP), which rarely supports any PPD-sponsored legislation (Torres Rivera 1991: 30).[20] The party's former secretary general, Carlos Gallisá, said that "[t]he recent law that converts Spanish into the official language, undoubtedly has as a feature national affirmation even when in practice that law does not notably alter the flow of Puerto Rican life" (Gallisá 1991: 11) [author's translation].[21] This separatist party, with strong ties to the Castro government in Cuba, only twice participated in the Puerto Rican electoral process (1976 and 1980 elections), quite frequently brands the Commonwealth as an illegitimate colonial status, and attacks the party that supports that status, the PPD. Nonetheless, Gallisá said: "The Popular [Democratic] Party and its leadership as promoters of said legislation should feel proud and confident that their action responds to the need to defend our language that is an essential part of what defines us as a Caribbean and Latin American nation" (Gallisá 1991: 11) [authors translation].[22] This kind of praise for the policies of rival political parties is extremely rare in the Puerto Rican partisan milieu.

If the 1991 law made no significant changes in the status of the Spanish language in Puerto Rico, why was it passed? Bill 417 was not the only attempt in recent decades to obliterate the 1902 law establishing official bilingualism. PPD Senator Sergio Peña Clos attempted to pass a similar bill in 1986 (Delgado 1991: 588). Nonetheless, his party, with a majority in both chambers of the legislature and control of the governorship, failed to take action on his proposal.[23] Assuming that the PPD's leadership is made up of "rational actors," there had to be a logical reason for them to take up this measure at that time.

The statute's defenders claimed that it was an attempt to back the local culture. Such an argument would tend to support the culturalist approach. However, Puerto Rico has lacked the "linguistic contact," a la Laponce, necessary to trigger such a response. There has been no significant influx of Anglophones to Puerto Rico. Its high population density and distance from the North American continent have served as perennial barriers to large inflows of American settlers to the island. Many ethnic Puerto Ricans born and raised in the United States, a significant proportion of whom are effectively English-language dominant, have returned to the island. Yet, they started to return in large numbers in the late 1960s and early 1970s, long before this language law was contemplated. Puerto Rico has also received large numbers of immigrants from neighboring islands in the region. But most of these newcomers are Cubans and Dominicans, both Spanish speakers. It is true that dozens of American companies have inundated the Puerto Rican market with their products and services. Few bother to translate labels and packaging into Spanish. Also American popular culture in the form of television and music have bombarded the insular airwaves. Yet, these processes are not new; they have been going on for decades without triggering any significant increases in nationalistic passions. Thus linguistic contact could not be the catalyst for this law.

Perhaps the answer can be found from Hechter's cultural-division-of-labor (CDL) argument. If Puerto Ricans were finding their social and economic ascendancy blocked, they could turn to the politics of nationalism, which would definitely include laws to protect elements of their culture. By protecting the culture they would be in fact safeguarding those individuals who shared in those cultural traits. Hechter's CDL perspective would explain this legislative action except that the elimination of the Americanization policy in the late 1940s meant that there was no longer any formal impediment to ascendancy for Hispanophones. All levels of the local bureaucracy, beginning with the 1950s, were filled essentially with Spanish speakers. It is true that fluency in English was required for a few positions with the Commonwealth government, and this was certainly the case with many private enterprises. However, even here most of these positions were filled with bilingual Puerto Ricans. There was certainly no change in that status in the late 1980s or early 1990s. So neither the culturalist or the CDL approaches adequately explain why the Puerto Rican legislature pushed an official language law at that time. There is, however, another explanation.

LANGUAGE AS A COMPONENT OF THE STATUS DEBATE

The answer to this puzzle lies in the intimate connection between language and the debate over Puerto Rico's final political status. Each of the island's three major political parties, the PNP, PIP, and PPD, align themselves not on a left-right axis so much as a center-periphery axis. As the champion of admitting Puerto Rico into the American Union, the PNP generally favors augmenting political, social, and cultural ties with the United States. It was the PNP's pro-statehood predecessors earlier in the twentieth century that favored the teaching of English in public schools as a step toward the eventual cultural assimilation of Puerto Ricans.[24] On the other end of the spectrum, the separatist PIP generally encourages stronger ties with Latin America at the expense of links with Anglo-North America. The autonomist PPD, as the defender of the commonwealth option, lies somewhere between these two points. These three parties and their respective leaders are aware of the intimate connection between Puerto Rican identity and the Spanish language (see chapter 6). Simultaneously they cannot forget the attachment most Americans have with their vernacular—English (see chapter 4). In effect the language debate in Puerto Rico is not about culture as much as it is about laying the groundwork for a plebiscite or referendum on the status question.

The 1991 language law was enacted during the administration of Governor Rafael Hernández Colón. This chief executive also served simultaneously as the president of the pro-commonwealth PPD. In the hostile partisan environment found in Puerto Rico, political actors of all persuasions attempt to discredit their adversaries and their preferred status options. With the PIP polling around 5 percent of the popular vote, the PPD had relatively little to fear, electorally, from separatists. On the other hand the pro-statehood PNP generally garners about the same number of votes as the PPD. Clearly the PNP and the statehood status alternatives present a more pressing concern to the PPD than separatism and the PIP. A noted poll published during the legislative debates over the language law, in the summer of 1990, indicated that the statehood option could obtain more votes than the commonwealth alternative.[25] Naturally polls fluctuate and political activists constantly rebuff surveys conducted by rival parties. What made these numbers so remarkable was that a strong statehood showing was reported in *El Mundo*, a daily newspaper associated with the PPD and the pro-commonwealth movement.

The PPD calculated that a change in the language law could make statehood a more difficult goal for the PNP to obtain (Vélez & Schweers 1993: 123-124). If the PPD changed the 1902 Official Languages Act it could force the PNP into one of two uncomfortable positions even if the PNP retook the governorship and a majority of the territorial legislature (which it did as a result of the 1992 general elections). One scenario, premised on the hegemonic role of the English language in the United States, posited that even if a majority of Puerto Ricans voted in favor of the statehood option in a future plebiscite, the U.S. Congress would be extremely reluctant to admit a formally Spanish-speaking jurisdiction into the Union. An alternative scenario could show a future PNP government changing the 1901 language law and restoring the linguistic *status quo ante*, thus restoring the statute from 1902. At that juncture autonomists and separatists could accuse the PNP of betraying the language of the Puerto Rican people.[26] Going one step further statehood opponents could brand the restoration of the 1902 law as a modern-day attempt at reintroducing the Americanization policy. The danger for the PPD was that by eliminating English as an official language it could be accused of trying to promote separatism. In order to counter such an attack Governor Rafael Hernández (1991: A25) printed an open letter in the *New York Times* in which he explained that with this law "[s]o as we reaffirm our Spanish language and culture today, we also reaffirm our unity with the United States."

Many of the assumptions underlying these two scenarios were openly expressed during the language law debates of 1991 and 1993 along with the proposed educational reforms of 1996 and 1997. Based on historic precedence University of Puerto Rico president Norman Maldonado said that under statehood Puerto Rico could be obliged to undergo a form of collective English-language immersion (Millán 1997a: 5). During the 1993 status debates, the organization English First a group that seeks to establish English as the official language of the United States and its respective "state" governments, published an advertisement in Puerto Rican newspapers[27] in which it stated that the adoption of English was a requirement for statehood in the case of jurisdictions with large non-English-speaking populations ("¡Aviso electoral!," 1993: 49). U.S. Congressman Gerald Solomon of New York, a supporter of making English the country's official language, jumped into the fray by stating that under statehood the Spanish language would disappear (Mulero 1993a: 13).[28] He reiterated the same opinion four years later (Mulero 1997a: 6). One of his fellow Republican congressmen, Randy Cunningham from California, said that a future law making English the official language would apply to Puerto Rico were it to become a "state" (Mulero 1996a: 7). His fellow Californian, Governor Pete Wilson, agreed with that opinion (Mulero 1996c: 5). The same view was shared by Mauro Mojica, president of the organization U.S. English, and Jim Boulet, the executive director of the group English First (Mulero 1997b: 12). In the eyes of conservative activist Pat Buchanan, the Spanish language, along with the existence of an active separatist movement, was reason enough to deny Puerto Rico statehood (Mulero 1996b: 10).[29]

The preceding opinions accept the "common sense" connection between membership in the United States and the English language. They uphold the idea that the American vernacular is hegemonic within the confines of the country, or at least within the "incorporated" parts of the United States. They assume that to enter into the Union a jurisdiction must be committed to linguistic assimilation. The PNP's predecessors earlier in the 1960s also accepted this ideal. However, the PNP assumed that statehood for Puerto Rico could be acceptable to Congress were the territory to accept official bilingualism (Martínez 1993b: 6). Former U.S. Senator Paul Simon from Illinois shared the belief that a bilingual territory could enter the Union as a full member (Mulero 1993b: 8). While the federal executive has not addressed the issue of Puerto Rican statehood directly, his spokesmen asserted that President Clinton would veto a federal English-only law (Fernández, J. 1997: 10). These statements would appear to boost the morale of statehood advocates in Puerto Rico. However, they do not endorse the admission of a "Spanish-speaking" territory into the Union, but instead offer the possibility to a "bilingual" territory. Even under these more liberal criterion, English is still an unwritten requirement for full membership.

It was with this understanding that the PNP, victorious in the 1992 general elections, abolished the 1991 language law. Governor Pedro Rosselló, who promised a plebiscite in late 1993, wanted to change the language law long before the vote on the status question. His new language law was both the first bill tabled by the PNP-dominated House of Representatives in 1993 and the first law passed that year.[30] His administration, in essence, decided to risk pursing the "second alternative" and take its chances with the Puerto Rican public rather than with the federal legislature in Washington. This law, like its predecessor from 1902, made both Spanish and English the official languages of the Puerto Rican government (both Commonwealth and municipal levels); its agencies, and departments.[31] Interestingly this law made allowances for the legislature and judiciary to determine how they would implement this law for their respective branches.[32] Representatives from the Teachers Federation, including its president Renán Soto Soto, expressed concern that the return to emphasizing English could open the door to a renewed effort at introducing the dominant language of

North America into the public school systems once more (Estrada 1993: 8). It would only take four years to justify their concerns with the advent of a proposed change in pedagogical policy.

Rosselló called the 1993 language law a success for the statehood movement (Martínez 1993a: 5). Autonomist leaders, such as Celeste Benítez (1993: 65), agreed with Governor Rosselló that the status question was the real impetus for this law. Separatist leaders also believed that *raison d'être* for the 1993 Official Languages Act was not to protect the English language *per se*, a language that was never threatened in Puerto Rico, but to prepare for the status plebiscite scheduled for the end of 1993 (Hernández, J. 1993: 3). Another statehood proponent who lauded the PNP's action on the language front attacked the 1991 statute as a scheme to make statehood more difficult (Fernández, I. 1993: 37). This was also the feeling of members of Puerto Rico's Federation of Municipalities, an association of PNP mayors. In fact this group threatened to violate the 1991 law while it was still in effect by carrying out municipal government business in the English language. Despite their threats such a protest was not very likely as a survey found that only a very small percentage of PNP mayors could even hold a basic conversation in the English language (Coss 1991: 5).[33]

Recently enacted language legislation in Puerto Rico, both the "promotion" of Spanish in 1991 and the restoration of official bilingualism in 1993, are indicative of an acknowledgment of the hegemonic role of English in the United States. In particular both the PPD's Bill 417 from 1991 and the PNP's Bill 1, written two years later, made the assumption that in Congress's eyes statehood and the English language walked hand in hand. The fact that the PNP has not returned to the official policy of the Partido Estadista Republicano (PER)[34] of openly promoting linguistic assimilation is indicative of its general acceptance that Spanish, the language of the "counter-hegemony," is the idiom of choice in Puerto Rico. But, a general acceptance is not the same as a complete acceptance.

Recent statements indicate that the PNP may be trying to inch its way back to those earlier policies. The Rosselló administration's secretary of education, Victor Fajardo, complaining about the poor level of fluency and reading proficiency in English from public school students, proposed strengthening English language instruction by introducing texts books written in that language (Rodríguez 1997: 6). Fajardo's ideas were controversial to say the least, but they caused an uproar when he suggested that the public school system employ teachers from the U.S. mainland, especially to teach in math and the natural sciences. As native speakers of English, it was presumed that they would be more successful in conveying the language to school children than non-native speakers (Millán 1997b: 10). In many ways the real audience for this policy proposal is not the people of Puerto Rico so much as it is the hallways of Congress. The PNP feels it must push such a policy because of the U.S. embrace of its language. While there have always been other languages in the United States, none has achieved the same level of social, political, and economic dominance as English. In the United States English towers over other languages. Examining its neighbor to the north, one sees that despite official bilingualism the same linguistic hierarchy that elevates English over other idioms prevails there as well.

NOTES

1. While the focus of this book is on linguistically distinctive ethnic minorities, many of the same principles apply to state majorities. When they feel threatened state ethnic minorities will often press the legislatures they control for relief. Recent examples of this phenomenon have been ongoing in the United States with the "English-only" and "English-first" movements. Such movements seek to fortify the hegemonic status of the English language, which they feel is threatened by the influx of non-English speakers. While English is clearly the dominant language of the United States, many federal policymakers have been reluctant to codify such a status in the form of a statute or constitutional amendment for fear of antagonizing recently naturalized citizens, many of whom are not native English speakers. Recent statements from White House officials highlighted President Bill Clinton's opposition to making English the official language of the country (Mulero 1997c: 4). Inaction at the federal level has galvanized these movements to promote their agenda at the "state" level (for more on these movements, see Baron 1990).

2. In one of the key cases defining the rights of Puerto Ricans under the U.S. Constitution, the federal Supreme Court held in 1901 that Puerto Rico, while a *possession* of the United States was not an integral *part* of it (*Downes v. Bidwell*, 182 U.S. 241, 287). By means of this ruling, the United States Supreme Court created a distinction between "incorporated territories" (which were both possessions and integral parts of the Federation, such as the District of Columbia) and "unincorporated territories" (which were not part of the Union, but merely property; belonging to it). Many contemporary scholars focus on Justice White's concurrent opinion in this case; he based his decision on the 1898 Treaty of Paris, which did not formally "incorporate" Puerto Rico. However, the formal opinion in this case was written by Justice Brown, who opposed extending the full protection of the U.S. Constitution to Puerto Rico because this island, along with the others conquered during the Spanish-American War were territories "inhabited by alien races, differing from us in religion, customs, laws, methods of taxation and modes of thought, the administration of government and justice, according to Anglo-Saxon principles" (*Downes v. Bidwell*, 182 U.S. 244, 287).

3. From the arrival of U.S. troops in 1898 until passage of the Foraker Act in 1900, Puerto Rico was ruled by the U.S. Navy.

4. In compliance with the United States Constitution (Art. 2, Sec. 2, cl. 2), these presidential appointments had to be confirmed by the federal Senate. Despite the American tradition of dividing legislative and executive responsibilities Congress created a legislative chamber (the "upper house") that also served as the "Executive Council" or Cabinet (Ramírez 1988: 64).

5. No ethnic Puerto Ricans were appointed governor of the island under the Foraker regime (1900-1917). This organic act was replaced in 1917 by the Jones Act, which was in effect until the promulgation of the 1952 Commonwealth Constitution. The only Puerto Rican appointed governor under the Jones Act was Jesús T. Piñero in 1946. The following year Congress amended the Jones Act to allow for an elected governor. Luis Muñoz Marín, the founder of the Commonwealth, was both the first elected governor in Puerto Rican history (in 1948) and the only chief executive elected under the Jones Act.

6. Official Languages Act (1902)—1 L.P.R.A. §51.

7. This law made allowances for either language in the territorial judicial system. Nonetheless, English was and still remains the sole language of the federal judiciary in Puerto Rico.

8. One should keep in mind that at this time Puerto Rico, while officially bilingual, was *de facto* a linguistically homogeneous society save for a few American bureaucrats who came to administer the territorial government.

9. *Cruz v. Domínguez*, 8 D.P.R 551, 555-556 (1905).

10. As discussed in chapter 6, pedagogues were able to link this language with Puerto Rican identity due to their access to large segments of the population, especially the future generations of adults. If the positions of teachers were threatened so would those of other Puerto Ricans who sought to enter the bureaucracy—a valued source of stable employment even in contemporary Puerto Rico.

11. Following the arrival of American troops in 1898, there have been a few established Anglophone enclaves on the island. But for the most part these are located inside or immediately surrounding military bases, which tends to isolate these communities from the general insular population. In addition, their connection with the armed forces means that most Anglophones inside these bases are stationed there for a limited period of time and thus few settle on the island.

12. The directive instating Spanish as the medium of instruction in the island's public schools did not abrogate the 1902 Official Languages Act. This law, formally asserting the equality of the two languages in all branches, departments, and agencies of the Puerto Rican government, was still on the books. Despite the existing legislation the Puerto Rican Supreme Court held in *Pueblo v. Tribunal Superior*, 92 D.P.R. 596 (1965), that henceforth Spanish would be *de facto* the sole language within the Puerto Rican judicial system. This ruling, however, had no impact on the federal court system on the island. Thus, at present, the two judicial systems in Puerto Rico (Commonwealth and federal) operate unilingually though the two do make provisions for translators.

13. Official Language Act of 1991—1 L.P.R.A. §5l, Ley Núm. 4 de 5 de abril de 1991, P. de la C. 417.

14. The label "Spanish Only" was intended to put this legislation in the same category as the various "English-only" laws passed in the past few decades in the U.S. at various local levels of government.

15. Official Language Act of 1991—1 L.P.R.A. §51, Art. 3.

16. Official Language Act of 1991—1 L.P.R.A. §51, Art. 3.

17. It is important to reiterate that under the first civilian regime in Puerto Rico under American suzerainty, the Foraker Act (1900-1917) created a bicameral legislature that was partially elected and partially appointed.

18. *Pueblo v. Tribunal Superior*, 92 D.P.R. 596 (1965).

19. Original: "No hay dudas, de que el eje de la cultura puertorriqueña es el idioma español. En esta hermosa lengua elaboramos todas las expresiones que nos caracterizan como colectividad nacional" (Delgado 1991: 603).

20. PSP—Puerto Rican Socialist party.

21. Original: "La reciente ley que convierte al español en el idioma oficial, no hay duda que tiene un carácter de afirmación nacional aún cuando en la práctica no se altere notablemente el curso de la vida puertorriqueña a partir de esa ley" (Gallisá 1991: 11).

22. Original: "El Partido Popular [Democrático] y su liderato como promotores de dicha legislación deben sentirse orgullosos y confiados de que su acción responde a la necesidad de defender nuestro idioma que es parte esencial de lo que nos define como nación caribeña y latinoamericana" (Gallisá 1991: 11).

23. PPD legislators tried to pass a bill promoting Spanish in the late 1970s (Delgado 1991: 588). However, this was a period when the legislative majority and the executive were in the hands of the pro-statehood PNP.

24. For further details see chapter 6.

25. The poll commissioned by the now defunct Puerto Rican daily *El Mundo* showed that if a plebiscite were held at that moment, the statehood option would garner 48.3 percent of the vote; commonwealth stood to win 40.6 percent; and independence about 8 percent ("Al frente la opción estadista" 1990: 3). The poll results were even more dramatic when there was a simple yes or no vote on statehood as opposed to presenting the three status alternatives. In such a yes/no plebiscite, the statehood option would win with 54 percent; 43 percent would say no to statehood; and 3 percent would be undecided ("Claman por una rápida solución" 1990: 4). This poll reportedly had a margin of error of 2.8 percent ("Se cuidaron todos los detalles" 1990: 7). The results of this poll were not that far from the results of the 1993 status plebiscite in which the commonwealth status was favored by 48 percent of the population, statehood by 46 percent, and independence by about 5 percent.

26. Within the American system Spanish remains the language of the "counter-hegemony." Nationalists in the periphery seek to make hegemonic their "counter-hegemony" within the confines of the periphery (in this case Puerto Rico) and not over the expanse of the state (in this case the United States).

27. Ironically, this organization had its advertisement published exclusively in the Spanish language.

28. Congressman Solomon's opinion on statehood and the primacy of English was publicly challenged by Luis A. Ferré, founder of the PNP and a former governor of Puerto Rico (Mulero 1993c: 11).

29. Governor Ferré also contested Buchanan's view that Puerto Rico's vernacular was an automatic impediment to statehood (Mulero 1996d: 5).

30. Official Languages Act of 1993—1 L.P.R.A. §59, Ley Núm. 1 de 28 de enero de 1993, P. de la C. 1.

31. Official Languages Act of 1993—1 L.P.R.A. §59, Art. 1.

32. Official Languages Act of 1993—1 L.P.R.A. §59, Art. 6. While it did not say so explicitly, the intent of this article apparently was to circumvent the Puerto Rican Supreme Court and its ruling in *Pueblo v. Tribunal Superior*, 92 D.P.R. 596 (1965), on the judiciary and the Spanish language.

33. This was a telephone survey of ten out of the thirty PNP mayors in office at that time. It found that most of these pro-statehood mayors and their staffs could not answer a few basic questions in English. The exceptions to this rule came from the mayors of the larger cities such as Alejandro Cruz, the chief executive of Bayamón.

34. Again, the PER, or Statehood Republican party, was the principal pro-statehood party in Puerto Rico from the 1940s through the late 1960s.

9

The Quebec National Assembly and the Promotion of French

The relative inexperience with language legislation in the Commonwealth of Puerto Rico stands in contrast to the long-term battles fought out in the Quebec provincial legislature. Debates over the standing of the French language in the public sector and private sphere have been an inherent and controversial component of Québécois political life for the past three decades. Outside of chronology and experience, there is another set of significant differences between the language laws in these two jurisdictions, and that is their social impact. Regardless of the intentions behind the 1902 and 1993 laws establishing official bilingualism, Puerto Rico remains over 95 percent Spanish speaking. The 1991 law, which presumably "promoted" Spanish, did not alter in any way, shape, or form the influence of English in the daily lives of Puerto Ricans. It did, however, succeed in fortifying the bond between Puerto Rican nationalists and the Spanish language. For the most part these Puerto Rican laws can be described as relatively "symbolic" pieces of legislation.[1]

They stand in stark contrast to the various language laws of Quebec that endeavored to enhance the role of French at the expense of English. The National Assembly became active on the language-law front, starting in the 1960s. Government involvement began with the establishment of the Office de la langue française in 1961, a provincial government agency that initially focused on "language purification" by replacing English terms with their French equivalents in various fields (Laporte 1981: 55). Then, starting in the late 1960s, the Quebec provincial legislature under various administrations passed four major pieces of legislation dealing with language: Bill 63 (1969),[2] Bill 22 (1974),[3] Bill 101 (1977),[4] and Bill 178 (1988).[5]

Prior to the 1960s Quebec's intervention in linguistic affairs was extremely limited (Laponce 1984: 51). The legislative assembly in Quebec City passed, despite strong objections from the Anglophone-dominated business community, a law in 1910 requiring public utilities to use both French and English when

communicating with the public. However, these same businessmen were successful in pressuring the provincial legislature in 1938 to repeal a law, passed the
previous year, that gave precedence to the French version of a provincial statute
over its English-language translation (Laporte 1984: 54-55; Levine 1990: 35). In
the first half of the twentieth century, entrepreneurs from this linguistic minority
effectively demonstrated the supremacy of the English language, even in a
French-majority province.

Regardless of their many differences, the language laws in both Puerto Rico
and Quebec do share one important trait. The two sets of laws recognize the hegemonic position of the English language in Anglo-North America. Both also
define their collective identities, at least partially, on the basis of the "other"
language—the language of the counter-hegemony. In their quest to fortify the
French language's standing, the National Assembly in Quebec City has drafted
laws affecting four major areas: the symbolic status of French in Quebec, public
signs, the language of the workplace, and schools. In each area the point of the
lawmaker was to enhance French by restricting English.

SYMBOLIC PRONOUNCEMENT OF "FRENCH" QUEBEC

Symbolism is one aspect that the language laws of Quebec and Puerto Rico
share. It may have little more than cosmetic value, but nonetheless it serves as an
admonition that the group in question is conscious of its existence and that its
uniqueness is based, at least partially, on certain cultural traits. Symbolic declarations represent the first step in the attempt to establish a counter-hegemonic
order. Two of Quebec's languages laws, Bill 22 (1974) and Bill 101 (1977),
have been the clearest with regard to defining Québécoisness on the basis of the
French language. The preamble to Bill 22 stated that the French language was a
national heritage and that the provincial government had a right to preserve and
promote it.[6] The first article of the statute established French as the province's
official language.[7] Government agencies would hereafter be designated strictly
by their French names.[8] It is rather interesting to note that this law embraced
French as the idiom of both the people and its government in contrast to the
Puerto Rican language laws that restricted their scope only to the governmental
sphere. Additionally, Bill 22 gave the French version of a statute precedence
over its English counterpart.[9] It mandated the publication of all official documents in the French language.[10] Contracts had to be drawn up in French though
they could be accompanied by an English translation.[11] Bill 22 was enacted by
the federalist Liberal party in an attempt to placate Quebec nationalists. As the
product of a nonseparatist party, the drafters of this law were reluctant to promote French any further, fearing the alienation of the province's influential Anglophone minority and their supporters in the federal parliament.

Bill 22 was followed by Bill 101, one of the earliest legislative products of
the Parti Québécois (PQ). In terms of legislation affecting language, this statute
represents the centerpiece of the PQ's cultural agenda. Like its predecessor Bill

101 also declared French the official language of the provincial government and its people.[12] However, Bill 101 went even further than Bill 22 by stating that only the French version of a bill was official.[13] Such provisions in Bill 101, coupled with those in Bill 22, clearly benefited those Francophone professionals whose work requires a thorough knowledge of the law. In terms of the language of the people, Bill 101 surpassed the scope of Bill 22 by enumerating a list of linguistic rights. They ranged from the right to receive government services, to obtain goods and services in the private sector, to speak, and to receive an education in the French language.[14]

In fact, at the time Bill 101 was enacted, these goods and services were already available in the French language. The incorporation of these particular provisions in Bill 101 was not designed to change the linguistic *status quo* but to provide an official podium from which the French language could be acknowledged as the common medium of the people and government of this jurisdiction. It was an act of defiance against Quebec's powerful English-speaking society. Bill 101 was also an attempt to codify the counter-hegemonic order, which asserted the French language's primacy within Quebec. Laws such as this one, which merely make pronouncements without intending to modify behavior, are little more than symbolic statements, designed to appease one segment of society or another. Again, this was as far as the Puerto Rican language laws went. In this case the societal segment that the Quebec lawmakers wanted to appease were the province's nationalists. It would be left to other statutory provisions to institute fundamental change.

THE PUBLIC FACE OF QUEBEC

Related to symbolic declarations is the issue of public advertisements and signs. On the one hand laws affecting the idiom used on public signs are symbolic in that they reassure linguistically based nationalists that the jurisdiction in question is "theirs." Evidence of their "ownership" is evident by observing the preponderance of their language. Whereas symbolic declarations restate the *status quo*, or project a hope for the future, restrictions on language usage on public signs are designed to institute change. Reforms of this kind not only affect selected individuals and the public expression of their ideas, but also the business community, which relies on public signs for advertisement. Mandates affecting public signs and the language of the workplace represent two areas in Anglophone-dominated corporate life that the Quebec provincial government endeavored to affect. Additionally, a Quebec covered in French language signs would serve as another incentive for Anglophones and others to acquire at least a working knowledge of French.

The first law altering the public face of Quebec was Bill 22. It required public signs to be drawn up solely in French: however, signs posted in English or other languages would still be legal so long as they were accompanied by French.[15] The one enumerated exception was newspaper advertisements, which could still be issued in a non-French language.[16] Bill 22's sign provisions, as was the case with many other areas, were overridden by Bill 101. The Charter of the French Language stated that signs, posters, and commercial advertising had to be published solely in French.[17] Exemptions to that rule were allowed for the media, religious messages, political advertising, or advertisements printed by nonprofit and humanitarian organizations.[18] Firms with fewer than five employees could erect signs in a non-French language so long as they were accompanied by a French-language translation that was supposed to dominate over the non-French version.[19] The point of Bill 101's sign provisions was to make Quebec "look French."

The constitutionality of these provisions was challenged by Quebec Anglophones in a case eventually heard by the Canadian Supreme Court. It was argued in *Ford v. Québec*[20] that the sign regulations contained in Bill 101 were a violation of Quebec's provincial Charter of Human Rights[21] and the federal constitution's Charter of Rights and Freedoms,[22] which protected an individual's right to free expression. The high court agreed.[23] Regarding the issue of language in general, the court said that the idiom one chose was a fundamental component of the basic right to express oneself: "Language is so intimately related to the form and content of expression that there cannot be the freedom of expression by means of language if one is prohibited from using the language of one's choice. Language is not merely a means or medium of expression: it colours the content and meaning of expression."[24] A requirement that signs be bilingual, even giving a "predominance" to the French version, would have been acceptable to the court,[25] but a ban on non-French languages was not. While the court asserted that its decision was based on a concern for protecting the rights of individuals, including corporations, one cannot escape the reality that the power of the English language in North America is such that even in a bilingual city, such as Montreal, English is still the hegemonic language. That point was not lost to French nationalists, who demanded that the Quebec provincial government counteract the high court's decision.

Quebec's chief executive, Premier Robert Bourassa, responded to the court's ruling on *Ford v. Québec* by enacting another piece of legislation—Bill 178.[26] Rather than accept the judiciary's holding on Bill 101, the legislature in Quebec City decided to alter it. This new law amended the Charter of the French language so that signs outside an establishment were still required be printed exclusively in French while signs inside an establishment could appear in both French and another language.[27] With this statute Premier Bourassa hoped to placate both French nationalists, with the "outside" provisions of the law, and English-language-rights activists by allowing their language on bilingual signs inside establishments. Based on the Supreme Courts earlier decision in *Ford v. Québec*, there was no chance that this revised version would pass constitutional scrutiny. What the provincial government did in order to avoid a court challenge was to invoke the *notwithstanding clause* of Canada's 1982 Constitution.[28]

The *notwithstanding clause* was designed to balance the principle of parliamentary supremacy found in the British model of governance with a written constitution that would invest the courts with the power of judicial review. Section 33 of the Constitution gave both the federal and provincial legislatures the capacity to enact laws that otherwise infringed on individual rights.[29] Once invoked the legislation in question would, after five years, cease to have effect.[30] At that time either the federal or provincial legislature would have the option of renewing the statute.[31] The Quebec provincial legislature invoked this clause in order to pass a law that knowingly violated the freedom of expression protections found in the federal Charter of Rights and Freedoms.

The invocation of this clause by a stridently separatist government might not be surprising. Yet, one of the most remarkable aspects of this law was its enactment by a National Assembly dominated by the Quebec Liberal party—a party openly committed to keeping Quebec within the Confederation. Despite its commitment to preserving Quebec's provincial status, the Liberals chose to draft a statute that openly defied a fundamental right entrenched in the federal constitution and in so doing alienated a core constituency in their party—Quebec Anglophones and allophones.[32] The actions taken by this non-separatist party indicate the grip that language has on Québécois society. Even non-separatists recognize the importance of defening the French language. Protecting the collective rights of Francophones took precedence over the individual rights of non-French speakers. This indicates that the French counter-hegemony within Canada is becoming hegemonic within the confines of Quebec's provincial boundaries.

THE LANGUAGE OF WORK

Besides symbolic declarations and public signs, Quebec language laws have been written specifically to augment the power of Francophones in the workplace, both in the private and public sectors, by mandating the use of their language in various fields. Most of the larger enterprises in postagrarian Quebec, even in Montreal, were owned and operated by Anglophones. Some professional positions were opened to Francophones in these businesses prior to the Quiet Revolution. However, most were reserved for Anglophones—a policy that maintained the elite status of Quebec's English-speaking minority at the expense of well-qualified Francophones. Privilege and economic mobility encouraged English-speaking families to preserve their language despite living in an overwhelmingly French-speaking province for generations (Kaplan 1994: 58). Thus, one of the goals of the new professional class in the 1960s was to overturn this historic arrangement and open the doors of corporate Quebec to French-speaking professionals. Analyzing the period known as the Quiet Revolution and its relationship to the language debate in Quebec, Levine said:

Inevitably, the central theme of the Quiet Revolution—to make Francophones *'maîtres chez nous'* (masters in our own house)—politicized issues of language in Montreal. Francophones could never be '*maîtres chez nous*' if Montreal, the urban center of French-speaking Quebec, remained as it was: a city in which Anglophones—and the English language—were a dominant force. Thus, the logic of the Quiet Revolution inexorably led to a movement to dislodge the Anglophone elite and 'reconquer' Montreal as the metropole of French-speaking Quebec. (Levine 1990: 40) [emphasis in the original]

Language came into the forefront of Quebec political life during this period. However, one should understand that this was a *reaction* to the linguistic barriers imposed by Anglo-Quebec.

The "Reconquest of Montreal," as Levine (1990) put it, acknowledged that one powerful sector—Canadian Anglophone and American businesses—operated under a system whereby their economic strength dictated language policies in the office and corporate boardroorn. Opening up opportunities for Francophones in these firms would require a champion with the strength and will to challenge corporate Quebec. Traditionally French Canadians turned to the Catholic church, which served as the great bodyguard that protected the interests of French Canadians. However, the Church was opposed to any policies that would promote further urbanization—a process that exposed French Canadians to "nontraditional" ideas. The Quiet Revolution would require another sponsor.

Quebecers could turn to the federal government in Ottawa. The advantage to any federal legislation is that it would apply throughout all ten provinces and thus strengthen the position of the portions of French Canada outside of Quebec's boundaries. Some pointed to the passage of the Official Languages Act of 1969, a statute that symbolically declared all of Canada officially bilingual and instituted bilingual policies at the federal level, as an example of concern at the federal level for protecting French language rights throughout the country.[33] Yet, appealing to the government in Ottawa had its drawbacks as this level of government was dominated by English-speaking Canadians. In the halls of Parliament, French nationalists would have to fight Anglophone Quebecers, their allies outside of the province, and English Canadian business interests. As evidence of their influence, the 1969 act, while it did provide greater opportunities for Francophones within the federal bureaucracy, did not institute any significant changes in the private sector workplace. After all, this was not a level of government that Francophones controlled. Passing any federal legislation would require compromising with various interests and in these negotiations Francophones had no guarantee of winning. On the other hand Francophones could turn to the provincial level of government in Quebec. At least here the French language was dominant and presumably these legislators would be more inclined to respond to the needs of a new upwardly mobile class bent upon challenging the supremacy of English as the corporate medium of communication.

The 1974 Official Language Act (Bill 22) set off to establish French as the language of the workplace within the public sector. The provincial government would conduct its day-to-day affairs in the French language. Such a legal mandate assured Francophones of one sector of the economy that they could monopolize. The provincial administration was required to use French when communicating with other governments within the province and with the Canadian federal government.[34] Appointment to the administration required an "appropriate" knowledge of French.[35] Keeping in mind that members of dominant groups rarely learn the languages of subordinate groups, these clauses in the 1974 law would, in fact, maintain the provincial government as a Francophone bastion.

Many of these same protections for French speakers within the provincial bureaucracy were reiterated three years later in Bill 101—the Charter of the French Language.[36] Where Bill 101 departed from Bill 22 was in expanding the use of the French language, deep into corporate Quebec. Traditionally large corporations conducted their daily affairs, including employer-employee relations, in English. Such a policy put the "bilingual burden" on Francophones since their ascendancy would require fluency in English, even in their own province. Bill 101 sought to reverse that encumbrance. As of 1977, even private sector employees could not be dismissed solely because they were monolingual Francophones.[37] On the other hand the statute extended no such protections to monolingual Anglophones.

Despite the protections that this legislation afforded Francophones, there are a few realities in the Quebec business world that provincial legislation cannot effectively alter. Commerce in Quebec involves interacting with English-speaking Canada, the United States, and many other countries. Add to that a provision that requires employer-employee communication, including job offers and promotions, to be conducted in French.[38] These stipulations in Bill 101 promoted Francophones into the private sector and protected them once inside from dismissal on account of their vernacular. But dealings with the English-speaking world obligated middle and upper management to have a fairly strong command of the English language (Miller 1984: 125). The power of the English language is such that even with statutory protection French speakers must still learn English if they want to climb the corporate ladder.

Again, the goal of Bill 101 was to make French hegemonic within provincial boundaries. Legislation is always limited to the furthest extent of a jurisdiction's territorial boundaries. Inevitably the protections afforded to Francophones by Bill 101 and its counterparts have no bearing on the Francophone communities in Ontario, New Brunswick, or other parts of Canada. As a result these laws, especially Bills 22 and 101, have strengthened the bonds between Francophones in Quebec and their provincial government—the only administrative level they could rely upon to protect and promote their linguistic interests.

FRENCH IN THE CLASSROOM

To the symbolic declarations, the public signs, and the stipulations for linguistic promotion within both governmental and nongovernmental institutions, one must add the elaborate efforts that various provincial regimes have made to expand the preeminence of the French language in schools. There are two major interrelated concerns that underlie the language and school debate. One is to protect the positions of Francophone teachers and the educational bureaucracy. The second is concern over the future of Francophones themselves. The two are related in that a decline in the number, or the proportion, of Francophones in the long run would diminish the need for French-language services, both public and private. A decreased need for French-language services invariably would reduce the necessity to hire personnel fluent in the language. Such a change could affect the current generation and would definitely impact the economic and social outlooks of the forthcoming generation of Quebec Francophones. Therefore, demographic changes have prompted the National Assembly to regulate the medium of instruction in school settings.

Population growth was not a concern of pre-Quiet Revolution Quebec. Until the mid-1960s Francophones had a higher birthrate than either Anglophones or allophones (Harrison & Marmen 1994: 52). Their demographic strength led many to suggest the possibility of a French reconquest of Canada, referred to as *la revanche des berceaux*, the revenge of the cradle. Not only did Francophones have a higher birthrate than all other major linguistic groups, but their numeric strength was fostered by the large number of allophones attending French-medium schools. Most allophone parents, until the 1950s, sent their children to schools that taught in the French language (Laporte 1981: 59). All of these factors benefited the Francophone community.

It was in the 1950s that this state of affairs began to change. A study of Italian immigrants in Montreal, the province's largest allophone community, detailed these changing patterns (Boissevain 1970: 38). Until the early 1950s about equal numbers of parents sent their children to French- and English-medium schools. However, by the middle of that decade, over 60 percent of Italian parents had decided to send their children to English-medium schools. By the early 1960s that percentage rose to 75 percent (Boissevain 1970: 38). When asked to explain their decision to send their children to English-medium schools, the two most frequent responses were that this particular language facilitated mobility and the search for employment (Boissevain 1970: 38). These parents recognized that education in this language facilitated fluency in a medium that would promote their children's upward mobility in Quebec and the rest of North America.

Coupled with this shift in school preferences was a change in birthrates. Immigrant birthrates did not rise, but the Francophone rate dropped. By the late 1960s the Francophone birthrate was still higher than that found in the Anglophone community; however, it was lower than that found among allophones (Harrison & Marmen 1994: 52). Francophone Quebec was looking at an enlarging allophone community that, due to its pedagogical choices, was acquiring English over French as its new vernacular. Some of the more pessimistic or alarmist studies indicated that without a radical change in the course of events the Francophone population of Quebec, which was over 80 percent, could fall to under 72 percent by the year 2000 (Caldwell 1974: 15). Public debate, starting in the late 1960s, talked about the possible *"minorisation"* of Francophones in Quebec and specifically in Montreal (Levine 1990: 62).

Given these concerns it should not be surprising that the first major conflicts over immigrant access to English-language schools erupted in St. Léonard, a heavily Italian suburb of Montreal (d'Anglejan 1984: 36). French nationalists were after assurances that more allophones would attend French-language schools. In their battle over educational policy these nationalists were confronted by a combined force of allophone parents and members of the Anglophone community who saw this as an issue of parental choice. The response of the Union Nationale, the governing party of the time, was the passage of Bill 63. Thanks to this law Quebec's minister of education was obliged to make sure that children who attended English-language schools had a "working knowledge" of French.[39] However, this statute would not force allophones to send their children to schools that taught in French. Immigrant parents "might" send their children to Francophone schools, but it was not mandatory.[40] The voluntary provisions of the law made this a purely symbolic piece of legislation in terms of its effect. But it also served as the first step towards mandating French language instruction.

Round two began with the educational provisions of Bill 22. Whereas allophone parents had the option of sending their children to English- or French-medium schools under Bill 63, they were now required to send their progeny to French-language schools.[41] Regardless of the language of instruction, pupils were still required to "acquire a knowledge of spoken and written French."[42] Premier Bourassa's Liberal government hoped to placate French nationalists with this legislation. But, as far as Quebec nationalists were concerned, Bill 22 did not go far enough since it provided allophones with an "escape" from the mandatory provisions of this law.

School choice was still an option if the child demonstrated "sufficient knowledge" in either of the two established languages, and that evaluation would be left up to the local school boards.[43] In order to bypass the intent of this law immigrant organizations set up "clandestine classes" so that four- and five-year old allophones would be able to pass the board evaluation, thus allowing them into English-language classrooms (Levine 1990: 105). In addition, liberal exemptions were made in many individual cases. Bill 22's ineffectiveness was demonstrated by the fact that the vast majority of non-English- and non-French-speaking pupils were still able to enroll in English-medium schools (Levine 1990: 105). Despite the fact that most allophones were still enrolling in English-medium schools, Quebec's English-language press attacked the Liberal party's law as an unfair restriction on individual liberties. In the end the controversy over Bill 22, while intense, did not last long as it was replaced only three years later with the Parti Québécois' Bill 101.

The Charter of the French Language represents the most recent change in Quebec's educational laws. This statute went much further than either one of its forerunners in terms of pedagogical policy. Unlike Bills 63 and 22, which began with the premise that the provincial educational system had two branches—one in each language—Bill 101 was founded on a unilingual assumption.[44] Elementary and secondary education would henceforth be in the French language.[45] There were a few exceptions.[46] But for the most part they were designed in such a way as to only exempt Quebec's established Anglophone community. Immigrants, even if fluent in English, would have to educate their children in the French language. The hope was that in time these allophones would become Francophones. In addition, school boards that did not provide instruction in English before this law went into effect were not required to subsequently introduce it.[47] Thus, English-language instruction would not necessarily follow any future Anglophone settlements in formerly Francophone areas. Bill 101's intent was not only to safeguard the standing of Francophones in the 1970s, but also to provide for a future Quebec that would be French.

In the area of education, Bill 101 represented the apex of French nationalist plans for the Francization of Quebec. It was passed in 1977 in the wake of two other language laws, both passed by non-separatist parties. Both Bill 63, passed by the autonomist Union Nationale, and Bill 22, enacted under the leadership of the federalist Liberal party, were designed to placate more militant nationalists while trying to avoid a direct confrontation with the province's powerful Anglophone community. In the end even the framers of Bill 101 decided not to tackle Quebec Anglophones. As manifested in their legislative actions, even a separatist regime could not ignore the backing this minority had in the rest of Canada. The Parti Québécois' assimilative plans were instead aimed directly at immigrants. After all, newcomers were socially, economically, and politically far less powerful than the established English-speaking community. In addition they also had higher birthrates; thus, they represented the greater source of a "potential demographic threat."

The point of these language laws was to strengthen the current role and future viability of the Francophone community. At the same time they underscored the tremendous influence of the English language not only in the other nine provinces but even within the *patrie*. Strengthening French in Quebec could only come about with the simultaneous weakening of English. In this sense the politics of language and nationalism is a zero-sum game. Yet even here French nationalists were aware that they could only push their English community so far. This was particularly evident in the battle over language in the classroom, which targeted *potential* Anglophones as opposed to current ones.

At the same time, the activism of the Quebec National Assembly (coupled with the accelerated linguistic assimilation of Francophones outside Quebec) has fundamentally redefined the language debate in Canada. In the past the battle over linguistic rights was a contest between English and French Canada. These two entities, while territorially concentrated, did not coincide with any established administrative units. Quebec may have constituted the single largest portion of French Canada but the two terms were not synonymous. To a large degree the struggle over linguistic rights is now defined in terms of Quebec versus the Anglophone provinces. In contrast to the language debates of the past, this conflict is defined in terms of cultural units that also coincide with administrative ones—provinces.

The importance of this redefinition is in facilitating the quest for greater autonomy. In the modern contest it is difficult to envision autonomy for a vaguely defined cultural unit, even less so independence. Autonomy, either in modest amounts or in the form of full-fledged sovereignty, requires a territorial and political base from which to operate. French Canada, in that sense, did not and could not constitute such a base. It cut across provincial lines, which also meant that discussing cultural autonomy or rights entailed negotiating with the federal government and several provincial regimes. Most of these governments had Anglophone majorities and a vested interest in maintaining the existing federal structure. Nationalism in Canada is now largely seen as a conflict between Quebec City and Ottawa. In this political game, one Francophone-majority government faces one Anglophone-majority government. The Province of Quebec provides that territorial and political receptacle that autonomy needs to function and flourish. At the same time the province, with an existing bureaucracy, has in place the administrative apparatus that would be needed to administer sovereignty.

NOTES

1. The 1902 Official Languages Act, a rather symbolic statute in and of itself, can be contrasted with the rulings of the Puerto Rican Supreme Court that promoted English over Spanish and the formal policy of Americanization, which was advanced by the federal government and its appointed bureaucrats on the island. For further details see the previous chapter.

2. Bill 63 (Act to Promote the French Language)—S.Q. 1969, c. 9.

3. Bill 22 (Official Language Act)—S.Q. 1974, c. 6.

4. Bill 101 (Charter of the French Language)—R.S.Q. 1977, c. C-11.

5. Bill 178 (Act to Amend the Charter of the French Language)—S.Q. 1988, c. 54.

6. Bill 22 (Official Language Act)—S.Q. 1974, c. 6, Preamble.

7. Bill 22 (Official Language Act)—S.Q. 1974, c. 6, Art. 1.

8. Bill 22 (Official Language Act)—S.Q. 1974, c. 6, Art. 11.

9. Bill 22 (Official Language Act)—S.Q. 1974, c. 6, Art. 2.

10. Bill 22 (Official Language Act)—S.Q. 1974, c. 6, Art. 6.

11. Bill 22 (Official Language Act)—S.Q. 1974, c. 6, Art. 17.

12. Bill 101 (Charter of the French Language)—R.S.Q. 1977, c. C-11, Preamble, Arts. 1 and 7.

13. Bill 101 (Charter of the French Language)—R.S.Q. 1977, c. C-11, Art. 9.

14. Bill 101 (Charter of the French Language)—R.S.Q. 1977, c. C-11, Arts. 2-6.

15. Bill 22 (Official Language Act)—S.Q. 1974, c. 6, Art. 35.

16. Bill 22 (Official Language Act)—S.Q. 1974, c. 6. Art. 36.

17. Bill 101 (Charter of the French Language)—R.S.Q. 1977, c. C-11, Art. 58.

18. Bill 101 (Charter of the French Language)—R.S.Q. 1977, c. C-11, Art. 59.

19. Bill 101 (Charter of the French Language)—R.S.Q. 1977, c. C-11. Art. 60.

20. *Ford v. Québec (Attorney General)*, [1988] 2. S.C.R. 712.

21. Charter of Human Rights and Freedoms, R.S.Q., C-12.

22. Section 2(b) of the Charter stated: "Everyone has the . . . freedom of thought, belief, opinion and expression, including freedom of the press and other media of communication" (Canadian Charter of Rights and Freedoms, Canada Act, 1982 [U.K.], c. 11, Schedule B, s. 2).

23. *Ford v. Québec (Attorney General)*, [1988] 2. S.C.R. 712, 767.

24. *Ford v. Québec (Attorney General)*, [1988] 2. S.C.R. 712, 748.

25. *Ford v. Québec (Attorney General)*, [1988] 2. S.C.R. 712, 780.

26. Bill 178 (Act to Amend the Charter of the French Language)—S.Q. 1988. c. 54.

27. Bill 178 (Act to Amend the Charter of the French Language)—S.Q. 1988. c. 54, Art. 1.

28. Bill 178 (Act to Amend the Charter of the French Language)—S.Q. 1988. c. 51. Art. 10.

29. Canadian Charter of Rights and Freedoms, Canada Act, 1982 (U.K.) c. 11, Schedule B, s. 33.

30. Canadian Charter of Rights and Freedoms, Canada Act, 1982 (U.K.) c. 11, Schedule B, s. 33(3).

31. Canadian Charter of Rights and Freedoms, Canada Act, 1982 (U.K.) c. 11, Schedule B, s. 33(4).

32. In reaction to Bourassa's policies, a group of Anglophone Liberals broke ranks with their party and formed their own—the Equality party (Levine 1990: 137).

33. Official Languages Act—S.C. 1968-1969, c. 53; R.S.C. 1970. c. 0-2.

34. Bill 22 (Official Language Act)—S.Q. 1974, c. 6, Art. 10.

35. Bill 22 (Official Language Act)—S.Q. 1974. c. 6, Art. 11.

36. Bill 101 (Charter of the French Language)—R.S.Q. 1977, c. C-11, Arts. 7-20.

37. Bill 101 (Charter of the French Language)—R.S.Q. 1977, c. C-11, Art. 45.

38. Bill 101 (Charter of the French Language)—R.S.Q. 1977, c. C-11, Art. 41.

39. Bill 63 (Act to Promote the French Language)—S.Q. 1969, c. 9, Art. 1.

40. Bill 63 (Act to Promote the French Language)—S.Q. 1969. c. 9, Art. 3.

41. Bill 22 (Official Language Act)—S.Q. 1974, c. 6, Art. 41.

42. Bill 22 (Official Language Act)—S.Q. 1974, c. 6, Art. 44.

43. Bill 22 (Official Language Act)—S.Q. 1974, c. 6, Art. 42.

44. The one minor exception to this norm was a recognition of the Cree and Kativik communities. These school boards would still be allowed to provide education in their respective indigenous languages. Bill 101 (Charter of the French Language)—R.S.Q. 1977, c. C-11, Art. 88.

45. Bill 101 (Charter of the French Language)—R.S.Q. 1977, c. C-11, Art. 72.

46. The exceptions referred to children whose parents received elementary instruction in English in Quebec, or whose parents received elementary instruction in English outside Quebec so long as they lived in Quebec at the time when the law came into effect, or who received instruction in English in Quebec in the last school year before the law took effect, or were a younger sibling of those who received instruction in English in Quebec in the last school year before the law took effect. Bill 101 (Charter of the French Language)—R.S.Q. 1977, c. C-11. Art. 73.

47. Bill 101 (Charter of the French Language)—R.S.Q. 1977, c. C-11, Art. 79.

10

Conclusion

Whether in the American Commonwealth of Puerto Rico or the Canadian Province of Quebec, the existence of strong nationalist movements in these jurisdictions serve to refute the notion that nationalism was confined to newly emerging states in the developing world. In and of themselves levels of social and economic development neither retard nor promote nationalism. Nationalism, the demand for rights and greater political autonomy based upon ethnic group membership, can exist just as easily in developed societies as in developing ones. Perhaps the greatest difference between these two sets of countries is the manner in which they respond to the nationalist challenge. Most advanced industrial societies, which are also liberal democracies, have shown in the last half of this century a greater tolerance toward nationalist movements, even meeting some nationalist demands, than is often the case with their counterparts in the developing world.

Trepidation by many governments to even hear the petitions of nationalist leaders stems from the very demands nationalists make on their respective states. In its more moderate manifestation, nationalists ask for some type of cultural autonomy within a specified region. Such regions have varying degrees of autonomy but remain under the ultimate jurisdiction of the host state. In more extreme circumstances the nationalist leaders in question may ask or demand the establishment of a separate, ethnically defined country, which would inevitably involve the dismemberment of the existing state. Over the years both the U.S. and Canadian governments have been compelled to contend with both autonomists and separatists in their respective cultural peripheries. Secessionist rebellions were crushed in both countries in the nineteenth century. However, the United States finally acceded to Filipino independence and the Canadian federal government has given aboriginal peoples in some parts of the country varying degrees of local rule.

The sentiment that binds members of a nation or ethnic group is a sense of common ancestry. This myth, promoted and perpetuated by elites within the group, alleges that group members pertain to one extended family; thus, fidelity to the ethnic group is a natural extension of loyalty to the family. While differing cultures and cultural traits can exist in isolation, ethnicity cannot. Ethnic classification is by its very nature a comparative endeavor. Ethnic consciousness exists where one group acknowledges that it differs from another. For there to be an "us," there must also be, simultaneously, a "them."

By the term "elite" we understand not just the members of the bourgeoisie but all those who hold a monopoly over, or dominate, vital social or economic resources. Members of the bourgeoisie by this definition, belong to the elite stratum of society as a result of their control over capital or land—both critical resources. By the same logic intellectuals are also elites in that they command the world of knowledge. Their expertise can be translated into an economic asset. However, their primary impact on nationalist movements is their critical role in disseminating the group's ethnic historical and genealogical "myths" to the masses. Their high social status, derived from their educational achievements, gives their version of past events a credence not shared by those belonging to the capital- or land-owning classes.

Intellectuals in general have been critical to the growth of nationalism in both Puerto Rico and Quebec. It should thus not be surprising that among the uppermost issues on their nationalist agendas has been pedagogical reform. The Teachers Association in Puerto Rico fought the U.S. government's policy of "Americanization," which put restrictions, and at times banned, the teaching of school subjects in Spanish. Top on the Parti Québécois' list of reforms was education whereby immigrants to the province were required to send their children to schools that taught in French. In both cases the resulting policy changes served not only to enhance the nationalist cause but also to safeguard the careers of these street-level bureaucrats whose positions were threatened by the domination of English—the dominant language in both the United States and Canada.

Elites turn to the nationalist ideology either when their upward mobility in society is hampered because of their group membership or when their group membership makes them a target of repression and discrimination. Elites point to one or more objective cultural traits as evidence of their group's uniqueness. Among the traits found in such lists are religion, folk traditions, physical traits, and language. In both the Puerto Rican and Québécois cases, language has become the most commonly touted characteristic used to distinguish locals from the dominant English-speaking community of North America in the twentieth century. The decision to embrace the Spanish and French languages by Puerto Rican and Québécois elites, respectively, was encouraged by their sense of discrimination—a discrimination based on the medium of communication. Neither Puerto Rican nor Québécois nationalists could have succeeded in promoting a nationalist agenda, based on protecting their respective vernaculars were it not for the discrimination they experienced—a discrimination based on their language.

Despite the importance of elites, the nationalist ideology cannot flourish without the participation of a broad spectrum of its society. For high-ranking members of an ethnic group, their privileges in social, economic, and political terms remain intact when they embrace the nationalist cause. Society's leaders become leaders of the nation, thus explaining their enthusiasm for the nationalist cause. By analogy, if the nation is an extended family then the nationalist leaders are its parents. Lower-ranking members of a society will embrace the nationalist cause when they are convinced that it is in their best interest. Nationalism does not change the class standing of the masses but does alter their social standing. Lower-class individuals under the nationalist rubric remain in the lower classes, but now acquire a higher social standing. After all, lower-class members of a given society usually command fewer technical skills, thus facilitating their replacement by equally experienced members of rival ethnic groups. Nationalism provides lower-class members of a society with a means of safeguarding their vulnerable positions and privileges.

Nationalism is more than an ideology, it is also a social contract. The crux of the *nationalist covenant* is that the group's elites shall continue to enjoy a guiding role in the course of the nation. The lower-class members of the same group promise their allegiance in exchange for preserving their access to the social and economic rewards that come with membership in the new "dominant" group—even if the group is dominant only in the state's periphery. In addition, the nationalist covenant offers lower-class members of the group the hope that their children might, with the appropriate education, join the ranks of the upper-class members of their ethnic group. Upwardly mobile elites were at the forefront of the Puerto Rican and Québécois nationalist movements as they sought access to rights and privileges that they deemed alienable. In both cases the respective nationalist movements were fueled by new waves of college-educated individuals whose upward mobility was hampered as a direct result of their language. Nationalism's champions were frustrated "new elites." Not only did they claim that the nation was at risk due to policies and practices from the elites in the dominant Anglophone society, but they also warned that future generations of Puerto Ricans and Quebecers were at risk from cultural assimilation and continued economic subjugation.

Elites commonly use language to define their group membership because of its rather unique properties. The standardization of a language requires the selection of one dialect over all others to become the official, and thus "correct," version. Elites in general, and members of the intelligentsia in particular, are among the most literate individuals in any society. They are also among the most affluent. Their literacy, combined with their financial capacity to publish newspapers and books, gives them the advantage in selecting their particular dialect as the official medium of communication. It is, in fact, a cultural trait that they control. Defining a group on the basis of its language promotes the group's intelligentsia just as characterizing a collective on the basis of its religion aggrandizes the power of its clerics.

Additionally, languages naturally act as barriers to communication. Communicating across groups will require fluency in at least two languages. Here again elites have the advantage. Access to education, which once more is associated with relative prosperity, affords one the opportunity to learn other languages. This condition is particularly beneficial to elites in the periphery or who belong to subaltern groups. Dominant society elites, due to their social and economic standing, have little incentive to learn the languages of subalterns. On the other hand peripheral elites must use their vernacular to communicate with the masses and must also learn the language of the dominant society's elites in order to speak with their class-counterparts. As a result, subaltern elites, more frequently than other segments of society, become the bilingual intermediaries between their masses and another group's elites. Well-educated Puerto Ricans and their counterparts in Quebec are much more likely to be fluent in English, the dominant language in North America, than their less-educated ethnic brethren. Despite their fluency in the dominant society's language, this bilingual coterie has been at the forefront of defending the linguistic rights and privileges of Spanish and French speakers, respectively.

Language, while frequently used to distinguish ethnic groups, is not an indispensable element in the definition of one group vis-à-vis another. Separate identities persisted among Serbian, Croatian, and Slavic Muslim communities despite the existence of a common medium of communication. There are many examples where nationalist sentiments persisted, contrary to the assumption of culturalists, despite the loss of a distinctive vernacular such as those in Britain's "Celtic Periphery." In the two cases highlighted here, language became a politically relevant issue only in this century. Catholicism was a far more important dividing line between Canada's two major linguistic communities than language in the eighteenth and nineteenth centuries. In nineteenth-century Puerto Rico both the local population and its colonial rulers from Spain shared the same vernacular. A linguistically based ethnic definition in both cases was fueled by policies from English speakers in both the United States and Canada.

Additionally, the rational choice argument, in particular its cultural-division-of-labor variant, has serious problems explaining the growth of nationalism in both Puerto Rico and Quebec. Throughout this century the Puerto Rican economy has remained peripheral to that of the United States. Yet, despite this consistently unequal economic relationship, nationalist sentiments have oscillated from one period to another. In contrast, Quebec has been an integral part of the Canadian economy. Notwithstanding its preeminent role in Canada's development and economic life, Quebec nationalism has also fluctuated in different periods. As one author suggested, it is not so much the division of labor between the center and the periphery as it is the division of labor *within* the periphery. In both Puerto Rico and Quebec, English speakers clearly outranked Spanish and French speakers, respectively.

The association between Americans and the English language began prior to their break with the British Crown. Early American political leaders helped in this effort by branding non-Anglophones as "outsiders" and even, ironically, disloyal to the empire. Their primary target was German-speaking leaders who refused to cooperate in military campaigns against various indigenous tribes. German legislative resistance hampered efforts at western expansion and in so doing threatened the financial enhancement of English-speaking elites. The response of these early American leaders was to embrace the English language as a group trait. This proposal became hegemonic at the point where no mainstream political actor dared to question the "common sense" nature of this proposal.

Evidence of the acceptance of this norm could be seen in laws requiring fluency in English in order to attain citizenship, the requirement that candidates for "statehood" be English speaking or be willing to implement linguistic assimilation programs, and finally the federal government's policy of exporting cultural and linguistic assimilation to non-Anglophone overseas territories such as the Philippines and Puerto Rico. To be American was to be English speaking. The country's Supreme Court rulings on the *Insular Cases* fortified this "us/them" distinction by relegating overseas territories as "unincorporated" and their mainland, English speaking counterparts as "incorporated" territories.

A parallel scenario was underway in Canada. In the eighteenth and early nineteenth centuries the *Canadien* label was used for French speakers. Anglophones referred to themselves as the *British*. The British of Canada distinguished themselves from the French both on the basis of their Protestant faith and the English language. In their words the French were not just a distinctive culture but constituted a different *race*. Among the most strident proponents of the division of the two communities were former Americans, the United Empire Loyalists, who migrated north where they would remain the King's subjects along with British businessmen in Upper Canada (modern-day Quebec). Their ire at the French was animated by the parliamentary tactics of the French—a series of actions designed to obstruct both Anglophone settlement of, and Anglophone investment in, Lower Canada. In the aftermath of the 1837 Rebellion, French Canada's ascending business elites were crushed. Their prestige and influence was inherited by the country's Roman Catholic clergy, who oversaw a rural society in which their Francophone parishioners played a subservient role in the Canadian economy. As the paramount elites of French Canada, clerics would help define their group identity more on the basis of religion than their vernacular.

Analogous to the American requirement that future "states" of the Union be English speaking, Canadian federal policies encumbered attempts at giving the French language an institutional foothold in the western provinces. The most blatant example of this policy was in Manitoba—a province originally designed as a homeland for the country's French-speaking *Métis* population. However, as opposed to the U.S. model, the Canadian version was not linguistically exclusive. English Canada accepted the principle of federal bilingualism so long as its language was on top. Unlike the U.S. case monolingual Francophone immigrants are not encumbered in terms of acquiring Canadian citizenship. But lacking fluency in English did block the ascent of Canadian French speakers. The Canadian linguistic hegemony was different from its American counterpart, but like its southern correlate, it ranked the English language, and by extension English speakers, over French.

Elites in both Puerto Rico and Quebec responded by contesting the established order with a rival regime—a counter-hegemony. If English were hegemonic in the heart of North America, then local notables would attempt to make their languages hegemonic within the confines of the periphery. Puerto Rico's newly emergent elites in the early twentieth century, a cadre of college-educated professionals who were discriminated against within the territorial bureaucracy, would extol the virtues of the trait that tainted them—the Spanish language. In like fashion a new wave of college-educated professionals in 1960s Quebec would redefine their ethnic identity more on the basis of their language than their faith. The success of their efforts to institutionalize a counter-hegemony could be measured in terms of the reaction of their non-nationalist rivals.

Puerto Rico's pro-statehood party, the Partido Nuevo Progresista, embraces a vision of joining the American Union as a bilingual state. It argues that even as a "state" of the United States, Puerto Ricans can continue to employ the Spanish language in all spheres of life, both private and public. This is a far cry from this party's predecessors earlier in the twentieth century that actively promoted the cultural and linguistic assimilation of islanders. Even this most pro-American of Puerto Rican parties was compelled to accept the links between Puerto Rican identity and the Spanish language—a clear sign that the nationalist counter-hegemony has taken root.

A similar pattern can be seen in Quebec where the federalist Liberal party defended the role of the French language in the face of strong opposition from Anglophones, one of the party's traditional sources of support. Reacting to a ruling from the Canadian Supreme Court that provisions of the province's Bill 101 violated the federal constitution's Charter of Rights and Freedoms, this party enacted a law, Bill 178, that effectively restored the most controversial aspects of the old language law. In order to do so the provincial legislature had to pass the law using an override provision of the federal constitution. The strength of the counter-hegemony, which endeavored to make the French language hegemonic within the provincial confines of Quebec, was so strong that a non-nationalist party felt the need to pass a statute that knowingly violated a fundamental principle of its federal constitution. The long term electoral viability of this party depended on accepting the nationalist paradigm that gave the protection and promotion of the French language precedence over the right to display signs in the language of one's choosing.

In the two cases highlighted here, the legislatures in both San Juan and Quebec City used their lawmaking powers to acknowledge the connection between the people and their vernacular while recognizing the hegemonic status of English in the rest of the United States and Canada. In 1991 the autonomist Partido Popular Democrático declared Spanish as the official language of the Puerto Rican government. Even when this 1991 statute was superseded a couple of years later by another one passed by the federalist Partido Nuevo Progresista, the new law still recognized the strong connection between the Spanish language and the islanders' government. As previously mentioned the 1993 law departed from the policies of previous pro-statehood parties in Puerto Rican history by promoting linguistic duality as opposed to Americanization.

Quebec's National Assembly has undergone a similar process. Provincial laws passed in 1974 and 1977 recognize French as the language of the government and its people. However, Quebec's laws have gone much further than their Puerto Rican counterparts, which remain symbolic declarations. The National Assembly has actively promoted the stature of the French language in the workplace, in public advertisements, and in the field of education.

The abolition of the Americanization policy in 1949 removed the only significant threat to the economic livelihoods of monolingual Hispanophones in the Puerto Rican bureaucracy. Lacking a perceived threat to their careers and ascendancy, Puerto Ricans have not pressured their local government to enact anything more than symbolic laws and declarations.

On the other hand Francophones in Quebec have had to contend with an Anglophone minority that is well entrenched in the upper and middle classes. To combat their economic prowess, the Quebec government used its legislative leverage to open up the provincial economy to Francophones. In Quebec's case the solidification of the counter-hegemony required not just officially defining the Québécois on the basis of their language but also smashing the barriers to Francophone ascendancy raised by its Anglophone elites. The decision by most immigrants to send their children to English-medium schools also raised the prospect of an expanding pool of Anglophones in Quebec. To counter this scenario Quebec's Bill 101 obliges immigrant families to send their children to French-medium schools. Quebec had to contend with an established, local English-speaking elite, something Puerto Rico never had to face.

Despite the many differences in the trajectories of nationalist movements in Puerto Rico and Quebec, these cases do suggest some common themes. While it is a mass movement, nationalism is highly dependent on elites not just to lead the group but also to define it and articulate its grievances. These elites are reacting to perceived injustices, whether subtle or gross, on the part of dominant groups in society. Ironically, the nationalist movements, which in so many cases threaten the preeminence of dominant or majoritarian groups, are in fact the result of their attitudes and policies. All too often it is an unanticipated byproduct of political and economic policies, and social attitudes. Their decision to exclude members of a peripheral society, especially elites from that peripheral society, thwart the possibility of either assimilation or accommodation. So long as they feel frustrated, peripheral elites can undermine the state's hegemony. Especially where they speak different languages, peripheral elites have the advantage of speaking the locals' vernacular and in that idiom they will convey their version of current events, history, and the myth of common ancestry. Escalating government repression only fuels their anger and intensifies the bitterness of their tales, which continue to drive a wedge between the groups. This suggests that government actions aimed at suppressing nationalist movements in the long run only fuel animosity toward the existing state and its dominant group.

Accommodating the concerns of differing ethnic groups does not come without a cost. Elites may not have the flexibility necessary to appease competing interests. Reconciliation between groups involves confidence-building measures that include not just constitutions, charters of rights, and other legal documents, but also the sharing of real power. That power will include political and economic resources along with its commensurate social standing or status. However, particularly during periods of economic decline, societies may not have the resources necessary to placate both ascending peripherals and members of their own group. Additionally, lower-class members of a dominant group must be persuaded to accept the new group definition, which now encompasses previously excluded individuals. In many cases the expansion of membership in the dominant group may jeopardize the privileges that lower-class members of the dominant group enjoyed. As key partners in the nationalist project, dissatisfied masses belonging to the dominant group could put their support behind rival leaders, or pretenders to the throne, and thus destabilize the regime as much as do disenchanted ethnic minorities. In the debate over nationalism, as in other political questions, leaders must weigh the risks of antagonizing peripherals or their base and determining which one of the two has the greatest potential to destabilize them. *Caveat Emptor!*

Bibliography

Aarebrot, Frank H. (1982). "Norway: Centre and Periphery in a Peripheral State," in Stein Rokkan & Derek W. Urwin, eds., *The Politics of Territorial Identity: Studies in European Regionalism*. London: Sage Publications, pp. 75-111.

"Al frente la opción estadista." (1990, July 23). *El Mundo*, San Juan, PR, p. 3.

Almond, Gabriel A. (1980). "The Intellectual History of the Civic Culture Concept," in Gabriel A. Almond & Sidney Verba, eds., *The Civic Culture Revisited*. Boston: Little, Brown & Co., pp. 1-36.

Almond, Gabriel A., & Verba, Sidney. (1963). *The Civic Culture: Political Attitudes and Democracy in Five Nations*. Princeton: Princeton University Press.

Anderson, Benedict. (1983). *Imagined Communities: Reflections on the Origin and Spread of Nationalism*. London: Verso Editions, Ltd.

Anderson, Charnel. (1984). "Was the U.S. Interested in Puerto Rico before 1898?" *Homines*, 8(1): 71-76.

"¡Aviso electoral!" (1993, November 11). *El Nuevo Día*, San Juan, PR, p. 49.

Azize, Yamila. (1984). "¿Interesaban los Estados Unidos a Puerto Rico antes de 1898?" *Homines*, 8(1): 77-81.

Banac, Ivo. (1984). *The National Question in Yugoslavia: Origins, History, Politics*. Ithaca, NY: Cornell University Press.

Banfield, Edward. (1958). *The Moral Basis of a Backward Society*. Chicago: Free Press.

Barnes, Barry. (1992). "Status Groups and Collective Action," *Sociology*, 26(2): 259-270.

Baron, Denis. (1990). *The English-Only Question: An Official Language for Americans?* New Haven: Yale University Press.

Barreto, Amílcar A. (1995a). *Nationalism, Linguistic Security, and Language Legislation in Quebec and Puerto Rico*. Ph.D. dissertation, State University of New York at Buffalo.

____. (1995b). "Nationalism and Linguistic Security in Contemporary Puerto Rico," *Canadian Review of Studies in Nationalism*, 22(1-2): 67-74.

Barth, Frederik. (1969). "Introduction," in Frederik Barth, ed., *Ethnic Groups and Boundaries: The Social Organization of Culture Difference*. Boston: Little, Brown & Company, pp. 9-38.

Benítez, Celeste. (1993, April 16). "Say It in English!" Editorial, *El Nuevo Día*, San Juan, PR, p. 65.

Berton, Pierre. (1987). *Why We Act Like Canadians: A Personal Exploration of Our National Character*. Markham, ON: Penguin Books Canada, Ltd.

Birch, Anthony H. (1989). *Nationalism & National Integration*. London: Unwin Hyman, Ltd.

Boissevain, Jeremy. (1970). *The Italians of Montreal: Social Adjustment in a Plural Society*. Royal Commission on Bilingualism and Biculturalism Studies, No. 7. Ottawa: Queens Printer.

Bothwell González, Reece B. (1971). *Trasfondo Constitucional de Puerto Rico: Primera Parte, 1887-1914*, Río Piedras, PR: Editorial Universitaria.

———. (1979a). *Puerto Rico: Cien Años de Lucha Política—Programas y Manifiestos, 1869-1952*. Vol. 1, Tomo 1. Río Piedras, PR: Editorial Universitaria.

———. (1979b). *Puerto Rico: Cien Años de Lucha Política—Programas y Manifiestos, 1956-1975*. Vol. 1, Tomo 2. Río Piedras, PR: Editorial Universitaria.

Bourhis, Richard Y. (1984). "Introduction: Language Policies in Multicultural Settings," in Richard Y. Bourhis, ed., *Conflict and Language Planning in Quebec*. Clevedon, UK: Multilingual Matters, Ltd., pp. 1-28.

Boyce, D. G. (1982). "Separatism and the Irish Nationalist Tradition," in Colin H. Williams, ed., *National Separatism*. Cardiff: University of Wales Press, pp. 75-103.

Brand, Jack A. (1985). "Nationalism and the Noncolonial Periphery: A Discussion of Scotland and Catalonia," in Edward A. Tiryakian & Ronald Rogowski, eds., *New Nationalisms of the Developed West: Toward Explanation*. Boston: Allen & Unwin, pp. 277-293.

Caldwell, Gary. (1974). *A Demographic Profile of the English-Speaking Population of Quebec: 1921-1971*. Québec: Centre international de recherche sur le bilinguism.

Carlson, Robert A. (1987). *The Americanization Syndrome: A Quest for Conformity*. New York: St. Martin's Press.

Carroll, Henry K. (1975). *Report on the Island of Porto Rico; Its Population, Civil Government, Commerce, Industries, Productions, Roads, Tariff, and Currency*. New York: Arno Press, Inc.

Chodos, Robert. Trans. (1994). *Quebec in a New World: The PQ's Plan for Sovereignty —National Executive Council of the Parti Québécois*. Toronto: James Lorimer & Company.

"Claman por una rápida solución." (1990, July 23). *El Mundo*, San Juan, PR, p. 4.

Clift, Dominique. (1982). *Quebec Nationalism in Crisis*. Kingston & Montreal: McGill-Queen's University Press.

Coleman, William D. (1984). "Social Class and Language Politics in Quebec," in Richard Y. Bourhis, ed., *Conflict and Language Planning in Quebec*. Clevedon, UK: Multilingual Matters, Ltd., pp. 130-147.

Comptroller General of the United States. (1980). *Experiences of Past Territories Can Assist Puerto Rico Status Deliberations*. GGD-80-26. Washington, DC: General Accounting Office.

———. (1981). *Puerto Rico's Political Future: A Divisive Issue with Many Dimensions*. GGD-81-48. Washington, DC: General Accounting Office.

Conner, Walker. (1994). *Ethnonationalism: The Quest for Understanding*. Princeton: Princeton University Press.

Cook, Ramsay. (1986). *Canada, Quebec, and the Uses of Nationalism*. Toronto: McClelland & Stewart, Ltd.

Coss, Manuel E. (1991, April 12-18). "Alcaldes PNP no hablan inglés." *Claridad*, San Juan, PR, p. 5.

Crawford, James, ed. (1992). *Language Loyalties: A Source Book on the Official English Controversy*. Chicago: University of Chicago Press.

d'Anglejan, Alison. (1984). "Language Planning in Quebec: An Historical Overview and Future Trends," in Richard Y. Bourhis, ed., *Conflict and Language Planning in Quebec*. Clevedon, UK: Multilingual Matters, Ltd., pp. 29-52.

del Rosario, Rubén. (1960). *Consideraciones sobre la lengua en Puerto Rico*. San Juan, PR: Instituto de Cultura Puertorriqueña.

_____. (1969). *La lengua de Puerto Rico: Ensayos*. Río Piedras, PR: Editorial Cultural, Inc.

Delgado Cintrón, Carmelo. (1991). "La declaración legislativa de la lengua española como el idioma oficial de Puerto Rico," *Revista Jurídica de la Universidad de Puerto Rico*, 60(2): 587-700.

Dinnerstein, Leonard, Nichols, Roger L., & Reimers, David M. (1979). *Natives and Strangers: Ethnic Groups and the Building of America*. New York: Oxford University Press.

Dufour, Christian. (1990). *A Canadian Challenge—Le défi québécois*. Halifax, NS: Institute for Research on Public Policy.

Durham, John, Earl of. (1905). *The Report of the Earl of Durham, Her Majesty's High Commissioner and Governor-General of British North America*. 2nd ed. London: Methuen & Company, Ltd.

Edwards, John. (1985). *Language, Society and Identity*. Oxford: Basil Blackwell, Ltd.

Eriksen, Thomas H. (1993). *Ethnicity & Nationalism: Anthropological Perspectives*. London: Pluto Press.

Estrada Resto, Nilka. (1993, January 15). "Imputa intereses partidistas," *El Nuevo Día*, San Juan, PR, p. 8.

Fernández, Ismael. (1993, January 25). "Demagogia y desinformación," Editorial, *El Nuevo Día*, San Juan, PR, p. 37.

Fernández Colón, José. (1997, March 6). "Corta Clinton el paso a la propuesta del 'English Only,' " *El Nuevo Día*, San Juan, PR, p. 10.

Fichte, Johann G. (1922). *Address to the German Nation*. Trans. R. F. Jones & G. H. Turnbull. Chicago: Open Court Publishing Company.

Flores, Juan. (1993). *Divided Borders: Essays on Puerto Rican Identity*. Houston: Arte Público Press.

Forbes, Hugh D. (1994). "Canada: From Bilingualism to Multiculturalism," in Larry Diamond & Marc F. Plattner, eds., *Nationalism, Ethnic Conflict, and Democracy*. Baltimore: John Hopkins University Press, pp. 86-101.

Frambes-Buxeda, Aline. (1980). "El papel de los grupos políticos y característisas de la cultura política," *Homines*, 4(2): 173-181.

Furtado, Charles F., & Hechter, Michael. (1992). "The Emergence of Nationalist Politics in the USSR: A Comparison of Estonia and the Ukraine," in Alexander J. Motyl, ed., *Thinking Theoretically about Soviet Nationalities: History and Comparison in the Study of the USSR*. New York: Columbia University Press, pp. 169-204.

Gallisá, Carlos. (1991, April 12-18). "La nacionalidad no se pone a votación," Editorial, *Claridad*, San Juan, PR, p. 11.

García Martínez, Alfonso L. (1976). *Idioma y Política: El papel desempeñado por los idiomas español e inglés en la relación política Puerto Rico-Estados Unidos*. San Juan, PR: Editorial Cordillera.

Gellner, Ernest. (1983). *Nations and Nationalism*. Ithaca, NY: Cornell University Press.

Ginorio, Angela B. (1987). "Puerto Rican Ethnicity and Conflict," in Jerry Boucher, Dan Landis, & Karen Arnold Clark, eds., *Ethnic Conflict: International Perspectives*. Beverly Hills, CA: Sage Publications, pp. 182-206.

Giraud, Marcel. (1986). *The Métis of the Canadian West*. Vol. 1. Trans. George Woodcock. Lincoln: University of Nebraska Press.

Glazer, Nathan, & Moynihan, Daniel P. (1970). *Beyond the Melting Pot: The Negroes, Puerto Ricans, Jews, Italians and Irish of New York City*. 2nd ed. Cambridge, MA: MIT Press.

González, José L. (1993). *Puerto Rico: The Four-Storeyed Country and Other Essays*. Trans. Gerald Guinness. Princeton: Princeton University Press.

Gramsci, Antonio. (1971). *Selections from the Prison Notebooks*. Trans. & ed. Quintin Hoare & Geoffrey N. Smith. New York: International Publishers.

Hamilton, Alexander, Madison, James, & Jay, John. (1961). *The Federalist Papers*. Ed. Clinton Rossiter. New York: NAL Penguin, Inc.

Hamilton, Richard, & Pinard, Maurice. (1976). "The Bases of Parti Québécois Support in Recent Quebec Elections," *Canadian Journal of Political Science,* 9(1): 3-26.

____. (1982) "The Quebec Independence Movement," in Colin H. Williams, ed. *National Separatism*. Cardiff: University of Wales Press.

Handler, Richard. (1988). *Nationalism and the Politics of Culture in Quebec*. Madison: University of Wisconsin Press.

Harrison, Brian, & Marmen, Louise. (1994). *Languages in Canada*. (CS 96-313E). Ottawa: Statistics Canada.

Hechter, Michael. (1975). *Internal Colonialism: The Celtic Fringe in British National Development, 1536-1966*. Berkeley: University of California Press.

____. (1985). "Internal Colonialism Revisited," in Edward A. Tiryakian & Ronald Rogowski, eds., *New Nationalisms of the Developed West: Towards Explanation*. Boston: Allen & Unwin, pp. 17-26.

____. (1987). *Principles of Group Solidarity*. Berkeley: University of California Press.

Hernández, Juan A. (1993, January 22-28). "Confirma la colonia, promueve la anexión," *El Nuevo Día,* San Juan, PR, p. 3.

Hernández Colón, Rafael. (1991, April 9). "An Open Letter to Fellow Citizens of the United States from the Governor of Puerto Rico," *New York Times*, p. A25.

Herzl, Theodor. (1988). *The Jewish State*. New York: Dover Publications.

Hobsbawm, Eric. (1983a). "Introduction: Inventing Tradition," in Eric Hobsbawm & Terence Ranger, eds., *The Invention of Tradition*. Cambridge, UK: Cambridge University Press, pp. 1-14.

____. (1983b). "Mass-Producing Tradition, 1870-1914," in Eric Hobsbawm & Terence Ranger, eds., *The Invention of Tradition*. Cambridge, UK: Cambridge University Press, pp. 263-307.

____. (1990). *Nations and Nationalism since 1780: Programme, Myth, Reality*. 2nd ed. Cambridge, UK: Cambridge University Press.

Huntington, Samuel P. (1968). *Political Order in Changing Societies*. New Haven, CT: Yale University Press.

Ignatiev, Noel. (1995). *How the Irish Became White*. New York: Routledge.

Inglehart, Ronald. (1988). "The Renaissance of Political Culture," *American Political Science Review,* 82(4): 1203-1230.

____. (1990). *Culture Shift in Advanced Industrial Society*. Princeton: Princeton University Press.

Inglehart, Ronald F., & Woodward, Margaret. (1967). "Language Conflict and Political Community," *Comparative Studies in Society and History*, 10: 27-45.

Jiménez de Wagenheim, Olga. (1993). *Puerto Rico's Revolt for Independence: El Grito de Lares*. Princeton: Markus Wiener Publishing.

Johnston, Donald, ed. (1990). *Pierre Trudeau Speaks Out on Meech Lake*. Toronto: General Paperbacks.

Joy, Richard J. (1972). *Languages in Conflict: The Canadian Experience*. Toronto: McClelland & Stewart, Ltd.

Kaplan, David H. (1994). "Population and Politics in a Plural Society: The Changing Geography of Canada's Linguistic Groups," *Annals of the Association of American Geographers*, 84(1): 46-67.

Katzner, Kenneth. (1995). *The Languages of the World*. New ed. London: Routledge.

Kedourie, Elie. (1993). *Nationalism*. 4th ed. Oxford: Blackwell Publishers.

Kohn, Hans. (1962). *The Age of Nationalism: The First Era of Global History*. New York: Harper & Brothers, Publishers.

Kuhn, Thomas S. (1970). *The Structure of Scientific Revolutions*. 2nd ed. Chicago: University of Chicago Press.

Lafaye, Jacques. (1976). *Quetzalcóatl and Guadalupe: The Formation of Mexican National Consciousness, 1531-1813*. Chicago: University of Chicago Press.

Laitin, David D. (1986). *Hegemony and Culture: Politics and Religious Change among the Yorubas*. Chicago: University of Chicago Press.

Laponce, Jean A. (1980). "The City Centre as Conflictual Space in the Bilingual City: The Case of Montreal," in Jean Gottman, ed., *Centre and Periphery*. Beverly Hills, CA: Sage Publications, Inc., pp. 149-162.

_____. (1984). "The French Language in Canada: Tensions between Geography and Politics," *Political Geography Quarterly*, 3(2): 91-104.

_____. (1987). *Languages and Their Territories*. Trans. Anthony Martin-Sperry. Toronto: University of Toronto Press.

_____. (1993). "The Case for Ethnic Federalism in Multilingual Societies: Canada's Regional Imperative," *Regional Politics & Policy*, 3(1): 23-43.

Laporte, Pierre E. (1984). "Status Language Planning in Quebec: An Evaluation," in Richard Y. Bourhis, ed., *Conflict and Language Planning in Quebec*. Clevedon, UK: Multilingual Matters, Ltd., pp. 53-80.

Latouche, Daniel. (1986). *Canada and Quebec, Past and Future: An Essay*. Toronto: University of Toronto Press.

Leibowitz, Arnold H. (1989). *Defining Status: A Comprehensive Analysis of the United States Territorial Relations*. Dordrecht, Netherlands: Martin Nijhoff Publishers.

Levine, Marc V. (1990). *The Reconquest of Montreal: Language Policy and Social Change in a Bilingual City*. Philadelphia: Temple University Press.

Levitt, Joseph, ed. (1970). *Henri Bourassa on Imperialism and Bi-culturalism, 1900-1918*. Toronto: Copp Clark Publishing Company.

Lijphart, Arend. (1968). *The Politics of Accommodation: Pluralism and Democracy in the Netherlands*. Berkeley & Los Angeles: University of California Press.

Lind, Andrew W. (1967). *Hawaii's People*. 3rd ed. Honolulu: University of Hawaii Press.

Lipset, Seymour M. (1990). *Continental Divide: The Values and Institutions of the United States and Canada*. London: Routledge.

Lustick, Ian. (1985). *State-Building Failure in British Ireland & French Algeria*. Berkeley: Institute of International Studies, University of California.

_____. (1993). *Unsettled States, Disputed Lands: Britain and Ireland, France and Algeria, Israel and the West Bank-Gaza.* Ithaca, NY: Cornell University Press.

Maldonado-Denis, Manuel. (1972). *Puerto Rico: A Socio-Historic Interpretation.* Trans. Elena Vialo. New York: Vintage Books.

_____. (1976). "Prospects for Latin American Nationalism: The Case of Puerto Rico," *Latin American Perspectives*, 3(3): 36-45.

Mallea, John R. (1984). "Minority Language Education in Quebec and Anglophone Canada," in Richard Y. Bourhis, ed., *Conflict and Language Planning in Quebec.* Clevedon, UK: Multilingual Matters, Ltd., pp. 222-260.

Martin, Ged. (1972). *The Durham Report and British Policy: A Critical Essay.* Cambridge, UK: Cambridge University Press.

Martínez, Andrea. (1993a, January 26). "Decidio a firmar el proyecto del inglés no empece a la marcha," *El Nuevo Día*, San Juan, PR, pp. 4-5.

_____. (1993b, July 10). "Con nombre y apellido la anexión," *El Nuevo Día*, San Juan, PR, p. 6.

Marx, Anthony. (1996). "Race-Making and the Nation-State," *World Politics*, 48(2): 180-208.

Mayall, James, & Simpson, Mark. (1992). "Ethnicity Is Not Enough: Reflections on Protracted Secessionism in the Third World," *International Journal of Comparative Sociology*, 33(1-2): 5-25.

McInnis, Edgar. (1969). *Canada: A Political and Social History.* 3rd ed. New York: Rinehart & Co., Inc.

McRoberts, Kenneth. (1979). "Internal colonialism: the case of Quebec," *Ethnic and Racial Studies*, 2(3): 293-318.

_____. (1984). "The Sources of Neo-Nationalism in Quebec," *Ethnic and Racial Studies*, 7(1): 55-85.

Meléndez, Edgardo. (1993). *Movimiento anexionista en Puerto Rico.* Río Piedras, PR: Editorial de la Universidad de Puerto Rico.

Michels, Robert. (1959). *Political Parties: A Sociological Study of the Oligarchical Tendencies of Modern Democracy.* New York: Dove Publications, Inc.

Migdal, Joel S. (1988). *Strong Societies and Weak States: State-Society Relations and State Capabilities in the Third World.* Princeton: Princeton University Press.

Millán Pabón, Carmen. (1997a, February 11). "Ineludible el inglés," *El Nuevo Día*, San Juan, PR, p. 5.

_____. (1997b, March 6). "Sin masticar el inglés en otras asignaturas," *El Nuevo Día*, San Juan, PR, p. 10.

Millán Pabón, Carmen, & Cabán, Luis A. (1987, March 6). "Reacciones diversas a alegato Webster," *El Mundo*, San Juan, PR, p. 7.

Miller, Roger. (1984). "The Response of Business Firms to the Francization Process," in Richard Y. Bourhis, ed., *Conflict and Language Planning in Quebec.* Clevedon, UK: Multilingual Matters, Ltd., pp. 114-129.

Morris, Nancy. (1995). *Puerto Rico: Culture, Politics, and Identity.* Westport, CT: Praeger.

_____. (1996). "Language and Identity in Twentieth Century Puerto Rico," *Journal of Multilingual Development*, 17(1): 17-32.

Morrow, James D. (1994). *Game Theory for Political Scientists.* Princeton: Princeton University Press.

Morton, William L. (1972). *The Canadian Identity.* 2nd ed. Madison: University of Wisconsin Press.

Moynihan, Daniel P. (1993). *Pandaemonium: Ethnicity in International Politics*. Oxford: Oxford University Press.

Mulero, Leonor. (1993a, October 29). "Romero le refresca la memoria a un congresista," *El Nuevo Día,* San Juan, PR, p. 13.

____. (1993b, November 5). "Simon 'vende' la estadidad," *El Nuevo Día*, San Juan, PR, p. 8.

____. (1993c, November 5). " 'Una fortaleza' el bilingüismo puertorriqueño," *El Nuevo Día*, San Juan, PR, p. 11.

____. (1996a, July 24). "Atan el inglés a la estadidad," *El Nuevo Día*, San Juan, PR, p. 7.

____. (1996b, August 15). "Bofetada a la estadidad," *El Nuevo Día*, San Juan, PR, p. 10.

____. (1996c, August 16). "Insiste Wilson en el 'English only,' " *El Nuevo Día*, San Juan, PR, p. 5.

____. (1996d, August 16). "Sin reversa la cruzada estadista," *El Nuevo Día*, San Juan, PR, p. 5.

____. (1997a, February 8). "Presto Solomon a debatir el inglés," *El Nuevo Día*, San Juan, PR, p. 6.

____. (1997b, March 10). "Bajo amenaza el lenguaje," *El Nuevo Día*, San Juan, PR, p. 12.

____. (1997c, March 20). "Desarma la Casa Blanca la bomba del inglés," *El Nuevo Día*, San Juan, PR, pp. 4-5.

Negrón de Montilla, Aida. (1975). *Americanization in Puerto Rico and the Public School System: 1900-1930*. Río Piedras, PR: Editorial Universitaria.

Nevitte, Neil. (1985). "The Religious Factor in Contemporary Nationalist Movements: An Analysis of Quebec, Wales, and Scotland," in Edward A. Tiryakian & Ronald Rogowski, eds., *New Nationalisms in the Developed West: Toward Explanation*. Boston: Allen & Unwin, pp. 337-352.

O'Brien, Connor C. (1988). *God Land: Reflections on Religion and Nationalism*. Cambridge, MA: Harvard University Press.

Olson, Mancur. (1971). *The Logic of Collective Action: Public Goods and the Theory of Groups*. Cambridge, MA: Harvard University Press.

Ortega y Gasset, José. (1960). *The Revolt of the Masses*. New York: W. W. Norton & Company, Inc.

Pareto, Vilfredo. (1991). *The Rise and Fall of Elites: An Application of Theoretical Sociology*. New Brunswick, NJ: Transaction Publishers.

Pattanayak, D. P., & Bayer, J. M. (1987). "Laponce's 'The French Language in Canada: Tensions between Geography and Politics': A Rejoinder," *Political Geography Quarterly,* 6(3): 261-263.

Pedreira, Antonio S. (1978). *Insularismo*. Río Piedras, PR: Editorial Edil, Inc.

Pei, Mario. (1984). *The Story of Language*. Rev. ed. New York: NAL Penguin, Inc.

Picó, Fernando. (1986). *Historia General de Puerto Rico*. Río Piedras, PR: Ediciones Huracán, Inc.

Pinard, Maurice, & Hamilton, Richard. (1984). "The Class Bases of the Quebec Independence Movement: Conjectures and Evidence," *Ethnic and Racial Studies*, 7(1): 19-54.

Quinn, Herbert F. (1979). *The Union Nationale: Quebec Nationalism from Duplessis to Lévesque*. 2nd ed. Toronto: University of Toronto Press.

Ramírez Lavandero, Marcos, ed. (1988). *Documents on the Constitutional Relationship of Puerto Rico and the United States*. 3rd ed. Washington, DC: Puerto Rico Federal Affairs Administration.

Rawkins, Phillip. (1981). "The Role of the State in the Transformation of Nationalist Movements of the 1960s: Comparing Wales and Quebec," *Ethnic and Racial Studies*, 7(1): 86-105.

Reid, Charles F. (1941). *Education in the Territories and Outlying Possessions of the United States*. New York: Bureau of Publications, Teachers College, Columbia University.

Rioux, Marcel. (1971). *Quebec in Question*. Trans. James Boake. Toronto: James Lewis & Samuel.

Robertson, Barbara. (1971). *Wilfrid Laurier: The Great Conciliator*. Toronto: Oxford University Press.

Rodríguez, Magdalys. (1997, March 5). "Por el libro el inglés," *El Nuevo Día*, San Juan, PR, p. 6.

Rogowski, Ronald. (1985). "Causes and Varieties of Nationalism: A Rationalist Account," in Edward A. Tiryakian & Ronald Rogowski, eds., *New Nationalisms of the Developed West: Toward Explanation*. Boston: Allen & Unwin, pp. 87-108.

Roosens, Eugeen E. (1989). *Creating Ethnicity: The Process of Ethnogenesis*. Newbury Park, CA: Sage Publications.

Scarano, Francisco A. (1996). "The *Jíbaro* Masquerade and the Subaltern Politics of Creole Identity Formation in Puerto Rico, 1745-1823," *American Historical Review*, 101(2): 1398-1431.

Schull, Joseph. (1971). *Rebellion: The Rising of French Canada 1837*. Toronto: Macmillan of Canada.

"Se cuidaron todos los detalles." (1990, July 23). *El Mundo*, San Juan, PR, p. 7.

Serrano Geyls, Raúl & Gorrín Peralta, Carlos I. (1979). "Puerto Rico y la estadidad: Problemas constitucionales," *Revista del Colegio de Abogados de Puerto Rico*, 40: 521-536.

Sheppard, Claude-Armand. (1971). *The Law of Languages in Canada*. Ottawa: Studies of the Royal Commission on Bilingualism and Biculturalism.

Smith, Anthony D. (1981). *The Ethnic Revival*. Cambridge, UK: Cambridge University Press.

_____. (1982). "Nationalism, Ethnic Separatism and the Intelligentsia," in Colin H. Williams, ed., *National Separatism*. Cardiff: University of Wales Press, pp. 17-41.

_____. (1989). "The Origins of Nations," *Ethnic and Racial Studies*, 12(3): 340-367.

Stalin, Joseph. (1935). *Marxism and the National and Colonial Question*. New York: International Publishers.

Steinberg, Stephen. (1981). *The Ethnic Myth: Race, Ethnicity and Class in America*. Boston: Beacon Press.

Stepan, Alfred. (1983). "U.S. Policy and Puerto Rico," in Jorge Heine, ed., *Time for Decision: The United States and Puerto Rico*. Lanham, MD: North-South Publishing Co., pp. 267-274.

Tocqueville, Alexis de. (1988). *Democracy in America*. Trans. George Lawrence. Ed. J. P. Mayer. New York: Harper & Row.

Toland, Judith D. (1993). "Introduction: Dialogue of Self and Other: Ethnicity and the Statehood Process," in Judith D. Toland, ed., *Ethnicity and the State*. Political Anthropology Series, vol. 9. New Brunswick, NJ: Transaction Publishers, pp. 1-20.

Torres Rivera, Alejandro. (1991, April 19-25). "Respaldo socialista al español," *Claridad*, San Juan, PR, p. 30.

Trotsky, Leon. (1978). *Leon Trotsky on Black Nationalism & Self Determination*. Ed. George Breitman. New York: Pathfinder Press.

Trudeau, Pierre E. (1968). *Federalism and the French Canadians.* New York: St. Martin's Press.

United States Department of Commerce. (1993). *1990 Census of Population and Housing: Summary Social, Economic, and Housing Characteristics—Puerto Rico,* 1990 CPH-5-53, Washington, DC: U.S. Government Printing Office.

United States-Puerto Rico Commission on the Status of Puerto Rico. (1966). *Report of the United States-Puerto Rico Commission on the Status of Puerto Rico.* Washington, DC: U.S. Government Printing Office.

Van Doren, Carl, ed. (1947). *Letters and Papers of Benjamin Franklin and Richard Jackson, 1753- 1785.* Philadelphia: American Philosophical Society.

Vallières, Pierre. (1971). *White Niggers of America.* Trans. Joan Pinkham. Toronto: McClelland & Stewart, Ltd.

Vélez, Jorge A., & Schweers, C. William. (1993). "The Decision to Make Spanish the Official Language of Puerto Rico," *Language Problems and Language Planning,* 17(2): 117-139.

Vojnić, Dragomir. (1995). "Disparity and Disintegration: The Economic Dimension of Yugoslavia's Demise," in Payam Akhavan & Robert Howse, eds., *Yugoslavia, the Former and the Future: Reflections by Scholars from the Region.* Washington, DC: Brookings Institute & Geneva: The United Nations Research Institute for Social Development, pp. 75-111.

Wade, Mason. (1968). *The French Canadians, 1760-1967.* Vol. 1. Toronto: MacMillan of Canada, Ltd.

Waters, Mary C. (1990). *Ethnic Options: Choosing Identities in America.* Berkeley: University of California Press.

Weber, Eugen. (1976). *Peasants into Frenchmen: The Modernization of Rural France, 1870-1914.* Stanford: Stanford University Press.

Weber, Max. (1958). *The Protestant Ethic and the Spirit of Capitalism.* Trans. Talcott Parsons. New York: Charles Scribner's Sons.

Weinstein, Brian. (1983). *The Civic Tongue: Political Consequences of Language Choice.* New York: Longman, Inc.

Williams, Colin H. (1984). "More than Tongue Can Tell: Linguistic Factors in Ethnic Separatism," in John Edwards, ed., *Linguistic Minorities, Policies and Pluralism.* London: Academic Press, pp. 179-219.

Wilson-Smith, Anthony. (1995, November 6). "A House Divided," *Maclean's,* pp. 14-16.

Woodcock, George. (1989). *A Social History of Canada.* Markham, ON: Penguin Books Canada, Ltd.

Woolard, Kathryn A. (1989). *Double Talk: Bilingualism and the Politics of Ethnicity in Catalonia.* Berkeley: University of California Press.

Zentella, Ana Celia. (1990). "Returning Migration, Language, and Identity: Puerto Rican Bilinguals in Dos Worlds/Two Mundos," *International Journal of the Sociology of Language,* 84: 81-100.

Index

162

Index

Language: bureaucracies, 34, 36, 39;
  dialects, 32-35, 40-42, 44 n.3, 83;
  diglossia, 43 n.2; elites, 36, 38-41,
  44 n.10, 82, 91, 143-44; ethnic
  identity, 5-6, 33, 35, 83-84; planning, 61 n.5; schools, 36, 37, 39,
  44 n.11; social hierarchy, 38, 40,
  41, 44 n.12, 91, 144; standardization, 6, 32-36, 39, 44 n.7, 50. *See
  also specific languages*
Language Laws in Canada: Official
  Languages Act of 1969, 134
Language Laws in Puerto Rico: Bill 1
  (1993), 123-24, 127 n.32; Bill 417
  (1991), 119-20, 123-24; Official
  Languages Act (1902), 116-20,
  122-23, 126 n.12, 139 n.1; symbolism, 117-18, 139 n.1
Language Laws in Quebec: Bill 22
  (1974), 130-32, 134-35, 137-38;
  Bill 63 (1969), 137-38; Bill 101
  (1977), 104, 130-32, 135, 137-38,
  140 nn.44, 46, 146-47; Bill 178
  (1988), 132, 146; education, 135-
  39, 140 nn.44, 46; public signs,
  131-33; symbolism, 130-31, 147;
  work environment, 133-35
Laponce, Jean, 39, 41, 43 n.2, 48, 55,
  103, 113 n.6, 120; Canada, 75 n.4;
  language contact, 37-38, 86; Quebec, 103-4, 129
Laporte, Pierre E., 129-30, 136
Latin, language, 33-34, 38, 43 n.2, 44
  n.8
Latin America: identity, 25, 78; indige-
  nous languages, 41
Latino identity, 82-84
Latouche, Daniel, 99, 108
Laurier, Wilfrid, 73
Leibowitz, Arnold, 57, 59-60
Lesage, Jean 110, 113 n.11
Levine, Marc V., 71, 102, 104, 130,
  133-34, 140 n.32, language and
  education, 70, 110, 137
Levitt, Joseph, 98-101, 113 n.3
Liberal party, Quebec, 113 n.11, 130,
  133, 137, 140 n.32, 146
Lijphart, Arend, 68
Lind, Andrew, 58-59

Lipset, Seymour M., 47-48, 63-65
López Galarza, Héctor, 119
Louisiana, 57-58, 71; statehood, 58,
  59, 112 n.2
Lustick, Ian, 25, 29 n.4, 29 n.10

Madison, James, 48
Maldonado, Norman, 122
Maldonado-Denis, Manuel, 24, 36, 77-
  79, 82, 85, 92, 95 n.25
Mallea, John, 102
Mandarin, 34
Manitoba: Catholic Church, 72-73;
  francophone minority, 4-5, 72-73,
  101, 145
Marmen, Louis, 104, 113 n.8, 136
Martínez, Andrea, 123-24
Martin, Ged, 71
Marx, Anthony, 29 n.9, 45 n.17
Mayall, James, 36
McCarthy, D'Alton, 73
McCarthy, Joseph, 62 n.13
McInnis, Edgar, 73, 101
McKinley, William 88
McRoberts, Kenneth, 21, 67-68, 98,
  109, 110
Meléndez, Edgardo, 85
Métis, 72, 75 n.10, 145
Mexico, nationalism, 25, 27-28, 30
  n.14, 78
Michels, Robert, 26-27, 40, 42
Migdal, Joel, 24
Millán, Carmen, 62 n.21, 122, 124
Miller, Roger, 135
Mojica, Mauro, 123
Montréal, 133-34, 136-37
Morris, Nancy, 77, 83-86, 90, 95 n.22
Morrow, James D., 19
Morton, William L., 71
Moynihan, Daniel P., 14-15, 58-60, 62
  n.13
Mulero, Leonor, 123, 127 nn.28, 29
Muñoz Marín, Luis, 96 n.26, 118, 125
  n.5
Murray, James, 67
Myth of common ancestry, 14, 16, 142

National Assembly. *See* Quebec government

About the Author

AMÍLCAR A. BARRETO is Assistant Professor of Political Science at Northeastern University. His articles have appeared in *Homines* and the *Canadian Review of Studies in Nationalism.*

ISBN 0-275-96183-4

90000>

EAN

9 780275 961831

HARDCOVER BAR CODE

DATE DUE
